She Came from Mariupol

She Came from Mariupol

Natascha Wodin

Translated by Alfred Kueppers

Michigan State University Press | *East Lansing*

Notes in the English version have been added by the translator.

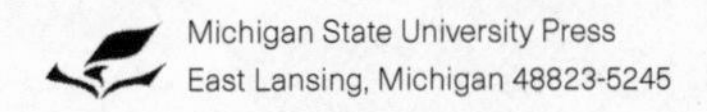

Michigan State University Press
East Lansing, Michigan 48823-5245

The translation of this work was supported by a grant from the Goethe-Institut.

The author would like to thank the Deutscher Literaturfonds e.V., the Berlin Senate, the Alfred Döblin Prize Foundation and the Robert Bosch Foundation for the support they provided during the writing of this book.

Library of Congress Cataloging-in-Publication Data
Names: Wodin, Natascha, 1945– author. | Kueppers, Alfred, translator.
Title: She came from Mariupol / Natascha Wodin ; English translation by Alfred Kueppers.
Other titles: Sie kam aus Mariupol. English
Description: East Lansing : Michigan State University Press, [2022] | Originally published in German as Sie kam aus Mariupol by Rowohlt Verlag in 2017. | Includes bibliographical references.
Identifiers: LCCN 2021017429 | ISBN 978-1-61186-423-6 (paperback ; alk. paper) | ISBN 978-1-60917-690-7 (pdf) | ISBN 978-1-62895-456-2 (epub) | ISBN 978-1-62896-450-9 (Kindle)
Subjects: LCSH: Wodin, Natascha, 1945—Childhood and youth. | Wodin, Natascha, 1945—Family. | Women authors, German—20th century—Family relationships. | Mothers of authors—Biography. | Women, Ukrainian—Germany—Biography. | World War, 1939–1945—Deportations from Ukraine. | World War, 1939–1945—Ukraine—Mariupol'.
Classification: LCC PT2685.O23 Z46 2022 | DDC 833/.914 [B]—dc23
LC record available at https://lccn.loc.gov/2021017429

Cover design by Erin Kirk
Cover art: Market old Mariupol, Wikimedia Commons;
and old vintage wallpaper, by Vadim Yerofeyev, Adobe Stock

Visit Michigan State University Press at www.msupress.org

Contents

For my sister

Natascha Wodin's Family Tree

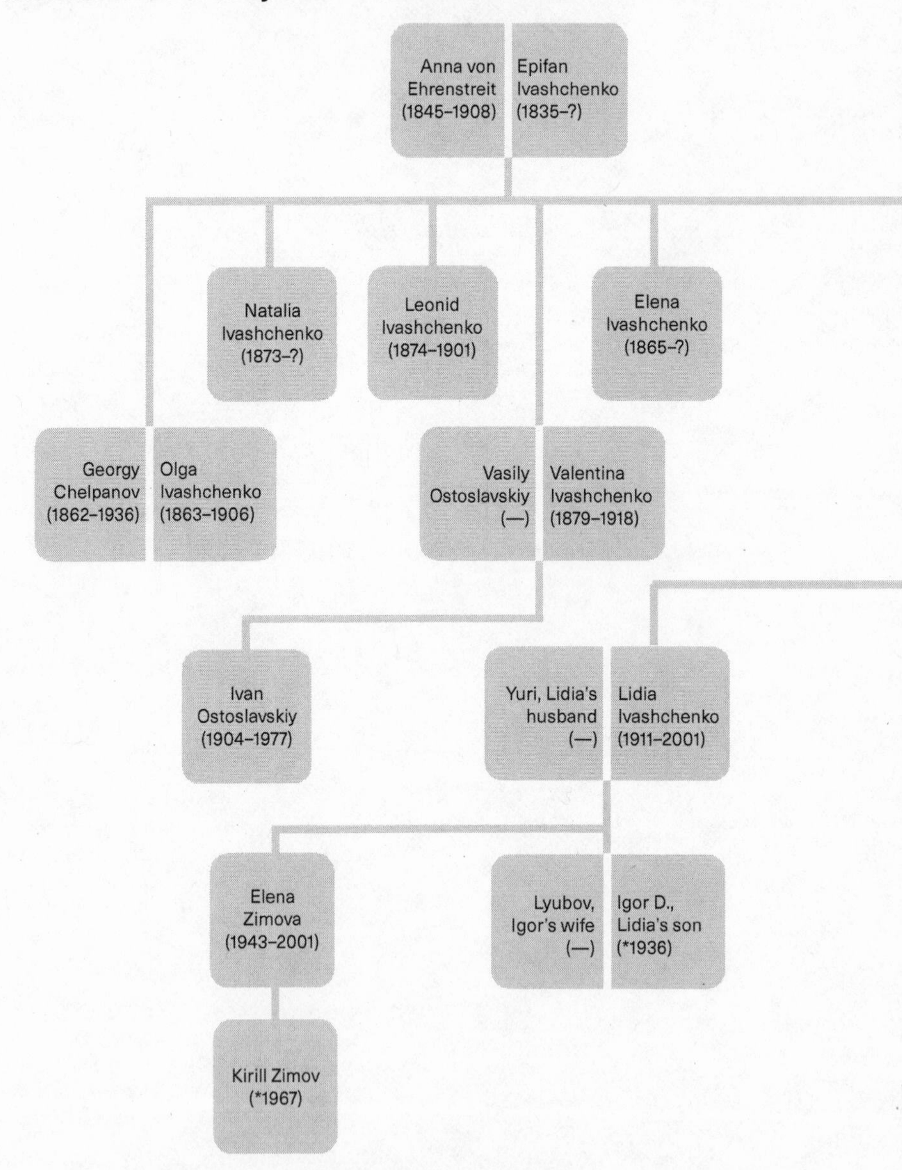

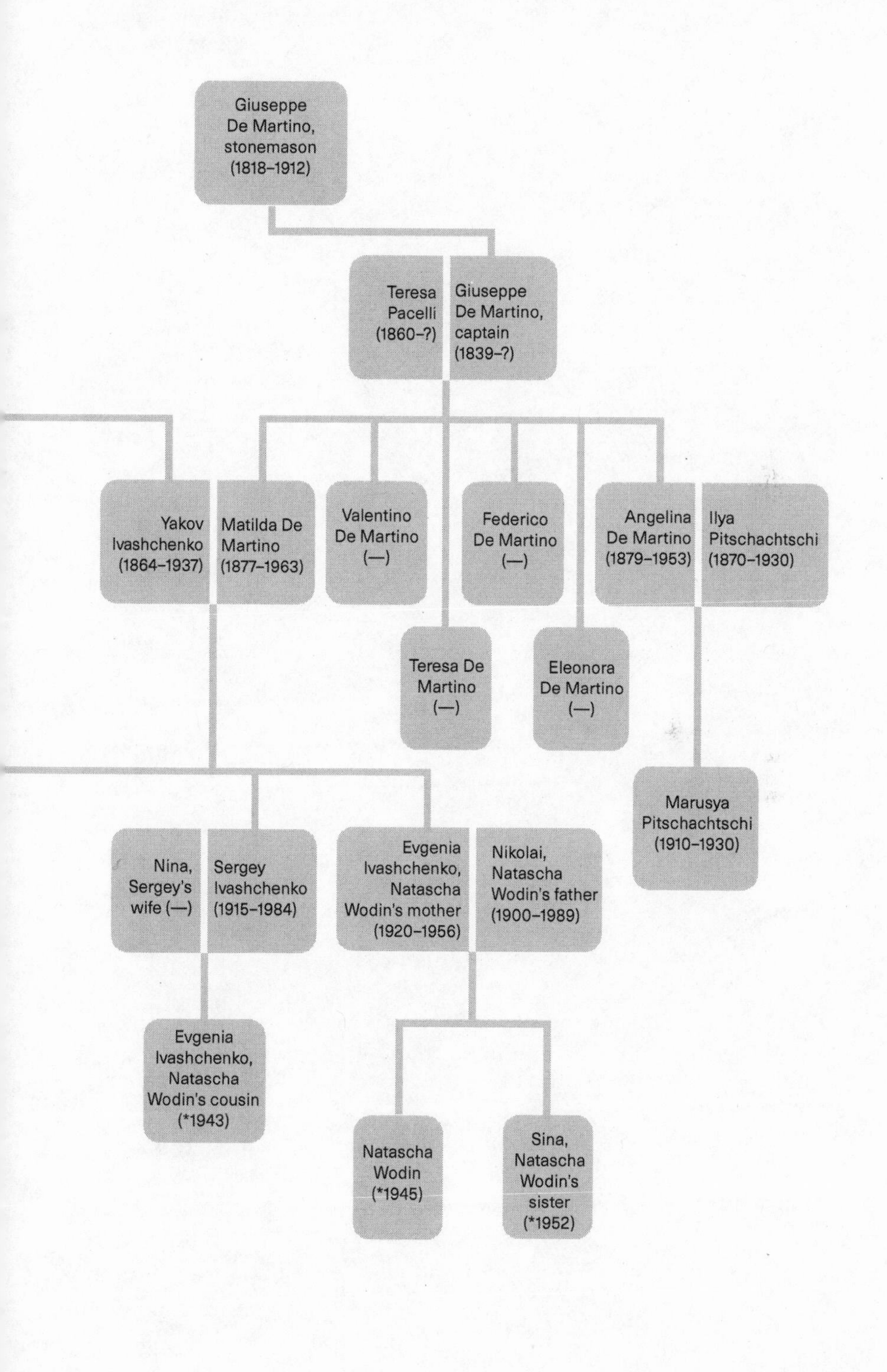
Giuseppe De Martino, stonemason (1818–1912)
Teresa Pacelli (1860–?)
Giuseppe De Martino, captain (1839–?)
Yakov Ivashchenko (1864–1937)
Matilda De Martino (1877–1963)
Valentino De Martino (—)
Federico De Martino (—)
Angelina De Martino (1879–1953)
Ilya Pitschachtschi (1870–1930)
Teresa De Martino (—)
Eleonora De Martino (—)
Marusya Pitschachtschi (1910–1930)
Nina, Sergey's wife (—)
Sergey Ivashchenko (1915–1984)
Evgenia Ivashchenko, Natascha Wodin's mother (1920–1956)
Nikolai, Natascha Wodin's father (1900–1989)
Evgenia Ivashchenko, Natascha Wodin's cousin (*1943)
Natascha Wodin (*1945)
Sina, Natascha Wodin's sister (*1952)

PART ONE

Answers in the Internet

I typed my mother's name into the Russian-language search engine on a whim, it really wasn't much more than that. I had tried to find a trace of her many times over the last several decades; I had written to the Red Cross and other organizations that searched for missing persons, the relevant archives and research facilities, even complete strangers in Ukraine and Moscow. I had searched faded lists of victims and registers, but I had never succeeded in finding even a trace of the trail, a vague sign of her life in Ukraine, of her existence before my birth.

When she was twenty-three, she had been deported together with my father from Mariupol to work as a forced laborer in Germany during World War II. I only knew that they were both sent to a Leipzig armaments factory that belonged to the Flick Group. My mother took her own life eleven years after the end of the war in a small West German town, not far from a settlement for stateless foreigners, as former forced laborers were called at the time. Other than my sister and me, there was probably not a single person left on earth who still knew her. And we did not actually know her either. We were children, my sister was only four and I was ten, when she left the house without a word on an October day in 1956 and never came back. I remembered her only as a shadow, more an emotion than a memory.

In the meantime I had long since given up looking for her. She had been born more than ninety years ago, and she only lived for thirty-six years. Not just any years, but the years of the civil war, the purges, and the famines in the Soviet Union, the years of the Second World War and National Socialism. She had been caught in the shredder of two dictatorships, first under Stalin in Ukraine, then under Hitler in Germany. It was an illusion to think that, decades later, I could find a trace of a young woman in the ocean of forgotten victims, about whom I knew little more than her name.

When I entered her name into a Russian internet site on a summer night in 2013, the search engine gave me a result right away. My astonishment only lasted for a few seconds. One aggravating detail that had always made my search more difficult was the fact that my mother had an extremely common Ukrainian name. There were hundreds, probably thousands, of Ukrainians with the exact same name. It's true that the person on the screen had the same patronymic as my mother, she was also a Evgenia Yakovlevna Ivashchenko, however, the name Yakov was also so common that my discovery did not mean anything.

I opened the link and read: Ivashchenko, Evgenia Yakovlevna, born 1920, place of birth Mariupol. I stared at the entry; it stared back. Although I knew very little about my mother, I did know that she was born in 1920 in Mariupol. Could it be possible that in a small city like 1920's Mariupol two girls with the same first and last names were born, whose fathers were both named Yakov?

I was not sure if I was actually reading my mother's name on the screen, or if it only appeared like a fata morgana in the desert, which is exactly what the Russian-language internet was for me even though Russian was my mother tongue (I had never entirely lost it over the

Figure 1. Evgenia Ivashchenko (1920–1956) with her mother Matilda Josefovna De Martino (1877–1963), roughly 1938. Author's private archive.

course of my life, and now spoke it almost every day since moving to post-reunification Berlin). They spoke a type of Russian online that was almost a foreign language to me, a Newspeak that changed rapidly and constantly introduced new vocabulary words and expanded daily with Americanisms, whose origin was hard to decipher after being transcribed into Cyrillic. The page that was now watching me from my screen also had an English name, Azov's Greeks. I knew that Mariupol was on the Azov Sea, but where did the "Azov Greeks" suddenly come from? I had never heard of any connection between Ukraine and Greece before. If I were British, I could say quite appropriately: It's all Greek to me.

At this time I knew next to nothing about Mariupol. While searching for my mother, it had never occurred to me to learn about the city where she came from. Mariupol was known as Zhdanov for forty years and only regained its old name after the collapse of the Soviet Union, and it remained an imaginary city for me, which I never exposed to reality's light. Ever since I can remember, I have been at home in the imprecise, in my own pictures and conceptions of the world. External reality threatened my inner world, so I avoided it as much as possible.

My original picture of Mariupol was shaped by the fact that in my childhood no one differentiated between the individual republics of the Soviet Union. All the inhabitants of the fifteen republics were called Russians. Even my parents spoke about Ukraine as though it were a part of Russia, although Russia emerged out of Kievan Rus,' the cradle of Russian civilization, in the Middle Ages. My father said Russia was a vast empire, that stretched from Alaska to Poland, taking up one-sixth of the world's total landmass. Germany was just a small dot on the map in comparison.

Ukraine merged into Russia in my mind, and when I imagined my mother's former life in Mariupol, I always saw her in Russian snow. She walked in her old-fashioned gray coat with a velvet collar and velvet cuffs—the only coat I had ever seen her wear—across dark, icy streets in some immeasurable expanse, through which a snowstorm had been sweeping for ages. The Siberian snow, which covered all of Russia and Mariupol as well, the eerie empire of eternal cold, where the Communists ruled.

My childlike conception of my mother's hometown survived for decades in the inner darkrooms of my mind. Even long after I knew that Russia and Ukraine were two different countries, and that Ukraine had absolutely nothing to do with Siberia, my Mariupol remained untouched, although I did not even know for certain if my mother really came from this city, or if I had imputed this to her because I liked the name so much. Sometimes I was not even certain if this city truly existed, or if, like so much else that had to do with my origins, I had simply invented it.

One day when I was flipping through a newspaper, I stopped at the sports page, and just as I wanted to go further, the word Mariupol caught my eye. A German soccer team, according to what I read, had travelled to Ukraine to play against Illichivets Mariupol. The simple fact that Mariupol had a soccer team was so sobering, that my imaginary Mariupol fell apart like a house of cards. Nothing on earth bores me more than soccer, but it, of all things, forced me to confront the real Mariupol for the first time. I found out that it was a city with a decidedly mild climate, a harbor city on the Sea of Azov, the shallowest and warmest sea in the world. It was said that there were long, wide, sandy beaches, vineyards and endless fields of sunflowers. The German soccer players groaned under the summer temperatures, which approached forty degrees Celsius.

Reality seemed far more unreal than my conception of it. My mother became a person separate from me for the first time since her death. Suddenly, I saw her walking along a street in Mariupol in a light and bright summer dress with bare arms and legs, her feet in sandals, instead of trudging through the snow. A young girl that grew up not in the coldest and darkest place on earth, but by a warm southern sea near Crimea, under a sky that might look similar to the one over the Italian Adriatic. Nothing seemed more irreconcilable than my mother and the South, my mother and the sand and the sea. I had to transfer all of my ideas about her life into another climate, another temperature. The old stranger had transformed herself into a new stranger.

Years later I read a Russian novel that included a realistic winter portrait of Mariupol from the time that my mother lived there, though I have forgotten the title: *Wet snow fell behind the window of the Hotel Palmyra. A hundred meters further, the sea, about which I do not dare to say that it roared. It gurgled and wheezed, the flat, insignificant and boring sea. The nondescript city, with its Polish churches and Jewish synagogues, was nestled up against the water. With its stinking harbor and storage sheds, the tattered tent of a travelling circus on the shore, Greek taverns and the lonely, dim lanterns by the entrance to the abovementioned hotel.* To me it seemed like a private message about my mother. She had seen it all with her own eyes. She had certainly walked past the Hotel Palmyra once, maybe in her gray overcoat, maybe in the very same wet snow, with the foul smell of the harbor in her nose.

Once again, I learned some surprising things about Mariupol on the internet site I found. During the time that my mother was born, the city was still heavily influenced by Greek culture. In the eighteenth century, Catherine the Great had given the city to Greek Christians who came from what was then the Khanate of Crimea. Other ethnicities were not allowed to settle in the city again until after the middle of the nineteenth century. A Greek minority continues to live in the city, and for some reason, my mother's name led me to a forum for Ukrainians of Greek origin. A vague suspicion stirred within me. I had only a very faint, almost indecipherable memory of what my mother told me about her life in Ukraine, but it had become fixed in my mind that her mother was Italian. Naturally, after all that time, I could not be sure if it was an actual memory, or whether I had accidentally stored it in my brain. Perhaps, and that seemed to me the most likely possibility, I had already concocted an Italian grandmother for myself when I was a child and made her the object of my adventurous fictions. Maybe the Italian grandmother sprang out of the burning desire I once had to shed my Russian-Ukrainian skin and become something other than what I was. Now I asked myself if I may have misremembered it only insofar as my mother's mother had not been an Italian, but a Greek. Was that not reasonable, considering what I had read now, only now, about Mariupol? Was it possible that the Greek subtly transformed herself into an Italian in my memory because, even in my youth, I had longed to travel there?

It seemed to me that I had discovered another enigma of my roots, as though I were suddenly digging in an even stranger, decidedly unrecognizable ground. I stared at my mother's name on the screen and had the feeling that the makeshift identity I had pieced together over the course of my life had burst like a soap bubble. For one moment, everything dissolved around me. I was only reassured later by the thought that the Greek roots of the Evgenia Yakovlevna Ivashchenko I had uncovered were only significant because they provided proof that she could not have been my mother. I was certain that I had never heard my mother utter the word "Greki." In those days, in the miserable and isolated world of the barracks, it would have stood out as something extraordinary and exotic. On the other hand, it was hard to imagine that my mother would have never mentioned her hometown's Greek past. After all, I had learned from the historical background information in the forum that a Greek presence still prevailed in Mariupol when she lived there.

I didn't make any promises to myself; all too often my investigations had come to naught, but since the Azov's Greeks also offered a platform where you could search for your relatives, I nonetheless decided to leave a message. However, I had to register before I could write anything. I had never done that on a Russian-language site before, and it struck me as unlikely that I would be able to master this technological hurdle, but to my surprise everything was very easy, much easier than on German-language sites. It only took a minute to get access.

I couldn't enter much more in the search engine than my mother's name and hometown. From her patronymic, Yakovlevna, it could be inferred that her father's name was Yakov, but I did not even know her mother's maiden name. I knew that she had a brother and sister, but I did not know their names either. I had a Ukrainian marriage certificate which showed that in July 1943, my mother wed my father in German-occupied Mariupol. On a work permit issued by the Leipzig employment office, it said that she was deported to Germany together with my father in 1944. That was all I knew about her.

And that begged the question, whom was I really seeking? It was almost impossible that her siblings were still alive, unless they had lived to a biblical age. Even their children, if they had any, would have reached an advanced age by now, much like me. My potential cousins could hardly have known my mother, and it was doubtful whether they even knew if she existed, if anyone had ever told them about her. At that time, and for decades afterward, it was dangerous to be related to a person like my mother; someone who may have willingly allowed herself to be deported to Germany, or who at least failed to avoid becoming a forced laborer for the enemy, by suicide if necessary, as Stalin demanded of true patriots. In order not to put them in danger, no one told their children about such relatives, since they were seen as traitors.

Previously, whenever I wanted to type a Russian text, my fingers had to adjust to a Cyrillic keyboard and make a cumbersome search for individual letters. Now, thanks to a wonderful program, I could type on the familiar Latin keyboard and it automatically converted the letters into Cyrillic. It's true, I doubted I would be able to transport the message I had typed with the transliteration program onto the Russian site—the route seemed too far to me—but after a few of the usual mouse clicks it actually jumped onto the Azov's Greeks site. I put my email address at the bottom of the message and sent it, without knowing where it would land. Maybe in a dead place, in an electronic void, where no one would ever discover my message in a bottle.

I had been living in my writing studio in Mecklenburg for a few weeks. I shared the small place on the Schaalsee with a friend, and we took turns using it. Almost the entire summer on the lake was mine that year. Gilla was an actress, abroad somewhere and up to her neck in a theater project; she would not be back until September. I was lazing about after finishing a book project. I couldn't remember when I had done that for more than half a day. My subjects were lined up inexorably, reminding me more and more of how little time I had left in life, which did not permit me to take any breaks. Ordinarily, I started working on a new book the day after I finished the old one; I couldn't hold out longer without writing, without engaging in the struggle with words. That is how the biggest part of my life passed by, I had hardly noticed it. Now I suddenly did not want to do anything other than sit out on the balcony and feel the silent movement of the air on my skin and look at the sky-blue lake. Toward evening, when the heat died down, I took long strolls with my Nordic walking sticks along the water's edge, where huge swarms of mosquitos attacked me in the lonely wetlands. On the way home I bought my dinner from the fisherman, who sold fresh whitefish and char from the lake.

The inner German border used to run through the Schaalsee. Part of the lake belonged to Mecklenburg, the other part to Schleswig-Holstein. A few kilometers away you now drove past a sign that said, *Germany and Europe were divided at this place until November 18, 1989, at 16:00*. In what used to be a closed border zone on the east side, flora and fauna had had more than forty years to thrive on their own, almost untouched by the human species, which only appeared here in the form of border guards. After reunification, this wild landscape was designated as a protected area and added to UNESCO's list of international biosphere reserves: a managed wilderness that had now attracted Hamburg's eco-elite. For the environmentally aware city people who moved here, or drove here on the weekends in their RVs, there were health food stores, health food restaurants, and regular health food markets. For fifty euros, you could buy a share for the protection of cranes, and in the town, there was a so-called Future Center for Humans and Nature. The old, established East German residents had become strangers, for the most part you only met them at Penny and Lidl.[1] They were onlookers to their own world, living in renovated little houses from the GDR[2].

The lake was the only thing I could see from the huge panorama window of my house. I felt a little tipsy all day from staring at the blue water that seemed bottomless to me; limitless cool depths, in which you would never cease sinking and drinking. From far away, the shouts and laughter of the children who splashed about in the water. Summer vacation, the sounds and smells, the splendor of a summer in childhood that you thought would never end. Luckily, motorboats were forbidden; the lake belonged to the many waterfowl that lived here. You only occasionally saw a rowboat or a dinghy with a small white sail drifting past. Hundreds of swallows sailed in the air, sometimes flying so low that they almost grazed me with the sharp tips of their wings while I sat with a book on the balcony and read or looked out at the water, countless mirrors dancing on its surface and casting silver reflections at each other. Wild geese flew across the sky in geometric patterns, as though tied together by an invisible thread; swifts took turns chasing each other, staging furious, bizarre games in the air. The waterfowl began their concert at twilight: the busy babbling of the ducks, the screeching of the whooper swans, and the excited trumpeting of the cranes, who came in from the fields where they feasted to gather on the lake for the night. Sometimes a sea eagle appeared, gliding motionlessly above the water with his powerful wings stretched out wide, the king of the lake, the terror of the fish and other lake dwellers. Once, someone told me that they watched from the lake shore as a sea eagle tore a crane apart. It was winter, and the cranes were standing up, asleep in the shallow water where they were safe from their enemies. One of them had frozen, its legs in the lake. He could not escape when the eagle swooped down on him, and he was torn to pieces, caught in the ice.

I loved this summer on the lake so much that I could not sleep. Sometimes I sat out on the balcony all night, bathing in the cool air, watching the line of light that the moon cast onto the dark water. I could not get enough of the silence, which was only occasionally interrupted by a soft, drowsy sound from one of the waterfowl hidden in the reeds.

I had never seen sunrises like those on this lake before. They announced their arrival on the horizon soon after 3 a.m., initially as a barely perceptible rosy tint to the sky above the water, then transforming increasingly into an unbelievably beautiful orgy of light. I was amazed that everyone else was asleep, that no one else seemed to attend these cosmic performances. The sky burned in every color from light green to gold, purple and flaming red, something different every day, something new: theaters of light, surreal paintings, that the sun cast onto the sky, and whose minute-by-minute transformations I followed on my balcony, as though from a loggia somewhere in the universe. I was deafened by the panicked sounding cries of the waterfowl, as though they were expecting an apocalypse, some event that was beyond human comprehension and had never occurred before. The colors intensified, exploded, and then began to fade, to quietly die out, to dissolve more and more into the blinding white light that gradually flowed over the lake. The animals grew quiet, the danger had passed, and a long, sweltering summer day began. I lifted myself out of the large old chair that I had pushed out onto the balcony, brushed my teeth, and went to my west-facing bedroom, where I had hung a bright awning to protect myself from the light and the heat. Even in sleep, I still heard the silence and dreamed all sorts of lucid, epic dreams. When I woke up around noon, I jumped out of bed right away and ran to the window in the other room in my nightdress in order to finally see the shining blue lake again.

Almost a week had passed since I sent my search query to Azov's Greeks. I had already forgotten about it when I received an email with unreadable characters in the sender line. I received many emails from Russians, but this time my email program did not recognize the Cyrillic letters. Someone named Konstantin with a Greek last name asked me to provide him with more details about my mother. He would try to help me, but to do this he needed a bit more information about her.

I had never made so much progress in my search. A man in Mariupol was ready to help me if I provided more information about my mother, and he apparently had the means to do so. Only I couldn't give him this information because I had already shared everything I knew. For some reason I felt ashamed to know so little about my own mother, as though it were a sign of poverty and disgrace. And at the same time, it was as though I had just found out something new about her. It seemed as though I could look at Mariupol with this stranger's eyes, as though he were a former neighbor of my mother's, who walked by her house every day and took me with him on streets that she once walked down, who saw houses, trees and places that she had once seen, the Sea of Azov and the Greek taverns, which perhaps still existed. In reality, there was not much left of the Mariupol that she had once inhabited. Germany's Wehrmacht had reduced most of it to rubble during the war. I thanked Konstantin with the Greek last name, who had been so kind and helpful, and sent my greetings to Mariupol. My mother, after this latest disappointment, sank eternally and forever into darkness, or so I believed.

In truth, it was not entirely by chance that I had asked the Russian-language search engine to find her name just then. I had entertained the idea of writing about my mother's life for a long time, especially the woman she had been in Ukraine and in the German labor camp before I was born. The only problem was that I knew next to nothing about this woman. She never spoke about her time as a forced laborer, and neither did my father, at least I could not remember anything about it. A few vague will-o'-the-wisps in my mind were all I could recall from what she told me about her life in Ukraine. I could only try to write a fictional biography, supported by the well-known facts and the historiography from the places and the time in which my mother had lived. For many years, I searched in vain for a book from a former forced laborer that I could use to guide my own writing. Concentration camp survivors had written world famous literature, books on the Holocaust filled entire libraries, but the non-Jewish forced laborers who had survived destruction through work were silent. Millions had been dragged to the Third Reich. Companies, businesses, workshops, farms, and private households across the entire country helped themselves as they saw fit to the contingent of imported slave laborers; the policy was maximum exploitation at minimum cost. They had to do the work of the German men who were on the front lines, under inhuman conditions that were often similar to those in the concentration camps. The villages and cities in their native lands were laid to waste, their families murdered. The number of men and women who were abducted and driven to death in the German war economy remains unknown to this day, but even decades after the end of the war, there were only brief, isolated reports in church circulars or Sunday newspapers about this crime against six to twenty-seven million forced laborers (the figures vary dramatically among different sources). They were mostly mentioned in passing together with the Jews, under the "also rans," as marginalia, an appendage to the Holocaust.

For most of my life I did not even know that I was the child of forced laborers. No one told me, not my parents, and not German society, where national memory did not include the large-scale phenomenon of forced labor. For decades, I did not know anything about my own life. I had no idea who all of the people were that lived together with us in various postwar ghettos and how they came to Germany: all of the Romanians, Czechs, Poles, Bulgarians, Yugoslavs, Hungarians, Latvians, Lithuanians, Azerbaijanis, and many others, who somehow managed to communicate with each other despite a Babylonian confusion of languages. I only knew that I belonged to a type of human refuse, to some sort of garbage that was left over from the war.

In the German school, we were taught that the Russians had invaded Germany, destroyed everything, and seized half of the country. I sat in the last row next to Inge Krabbes, who everyone also shunned, even though she was a German, because she smelled and wore filthy clothes. The teacher in the front at the lectern told us how the Russians burned her fiancé's eyes out with glowing coals and crushed small children with their boots. All heads turned to me, even Inge Krabbes moved away from me a bit, and I knew that the chase would begin again after school.

It had been a long time since my lies were of any help to me; I was not only counted as one of the Russian barbarians, but I had long since been exposed as a fraud. To improve my standing in the eyes of the German children, I had told them my parents, of whom I was so ashamed, were not my actual parents at all—they had found me in a roadside ditch while fleeing from Russia and taken me with them. In reality, I came from a wealthy noble Russian family that owned castles and estates, though I neglected to mention how I, as the child of nobility, wound up in the ditch. But for a day or for a few hours I was a misjudged, mysterious creature, who enjoyed the stunned admiration of the German children. Naturally, at some point, they saw through me, and then they persecuted me all the more, the small avengers of the vanished Third Reich, the children of the German war widows and Nazi fathers; when they pursued me, they pursued all Russians. I was the embodiment of the Communists and Bolsheviks, the Slavic *untermenschen*; I was the embodiment of the global enemy, who had defeated them in the war. And I ran, ran for my life. I did not want to die like Jemila, the Yugoslavs' little daughter, who the German children also chased and, one day, pushed into the Regnitz, where she drowned. I ran, and drew a wave of war cries along with me, but I was a practiced sprinter and by then I did not even get stitches anymore, so that I was mostly able to shake off my persecutors. I only had to reach the gravel pit which marked the border between the German world and ours. Behind the gravel pit, our territory began, our terra incognita, where no German had ever set foot except for the police and the mail carriers. German children were also afraid to go there. In front of the gravel pit, a dirt path split off from the asphalt road that led to the "houses." I did not know why the Germans called our stone apartment blocks like that, houses; maybe it was the distinction between us and the gypsies, who lived even further away in wooden barracks. They were one step below us and aroused a similar feeling of horror in me as we probably triggered in the Germans.

Once I had crossed the magic border I was safe. Around the bend, where my pursuers could no longer see me, I let myself fall into the grass and waited until my racing heart had calmed down, until I could breathe again. On this day I had made it, and I was not thinking about the next one yet. I dawdled for as long as I could, roamed around in the river meadow, skipped flat stones over the surface of the Regnitz, stuffed sorrel into my mouth and gnawed off the raw field corncobs which I stole. I never wanted to go home. I wanted to get away, always just away, ever since I could think. For my entire childhood I only waited to grow up, so that I could finally get away. I wanted to get out of the German school, out of the houses, away from my parents, away from everything that defined me and struck me as a mistake, in which I was trapped. Even if I could have known who my parents and all the other people were, to whom I belonged, I would not have wanted to know. It did not interest me, nothing less than that; I had nothing to do with it. I only wanted to get away, just out, to leave everything behind forever, to finally break free to my own and actual life, which was waiting for me somewhere out in the world.

I remember my first conscious image of my mother: I am about four years old; we are living in the storage shed of an iron works where my parents have found temporary asylum in Germany. I am forbidden under threat of punishment from leaving the factory grounds, but even then, I always try to escape. Behind the factory grounds, on broad Leyher Street, another, unknown world begins. There are stores there, a streetcar; I don't remember any war ruins, only houses that seem like palaces to me, houses of stone with big heavy doors and high windows with curtains hanging in them. And there is a meadow with wild pear trees. I have never eaten pears; I want to know what they taste like. But I am too small, I can't reach the branches from which the fruits hang. I try it with a stone which I throw into the tree. It ricochets off a branch and shoots back down on me, a boomerang that knocks a hole into my face, missing my left eye by a hair's width. I no longer know how I got home; I only remember that I am standing on the factory grounds, and I don't have the courage to enter our dwelling. Warm blood runs over my face and drips onto my dress. My mother is behind the shed's open window. Her head is bent over a washboard, and she is scrubbing the laundry, a dark strand of hair falls onto her face. She raises her head and sees me. And I see her, an image, which is my first memory of her. She starts with a cry, the rest consists only of her eyes. Eyes which hold a horror that will come to embody her for me. A horror from far away, from far beyond me, incomprehensible, bottomless. The horror that she means when she says, "If you had seen what I have seen." Over and over, the refrain of my childhood, "If you had seen what I have seen."

I have two photos of her which she brought from Ukraine, portraits, taken in a studio. In one, she is a young girl of about eighteen; next to her is a tender woman with white hair whom I do not know. My very thin, probably undernourished mother is wearing a simple summer dress, her thick, black hair is cut in the pageboy style, which was probably in fashion at the time. Apparently the photographer wanted to bring his artistic skills to bear by depicting her somewhat enigmatically, because the left side of her face is darkened by a shadow. She looks like a child, but the innocence and defenselessness in her face are combined with a terrible knowledge. It is hard to believe that a person of such fragility could endure such knowledge—as though a one-ton weight were hung from a thread. The white-haired woman next to her has something masculine about her, despite her tenderness, judging by her age she could be my mother's grandmother. A grey dress with a white lace collar, upright posture, severe, on her face the pride of the humiliated and insulted. It must be around 1938, the height of Stalin's Terror, hunger and fear.

In the second photo my mother is probably a bit older, maybe this picture was taken during the war, shortly before her deportation. Here her eyes look entirely inward, onto some distant, inscrutable landscape; the gloom in her features mixes with a hint of a smile. Her face is framed by a headscarf in the Ukrainian folk style, which she has thrown loosely around her head. Maybe she went to the photographer to have a final picture made of herself in Ukraine, a souvenir photo.

"What a beautiful woman," everyone who sees this old black and white picture says. Even in my childhood, my mother's beauty was legendary. "What a beautiful woman," I always heard people say. And "What an unhappy woman." With my mother, beauty and misery seemed to belong together, to give rise to each other in a mysterious way.

There is also a third photo from Ukraine in my archive. It depicts a well-dressed older gentleman with intelligent, melancholy eyes, a high forehead, and a short, graying beard. He stands behind two seated women, one in a severe, high-necked dress, with the face of an intellectual and a pince-nez on her nose. The younger one is in a white blouse, girlishly shy, a look of futility in her eyes. On the back it says, "Grandfather and two acquaintances" in my mother's handwriting. I don't know whose grandfather she means, mine, or my mother's. I don't know why she has labeled this photo in German, though she was always opposed to speaking German with me and stubbornly spoke Russian.

In addition to these three photos, I also possessed the two aforementioned official documents. In order to read my parent's wedding certificate, I have to hold the postcard-size piece of paper up to a mirror. It is a mysterious copy with backward white handwriting on a black background. In the mirror I can read that my mother, Evgenia Yakovlevna Ivashchenko, married my father in Mariupol on July 28, 1943. The document is in Ukrainian and the stamp is faded, but the German word "Standesamt"[3] can be seen clearly. I stumble over this word every time. What did the Germans lose at the Mariupol registry office? A detail from the daily life of the occupation, which I find very difficult to imagine. It always seems like a miracle to me that this nondescript document survived not only war, deportation, the labor camp, and the subsequent odyssey through the postwar camps, but also my later relocations, of which I have completed more than a few. A more than seventy-year-old, apparently indestructible, piece of evidence from a fairly short and disastrous marriage.

My mother's German employment card is missing, it may have crumbled into dust at some point in a dark, airless corner of my desk, but I know that except for the name, it was identical to my father's, issued on August 8, 1944, in Leipzig, which still survives. A soap-bar sized piece of paper, folded twice, yellowed and worn. Name, date of birth, my father's place of birth, which is called Kamyshin, but was transformed into Chanushin on the way from his mouth to the German typist's ear. It reads as follows:

Citizenship: unresolved, Eastern worker
Country of Origin: Occupied Eastern territories
District: Marienpol
Resident:—
Employment: unskilled metal worker

Place of Employment: ATG Maschinenbau GmbH
Leipzig W 32, Schönauer Str. 101
Employed since 5.14.44

Two stamps with the imperial eagle, one from the police headquarters, one from the Leipzig employment office, in addition a photo of my father with a number affixed to the lapel of his suit. On the back, two fingerprints, left index finger, right index finger. Underneath: *This employment card only authorizes employment with the designated plant manager and is invalid upon departure from this workplace. The bearer must have the employment card in his possession at all times. Valid until further notice. Subject to revocation.*

My entire family inheritance consisted of these two historic documents, the marriage certificate and the employment certificate, the three black and white photos and an old icon which my mother took with her in her bundle on the long journey. The icon, hand painted on a gold background, showed a multitude of the most important Russian-Orthodox saints. Every detail was elaborated so skillfully that you could even see the saints' fingernails.

If I remember anything precisely, then it is how my mother spoke about her family's poverty in Ukraine, the constant hunger. In my memory, the fear of Stalin and poverty were the things that dominated her life in Ukraine. But how was it possible to reconcile the poverty with the valuable icon that she had brought with her? It had also miraculously survived deportation and the labor camp, it was not lost on the way, was not damaged, and no one took it from my mother or stole it. In each of our barracks, it hung in the corner, silently and secretively shimmering. I had sent my most passionate childhood prayers to it, the desperate pleas for my mother's life when she said goodbye to me and my sister once again and lay down to die. Now the icon hung in my Berlin apartment above an old Catholic church pew, which I had once found in an attic. It was probably the most valuable thing that I had ever owned.

I could only add a few hazy, uncertain memories to this meagre archive, a child's memories which perhaps were not memories at all anymore but mere foam left behind by time's decades-long fermentation process in my mind:

I found the Russian word *advokat* inside myself—my mother's father was apparently such a person. She always worried about him; he had heart disease, and when she was taken out of class one day at school, she knew right away that he had died.

I found the name "De Martino"—apparently this was my mother's mother's name. She was a woman from a wealthy Italian family; I did not know what could have brought them to Ukraine in the last century, or the century before that. The family fortune was explained by the words "coal business," which had settled in my mind next to the name "De Martino."

I found the name Medvezhya Gora, or Bear Mountain—in my memory this was the name of the place where my mother's sister had been exiled. I did not know anything more about her. My mind had only saved the fact that one day my mother's mother left for Medvezhya Gora to visit her daughter in the camp. During this time, World War II broke out, and she never came back. That seemed to be the greatest catastrophe in my mother's life: that she lost her mother, that she did not know what happened to her—if she was still alive or if she had found her death in a hail of German bombs.

I also found a brother, who had apparently been a famous opera singer and who was bound to my mother through an especially fervent love. She cried almost as many tears for him as she had for my mother.

At bottom, I believed almost nothing of this. The wealthy Italian family, a grandfather, who had been a lawyer, the famous opera singer, even the coal business was suspiciously similar to my childhood longing for a respectable background, which, when seen from my perspective at that age, a coal trader possessed. The opera singer probably came from a later time, when, still just a girl, I discovered opera completely by surprise and dreamed up an uncle who sang my favorite arias from Bellini and

Handel. And my aunt's exile probably originated in my childish longing for tragic significance, or maybe just from the fear-inducing words "Bear Mountain," which I may have heard from my mother in an entirely different context, perhaps in one of the many fairy tales that she told me.

I really only remember one of my mother's stories clearly, about a friend of hers. She spoke about her, time and again, with that look of horror in her eyes which I so dreaded. The Nazis hunted the Jews in Mariupol too, during two days in October 1941 alone, eight thousand Jews were shot in the city. What reached its peak at Babi Yar happened everywhere in Ukraine, with its large Jewish population. My mother's friend was Jewish as well, and one day she was also seized. She was forced to dig a long ditch together with the other Jews and then stand with her back to the German machine guns on the edge of the ditch. She managed to forestall the bullet that was supposed to hit her by dropping into the ditch a second before it came. She waited until it was dark and worked her way out from the pile of corpses that she was buried under and ran to my mother. Covered in blood, she stood at her door.

For a long time, I had racked my brains over my mother's relationship to the German occupiers during the war. In those days, the entire population of the occupied territories had to work for the Germans; there was no alternative. Only those who worked received ration cards, and no one could survive without them. But my mother, who was only twenty-one when the war began, had a special job. A future forced laborer herself, she, of all people, worked for the German employment office that recruited forced laborers and transported them to Germany. It was as though she had been tasked with deporting herself. Moreover, the employment offices were essential institutions of power and control for the German occupiers. Everyone had to register there; no one could avoid the German employment offices. What sort of assignments could my mother have had there? Did she stand with the Germans because she saw them as liberators who would defeat Stalin's regime? Did she work at the employment office out of conviction, or was she merely a random cog in the German war machine? Was she deported in the end just like all the others, or did she voluntarily register for a transport? Was she a victim of the omnipresent propaganda that promised a paradise in Germany to gullible and impoverished Soviet citizens? Did she still believe this propaganda in 1944, the year she was deported, when everyone already knew what awaited those who were seized every day by the thousands and brought to Germany in freight cars? No small number had already come back by this time, sick, physically and mentally destroyed by the brutal working and living conditions, slave laborers who were no longer fit to work, whom the Nazis could no longer use. Maybe my mother, if she had really gone voluntarily, knew all of this, but had no choice. When it became clear that the Red Army would reconquer Mariupol, escape was her only option since anyone who worked at the German employment office would probably have been shot on the spot as a collaborator and a traitor to the fatherland. And possibly, my father would have had even more profound reasons than she did for leaving the Soviet Union. Maybe she simply followed him, a man who at that time was her protector, the only one she could turn to when she was in trouble. She was probably much too young, too inexperienced and distraught to take decisions of such significance, to oppose the forces of her place and time.

Now, during this magical summer by the lake, I became aware, with increasing horror, of what I had gotten myself into. My first book, which I published decades ago, was a sort of attempt at an autobiography, but at that time I knew nothing of my own history, I did not know my biography and its context. My mother had always remained an internal character for me, part of a vague CV of my private life that established itself in the approximate; I had concocted it beyond political and historical contexts, in a no man's land where I was a rootless individual of unknown origin. It was not until much later that I began to understand who my parents were and what sort of "material" they had left behind for me. Now I was facing the task of making up for what I had missed, of saying in maybe a last book what I should have said in my first. Only I still knew next to nothing about my mother's life before I was born, and absolutely nothing about her time in a German labor camp. I stood empty handed, with only the historiography and my imagination, which was not equal to the depths of the subject.

When the so-called "eastern workers" (a term coined by Hermann Göring)[4] began to submit their long-delayed compensation claims in the 1990s, the topic shifted into the limelight, or at least the half-light, of the German public at large. Now there were nonfiction books, reports, and documentaries about forced labor in the Third Reich; I could read and educate myself. By then, I had even found the literary voice I had long sought in vain; it was a book by Vitaly Semin called *Zum Unterschied ein Zeichen* in the German translation that appeared in the 1970s.[5] In the book, the Russian author tells the story of a teenager who had been abducted from Rostov-on-Don and only survived forced labor in Germany because he was convinced that what he saw and was forced to experience must not die with him, that he was obligated to bear witness for future generations. In the labor camp, he writes, it was better than in the death camps, though only insofar as you were not immediately murdered, but slowly destroyed through an inhuman workload, hunger, beatings, constant harassment, and lack of medical care.

I was surprised to find out that the book's translator was Alexander Kaempfe; in the 1970s, I had been connected to him by a friendship. He often read parts of his translations to me, and it was quite possible that he read to me from Vitaly Semin and that I didn't remember it simply because at that time, I did not know that it was a book about my parents, that they also once wore *a distinguishing mark*, a patch with the word "OST," which differentiated them from the racially higher-ranking Western European forced laborers.

The longer I researched, the more atrocities I came across that hardly anyone seemed to have heard about up to now. I was not the only one who was in many ways ignorant; among my German friends, whom I considered to be enlightened people with a sense of history, no one knew how many Nazi camps once existed on the territory of the German Reich. Some thought that there were twenty, others two hundred, a few estimated that there were two thousand. According to a study by the Holocaust Memorial Museum in Washington, DC, the figure ran to 42,500, not including the small and secondary camps. Thirty thousand of them were labor camps. In an interview that appeared in *Die Zeit* on March 4, 2013,[6] the American historian Geoffrey Megargee, who contributed to the study, noted: The shocking number of camps confirms that nearly all Germans knew about their existence, even if they did not grasp the scale of the system that stood behind it, or if they did not know about the conditions that existed in the camps in every case. It was the old story: no one knew anything. Even though the entire country, covered with more than 42,500 camps, must have been one single Gulag.

I sank ever deeper into world history, into the ghostly tragedies of the twentieth century. Reports about forced labor in the Third Reich were full of blind spots, inconsistences, and contradictions. My topic slipped noticeably out of my control and became too much for me to handle. Was it not anyhow already too late, I asked myself, would I still be breathing long enough to do justice to this powerful material? And were there even words for all of that, words for the life of my mother, forgotten in anonymity, her fate representing millions of others?

I had long since forgotten about the Azov's Greeks when once again an email reached me with the strange hieroglyphics in the return address which Konstantin with the Greek last name hid behind. I read the following:

> Dear Natalia Nikolaevna,
> After checking one more time I have come to the conclusion that it is highly likely that the Evgenia Yakovlevna Ivashchenko listed in our archives is your mother. Let me begin in the distant past. In the nineteenth century, a wealthy Ukrainian landholder from the Voivodeship of Chernigov,[7] a nobleman by the name of Epifan Yakovlevich Ivashchenko,

lived in Mariupol. That was your great-grandfather. He was probably one of the first non-Greeks that settled in Mariupol at that time; back then, it was still a small merchant city on the Black Sea with barely five thousand inhabitants. He bought a house on Mitropolitskaya Street for himself and his family, became a city councilor, shipowner, and director of the port customs agency. Over the course of time, he acquired a significant amount of property in the city, founded several businesses, and was held in great esteem. He married one Anna von Ehrenstreit, about whom we only know that she was descended from Baltic landed gentry and, according to the parish register, that she lived from 1845 to 1908.

Your great-grandparents had six children, two boys and four girls. The oldest son was Yakov, your grandfather, your mother's father. His younger brother Leonid died at the young age of twenty-six from epilepsy, according to the parish register. We don't know anything about the sisters Elena and Natalia, but we know that Olga, the third sister, married the famous psychologist Georgy Chelpanov, who had Greek roots. This also explains why not only your mother's name but also information about all of Chelpanov's relatives by marriage landed in our archive. Your grandfather's fourth sister, your great-aunt Valentina, belonged to the crème de la crème of the Mariupol intelligentsia; she is still well known in the city today. You can read more about her in the attached article.

Unfortunately, we don't know anything about your grandmother, only that her name was Matilda Josefovna. Your mother's sister's name was Lidia, and she was born in 1911, according to the parish register. Her brother was named Sergey; he entered the world in 1915. He was an opera singer; during the war, he sang at the front and was awarded a medal. You can also find a digital version of the certificate in the attachment.

Recently, a book about Georgy Chelpanov appeared in which his wife's family is mentioned numerous times. Your great-aunt Olga apparently suffered from a mental illness and jumped out of a window in Moscow when she was forty-three years old. We will ask the author of the book for a copy for you.

> Your mother's siblings are presumably no longer alive. But it will also not be easy to find their descendants, especially since the name Ivashchenko is extremely common and we don't know any more about your Aunt Lidia than her birth name. Searching for women is always much more difficult if you don't know the husband's name. Therefore, I suggest that we first concentrate our search on your Uncle Sergey, or rather his descendants. To start with, we could contact the producers of the television program *Wait for Me*. It is a very well known show where people search for their relatives that is broadcast in Russia as well as Ukraine.

I did not understand what I was reading. Who was this Konstantin? Some sort of internet-apparition, a lunatic, a gambler? Now that it was back in fashion in Russia to have at least a drop of blue blood in your own veins, did he want to bait me with noble ancestors so that he could send me more installments of his "knowledge" after an advance payment? To me it seemed completely out of the question that my mother came from the background that he described, from the upper classes. The woman I knew did not even belong to the lowest class, to say nothing of the upper classes. She was outside all classes, a Slavic *untermensch*, a poor, wretched figure at whom the man on the street threw stones. If she had ever merely hinted at her noble origins, then I would have greedily snatched it up in my frustrated, childish desire for a higher social standing. It was as though the author of the email had read into the delusions of my childhood, as though he was reciting the tall tales I had told back then. Apparently, I was dealing with a particularly mysterious flower in the digital jungle.

I opened the first attachment and read the headline of an article in boldface: "Valentina Epifanovna Ostoslavskaya—a daughter of our city who has not been forgotten." Beneath it, an oval, medallion-shaped portrait photo of a woman. It took my breath away. I knew this woman, I had known her ever since I could think. She was pictured on the photo printed on thick paper that lay in my desk drawer and on the back of which my mother had written, "Grandfather and two friends." The woman, who now stared at me from my screen, was a bit younger and a bit thinner, but it was quite obviously the same face: an intellectual with high cheekbones, stern features, and a somewhat arrogant mouth. In this photo, she also wore a dark, high-necked dress and a pince-nez on her nose.

It seemed to me that the lake was trembling outside my window. Everything around me was suddenly new and strange. I stared at the face of the woman on my screen, and slowly, as though in slow motion, it dawned on me what it meant. This photo was the unbelievable, phantasmagoric proof that the Evgenia Yakovlevna Ivashchenko whom I stumbled onto in the Azov's Greeks forum was truly my mother. And that woman in the photo who looked so familiar to me, whom my mother had called a friend, was in reality her aunt, a sister of her father's.

Breathless, I skimmed the article. I found out that Valentina Epifanovna, born in 1870, had founded a private lycée for girls from poor families. All of her life she fought for social justice, it said, and thanks to her commitment countless Mariupol girls were able to gain access to higher education and escape a life of ignorance and poverty. Spiritually, she was close to her brother Yakov, my mother's father, who studied law and history and had already worked with the Bolsheviks in the underground as a student. When he was twenty-three, he was arrested by the czar's secret police and exiled to Siberia for twenty years.

Valentina Epifanovna, my mother's aunt, was married to Vasily Ostoslavskiy, a man from an extraordinarily wealthy Russian noble family, which was well known for its erudition, open-mindedness, and liberalism. After the revolution, so it said, this man died from hunger, together with millions of others who lost their lives in the disastrous famine in Ukraine. Valentina's lycée burned down during the civil war, and she died at the age of forty-eight from the Spanish flu, which was raging at the time. Her son, Ivan Ostoslavskiy, became a famous aerodynamics expert, whose books were required reading for students of flight and space technology across the entire Soviet Union. A photo showed an older man who looked like a Saint Bernard, with coarse facial features and bright, flashing eyes. Valentina's daughter, Irina Ostoslavskaya, made it all the way to deputy minister of public education, but was arrested as an enemy of the people under Stalin and exiled to Siberia.

And I also found out something else. My great-grandfather, Epifan, the major landholder from the Voivodeship of Chernigov, was reported to have gradually become addicted to alcohol and lost his entire fortune. At some point, so the story goes, he disappeared without a trace and left his wife, Anna von Ehrenstreit, behind with their six children, alone and destitute. One rumor holds that he fled to India on one of the cargo ships that once belonged to him.

It seemed to me that I needed two heads in order to grasp everything, to understand it. In my experience so far, the truth always turned out to be a lie; now, the ridiculous thing was that the lies I told in my childhood turned out, at their core, to be true.

My mother's dramatic fall, which I had never suspected, shook me the most. Why had she never spoken about her background before, never said a single word about it? Why did she even deny her relationship to her Aunt Valentina and call her a friend? In my eyes, my mother was always a woman who came from the people, from a poor background. Her true origins, which still seemed like an inscrutable invention to me, lent an entirely new, and incomprehensible, dimension of brutality to her fate.

My fingers numb, I opened the second attachment which arrived with the email from Azov's Greeks. A digital copy of a weather-beaten, foxed document appeared on my monitor; I had to enlarge it several times before I could decipher the deeply faded Russian typescript. I read the following:

> The Order of the Red Star is hereby awarded to Ivashchenko, Sergey Yakovlevich, born in 1915 in Mariupol, party member, in the Red Army since 1939, sergeant, on the front from the first days of the war, called up from Kyiv, not wounded.

As a soloist in the Red Banner ensemble, Comrade Ivashchenko rendered a great service with classical Russian music, performing arias from Russian operas for soldiers and officers on the front. "The Song of India" from Rimsky-Korsakov's opera *Sadko* and the "Aria of Galitsky" from the opera *Prince Konstantin* by Alexander Borodin became favorite melodies in the units and formations for which Comrade Ivashchenko performed.[8] He was not frightened by any dangers or tribulations, and he continued his performances under the most adverse circumstances, occasionally under mortal danger. His recitals were always of the highest artistic quality, and the soldiers at the front loved and revered him for this. The comrade distinguished himself through his exemplary work ethic and discipline; he was loyal to the party of Lenin and Stalin and selflessly served his socialist homeland. He was previously awarded the medal of merit "For the Defense of Stalingrad." With this, the Soviet government awards him the Order of the Red Star.
Director of the Department for Press,
Propaganda, and Political Agitation.
Colonel B.F. Prokofiev

I spent several days in a state of shock. I did what I always did; I sat outside on the balcony, I walked along the lake, I cooked something to eat, but that was not me—I watched a stranger going about her daily routine. I watched her as she stared at a wall for hours, lost in thought, or suddenly broke out into laughter for no reason at all. It went so far that I suddenly began to gesticulate to unseen people in internal conversations that I could not understand, contradicting them furiously or nodding in agreement. An outside observer would have taken me for a lunatic.

I read Konstantin's email and the attachments over and over; I had to keep reassuring myself that I was not dreaming. My eyes lingered on my grandmother's name with astonishment. That's how she had been called, my mother's mother: Matilda Josefovna. One Matilda, whose father was named Josef. It was a woman's name that I had never heard before in Russian. Konstantin had access to a digitalized parish register from Mariupol; he informed me that Matilda Josefovna's religious affiliation was listed as Roman Catholic. Taken together with the name Matilda, this was a clear indication of my mother's Italian origins, particularly as there was some evidence that her patronymic, derived from the name Josef, was the Russified form of Giuseppe. But there was no room in my consciousness for any of this, there was too much raining down on me at once.

It seemed to me that by finding the name of my mother's mother, I had found her. Matilda Josefovna, the woman for whom my mother had cried so many tears, who had made her way on the long journey to her exiled daughter Lidia and never returned. It seemed as though my discovery had annulled part of my mother's misfortune, which survived in the pain she felt because of her long-lost mother, and contributed to the fact that she could no longer live. Again and again, I imagined running to my mother and delivering the news: Matilda Josefovna, your mother, I have found her again; Matilda, do you recognize her? I have really found her; here she is, look . . .

The magic of names. My mother's siblings had suddenly become real people. Lidia and Sergey. It was completely obvious to me that they could only have had these names and no others; I was surprised that I did not think of them myself. Lidia and Sergey, two names that sounded like a natural complement to my mother's name. My Aunt Lidia and my Uncle Sergey. I read Sergey's certificate again and again, the proof that he was awarded the Order of the Red Star; I searched for clues about his life, which also would have been clues to my mother's life.

Every time I thought about what my imagined uncle, the opera singer, was like, I heard a tenor who sang such radiant arias as "Lunge da Lei" or "Care Selve," but the parts mentioned in the certificate revealed that he had been a bass. Immediately, an entirely different man appeared in front of my inner eye, with a massive, corpulent stature and a dark, voluminous voice. A lead singer, a party member, a soloist in an ensemble called the Red Banner. The certificate took away the glow from the uncle that opera singers held for me. Apparently, he received the state order more for his loyalty to the party line and for being an exemplary Soviet citizen than for his achievements as a singer. Konstantin considered it highly unusual that someone from a noble family would be admitted into the CPSU in those days and decorated with a state order;[9] in his opinion it was easier for a camel to pass through the eye of a needle. Who, then, was my mother's brother? What did he do to pass through the eye of a needle? As his sister Lidia was exiled to a prison camp and therefore undoubtedly counted as an enemy of the people, the eye of the needle must have been twice as narrow for Sergey. And how was it possible that my mother had loved her brother with such fervor, although the CPSU, as I know for certain, was the embodiment of evil to her? If I remember anything precisely, then it is my parents' hatred for Soviet authority, for Stalin; this hatred was probably the main thing they had in common. My mother never lost her fear of the long arm of the regime, from which, in her eyes, you were never safe anywhere on earth. The Soviets were to blame for the fiasco of her life, they had killed an uncountable number of people, they had destroyed her homeland and forced her to live in a foreign country.

So now it had turned out that her father had also been a socialist, one of the first Bolsheviks, who was sent into exile for twenty years by the czarist regime for his political convictions. My confusion grew. What sort of family was it? My mother's father a Bolshevik revolutionary who had been exiled for many years, her brother a decorated party member, she and her sister renegades, one exiled to a Soviet labor camp, the other a forced laborer with the German war enemy, a potential collaborator. Mustn't a chasm have divided the family? How could my mother have hated the Soviet authorities at the same time that she loved a father and a brother who had both offered their services to this power?

My image of my mother's family, as vague as it had been, had turned out to be entirely unreal and mistaken. Now I knew less than ever. I only knew that my mother was someone completely different from the person I had always assumed her to be, and that I was not the person I thought I was.

That her father had studied history and law matched the word *lawyer* in my memory, although I had always associated this word with an upstanding bourgeois gentleman who sat in his cabinet all day, drank tea from a samovar, received clients, and studied court records with a lorgnette. Twenty years in exile changed my image of this "gentleman" tremendously. Apparently he had not been a respectable student who crammed paragraphs and prepared for his professional career, but a young rebel who agitated in the Bolshevik underground, the brother of a woman who had opened a lycée for girls from poor families—a brother and sister who stood for the fight for social justice, for solidarity with the masses enserfed by the czarist regime, for the abolition of their own aristocratic class. My grandfather paid a heavy price for this, twenty years somewhere in the Siberian wilderness, most likely with much of his vitality. A man with a terrible fate, who could not have had anything in common with the imagined lawyer of my childhood.

According to the church register, he was born in 1864. If he had been exiled at the age of twenty-three, he was not released until 1907, at forty-three. And my mother was not born for another thirteen years, when he was already fifty-six. It was a conspicuous parallel between me and her: I had also had an old father, who was twenty years older than my mother. And her father, like mine, must also have been married to a considerably younger woman, or else my mother could not have been born. After he returned from Siberia, he had probably married Matilda Josefovna, who was still young at the time; four years later, Lidia was born, my mother's sister, and four years after that, Sergey, her brother. My mother was the youngest of the three siblings, a late arrival, perhaps the favorite of the nest. Although at that time, in the year 1920, there could not have been a nest anymore; the family must have long since been dispossessed and had probably suffered from serious reprisals.

My mother's siblings had at least experienced the final years before the revolution, for a short time they had enjoyed the privileges of their background. My mother, on the other hand, only knew the destruction of that from which she had never benefited herself. She was born right in the middle of the civil war, the Terror, the hunger, and the persecution. This defined Ukraine at the beginning and at the end of her time in the country, she had never known anything else there.

Little by little, I understood why she had never mentioned her background. During her time in the Soviet Union, there was nothing worse than being a member of the nobility. It was an offense, a hereditary crime, the worst affront, grounds for murder. And probably fear mixed with contempt and shame inside her, because she gradually began to believe that people like her were an inferior societal offshoot with no right to exist, consigned to the dustbin of history. Germany was not the first place where she had been labeled an *untermensch*, she had already been one in Ukraine; my poor, tiny, crazy mother, who had emerged from the deepest darkness of the bloody twentieth century.

I also considered another possibility. No one had told her who she was; it was kept from her in order to protect her. Maybe, like me, she had not known what her roots were for her entire life. Maybe she did not even know the world of her ancestors from hearsay because they had eliminated listening and speaking in Soviet Ukraine, and because, already in childhood, her social class had been so thoroughly eradicated that she no longer existed in the society.

Maybe she had just written "Grandfather and two acquaintances" on the photo from Ukraine because she did not know who the two women were; the second, the younger one with the shy smile on her face, may have also been one of her aunts, another of her father's sisters. Perhaps the tremendous upheavals of her time threw people into such chaos, uprooted and scattered them to such an extent, that all bonds were sundered, that no one knew anyone anymore. Or, when she was labelling the photos, she must have simply thought that the two women did not have any meaning for my sister and me since we did not know them, and never would, because nothing from the world in which she had lived could be salvaged in the alien German land.

But according to everything that I now knew, one thing was clear: the man in the photo was not my mother's grandfather. It was her father and *my* grandfather. My mother was thinking of my sister and me when she labeled the photo. However, my mother's father looked much more like my previous image of him than my new one. I could not see any trace of a former revolutionary and Siberian prisoner in him; indeed, he looked very much more like that respectable, bourgeois lawyer whose picture I had seen in front of me in my childhood. He exuded calm and warmth, had soft, intelligent facial features and my mother's sad eyes. It probably was not just his age and his heart disease that caused my mother to worry about him. There was also a third risk that may have been more unpredictable than all the biological factors: a political person could get caught up in Stalin's deadly machinery at any time. No one was safe, especially not someone like him, who not only carried the inherited burden of the nobility but also had proven to be a rebellious, insubordinate spirit during czarist times. For Stalin, every act of rebellion against the state was suspect, no matter what it was about. When I once again opened up the digitized church register to which Konstantin had given me access, I noticed a telling detail. For the other family members, whose dates of death were recorded, the relevant cause of death was also listed. My mother's father was the sole exception. Only the year of his death was listed: 1937. It was probably the most terrible year in Soviet history, the zenith of the purges, which are counted among the greatest political massacres in human history. My mother was seventeen years old at that time.

Later, when I attempted to orient myself in the thicket of family relations, which had been completely unknown to me all my life, and I compared the dates, I understood that my mother, as a late arrival, was born not only into a surfeit of violence and destruction but also

Figure 2. Yakov Ivashchenko (1864–1937), Evgenia's father, with his sisters Elena, Valentina, and Natalia, roughly 1915–1920. Author's private archive.

into a great void. Not only had the world of her ancestors vanished by this time—the ancestors themselves were also gone. Almost nothing remained of the many branches of the large Ukrainian-Italian family. Her Aunt Valentina, the founder of the girls lycée, died from the Spanish flu two years before she was born; her Aunt Olga had already jumped out of a window fourteen years previously. Her Baltic German grandmother Anna von Ehrenstreit had already been under the earth for twelve years; her grandfather Epifan, the erstwhile estate owner from the Voivodeship of Chernigov, must have run off some time ago; her Uncle Leonid died of epilepsy almost twenty years before her birth. No death records for her aunts, Natalia and Elena, survived; the church register only contained information about their dates of birth. According to these records, they were both born so many years before my mother that she could only have known them as older women, if she knew them at all.

A strange wonder had occurred. The black box of my life had opened in my declining years, and if I did not see anything inside it until now other than a new black box, in which perhaps another and yet another were hidden, like a matryoshka—the Russian dolls within a doll—for the first time in my life it seemed possible that I was not outside human history, but that I belonged to it just like everybody else, even if I had not yet reached the end of my inquiries, but was only at the start. However, everything which I had found out thus far was related to the family of my mother's father. Konstantin and I had thus far searched in vain for a clue about her mother. Neither her maiden name nor her birth year were recorded in the church register, only her name, her patronymic and religious affiliation. A Roman-Catholic Matilda Josefovna, presumably an Italian, was the great unknown in my equation.

At the lake, autumn announced its arrival with an unexpected yellow leaf on my balcony, with the sudden disappearance of the trail of ants in the kitchen, which I had fought for weeks without success. In the evenings, when the soft, drowsy light lay on the smooth glassy surface of the lake, when the air became so still that not a single leaf stirred, and even the chatty waterfowl no longer made a sound, a peace reigned that was so shocking and unreal it seemed I was no longer located in the developed world.

There was an inexplicable fear inside me as I carried my luggage to the car. It seemed that with my departure I was leaving behind everything I had found here. I could not imagine being able to take it home within some chips and electrodes inside the flat, unremarkable box known as a laptop. It also seemed that I was losing Konstantin by departing from the place of our correspondence, the Ukrainian Konstantin with Greek roots, who did not even live in Mariupol, as I had since learned. It's true that he was born in Ukraine, but he had been living in the northern Russian city of Cherepovets for many years, where he worked as an engineer in a steel plant and ran a forum for Ukrainians with Greek roots in his spare time. He was married with four children and countless grandchildren. One of his sons was a historian in the United States.

Why he had dedicated himself to the search for my mother, I did not know. Finding him was the most unbelievable stroke of luck that a person could have. Not only did he possess an outstanding knowledge of Russian history, he was not only what you would call a computer freak, but also a passionate genealogist. Even as a child, his favorite activity was drawing family trees with as many branches as possible. He had traced his own family tree back to the sixteenth century, if not further, the number of relatives he found filled several meters of paper.

His masterstroke of detective work consisted of finding a broken off, shot-up aircraft wing sixty years after the end of the war on which the fighter plane's serial number was still visible; it had been flown by his long-lost uncle. Like everyone who went missing in the Soviet Union during the war, he was suspected of desertion. With his belated and spectacular find, Konstantin had brought the truth to light. The uncle was rehabilitated postmortem, and his son, who eked out a miserable existence as a farmer in a Ukrainian village (since descendants of suspected deserters could not find work), received a modest restitution late in life, which made it possible for him to afford dentures. Konstantin even found out that the German fighter pilot who shot down his uncle's Ilyushin was a recipient of the Knight's Cross named Hubertus von Bonin, one of the most successful combat pilots of the Second World War, who was later killed in another dogfight. I quickly found a nephew of his online and served as a translator for a brief email correspondence between him and Konstantin. The German descendant of the Knight's Cross recipient appeared to not really grasp what the Russian wanted, perhaps he suspected that the stranger who appeared from nowhere wanted to blame him for the fact that his uncle killed one of his relatives in a dogfight seventy years ago; possibly he even believed Konstantin had some sort of private compensation demands in mind. In any case, all of Konstantin's efforts to speak with him were blocked by Prussian pleasantries. I felt sorry for Konstantin, who only wanted to chat a bit; he would have liked to have known what sort of person had fired the deadly shots at his uncle's airplane and a question about his uncle would certainly have made him happy. But this question was not asked. Nevertheless, the detective in Konstantin had still triumphed. After more than seventy years, he found a descendant in Germany of the man from whom the bullet holes in his uncle's Ilyushin originated, and he even exchanged a few emails with him. Now the man who could not rest until he found the final piece of the puzzle was only missing the so-called official confirmation of the kill. He had already inquired at the German military archive many years ago and received no reply. Now I contacted the archive. Two months after I filled out a complicated form with Konstantin's assistance and paid thirty euros, I received a small package with a sealed film reel inside it. They had bought back the film material from an American military archive after the war, and now it was returning to the place where it had been created. The picture quality was poor, but Konstantin saw everything that he had wanted to see, the final piece of evidence had been furnished.

I think that I was not the only one whom Konstantin helped with the search. As soon as he came home from work, he sat down at his digital console and connected loose ends—that was his passion, his obsession, his inner need. He returned the disappeared to earth, drew up large, complex family trees, as he had done as a child, only now he used a computer to do it. I believe that for him, the internet replaced the world; for his entire life he had not been allowed to travel, and when it had been permitted, he was too poor. In the virtual world, he could travel to any place that was part of his quest unhindered. In the end, he had also made a family tree for me that was not a tree, but a forest in which I constantly got lost. I, who had never had any relatives, suddenly had so many of them that I got them all confused and often did not know what all the cross-links and degrees of relationship were about. I had enlarged this family tree and pinned it to the wall above my desk, and now and then, I sat in front of it and studied it as though it was a map of the world.

Meanwhile, I learned that I was certainly not the only one who was searching. After the revolution, the nobility and the landholders had been murdered or driven out of the country, the farmers had been dispossessed and put in camps, countless intellectuals disappeared in the Gulag or in exile, and twenty million more died in the war, though some estimates ran considerably higher. All of this severed the natural ties between the generations in the twentieth century. Now, after almost one hundred years of fear and silence, entire nations had started looking for relatives, the missing, the arrested, and those who never returned; they were looking for their ancestors, their identity, and their roots. My mother, born in 1920, was the last person listed in the family history of the Ivashchenkos. With her, the family history broke off. She was the final addition to the family before the great disappearance; even her siblings' children were no longer mentioned, to say nothing of their children.

There could be no one who was now more in demand than such an obsessive detective as Konstantin. He cleared open strips in the jungle; I followed him. And he followed me, that was the most inexplicable part. He followed me to all the heights and depths of the quest; he shared my fervor and my disappointment when a newly discovered track once again vanished into nothing. Sometimes I thought that he was my greatest discovery. Without him, I would have gotten lost very quickly in the jungle of the Russian-language internet; without his perseverance, I would have given up the search at one of its dead ends. But Konstantin never let up, he always pressed on; he was the driving force of the quest, and he pulled me along. He was the sorcerer, and I was the apprentice, the master detective's helper. He was a riddle, the only part of my quest that he did not help me to solve.

The book that he had promised to send awaited me at home: the book about Georgy Chelpanov, the Ukrainian philosopher and psychologist, whom Olga, one of my mother's aunts, had married, and whom I had to thank for the internet entry about my mother. I already knew from his German-language Wikipedia article that he lived from 1863 to 1936 and that he was a neo-Kantian who founded the first Russian research facility for experimental psychology. A number of books flowed from his pen: *Mind and Soul, Textbook of Logic, Introduction to Experimental Psychology,* and many others. It is possible that my mother had still known him, since he apparently traveled to his hometown of Mariupol frequently after his wife Olga's suicide, and he may have visited his brother-in-law, my mother's father, on these occasions.

The small package with the book inside was only held together by a string, and covered from top to bottom on one side with postage stamps of little value; apparently, they did not have any others at the Cherepovets post office at the time. I recognized the font that I used to write emails on the small white paper square. In order not to make any mistakes, Konstantin had not written the address by hand, but printed out my email, cut out the address, and glued it onto the grey packing paper. Awkwardly, I untied the string. It would have seemed like a sacrilege to me if I had cut it, a frayed piece of jute twine which had been used many times, the type I only knew from my childhood. A book of average thickness with a glossy cover in the Ukrainian national colors of sky-blue and the yellow of a wheat field appeared. The title stood above small randomly assorted photos of Mariupol and Moscow, *Georgy Chelpanov: Life and Work.*

I had already found out from Konstantin that my mother did not appear in the book, but I was so close to her world that I felt dizzy. As I opened the cover, my eyes fell on the frontispiece that did not show Chelpanov's relatives, but those of his wife Olga Ivashchenko. I looked right into a room belonging to my mother's grandparents, on whom I had not wasted a single thought in my entire life. At first glance I recognized Valentina, the founder of the lycée for girls, and when I looked closer I recognized another familiar face. It was the woman who is seated next to Valentina in the photo print from Ukraine. The caption in the book tells me, as I had already guessed, that it is another one of my mother's aunts, her Aunt Natalia. There was no information about when the photo was taken, but I could make a rough estimate. Since Leonid, my mother's only uncle, was pictured in the photo, it must have been taken before 1901. In that year Leonid died of an epileptic seizure at the age of twenty-six.

Here he stood in a dark suit and tie behind his sisters, with something in his hand that could be a cigarette holder, without suspecting a thing about his impending death.

I was surprised by how much I already knew about the family. It was clear to me that three people were missing from the photo. It is extremely likely that Epifan, my mother's grandfather, had already left his wife by this time and had sailed off on one of his ships. Olga, my mother's oldest aunt, had also turned her back on Mariupol and lived with her husband Georgy Chelpanov in Moscow. And my mother's father, whom I would have been so glad to have seen once more in a different moment of his life, found himself in a distant, Siberian camp at the turn of the century. Apparently, the part of the family that was still based in Mariupol was assembled in the photo. The valuable old furniture and carpets must have come from better days, before Epifan became impoverished and disappeared for good, never to be seen again. An indoor palm, which stood in the background on a console table, towered over the people who had been carefully arranged on the furniture.

Natalia, who I knew from the photo print from Ukraine, did not have any sign of the futile smile on her face here; she was noticeably younger and appeared girlishly carefree. Her hair was drawn up loosely in a bird's nest; she wore a long dress with gigot sleeves and held a fan in her hand. Valentina was outfitted according to the dress code for a headmistress, which I had already come to expect from her; lean and with a proper, straight back, she sat next to her mother on a chaise longue. On an armchair next to her, her husband, Vasily Ostoslavskiy. He was young, good-looking, and regally dressed; the wealthy Russian aristocrat in whom one saw nothing less than his eventual death by starvation. My mother's third aunt, Elena, whom I saw for the first time in this photo, was the most elegant of them all. She wore a tight, brocade dress with a Medici collar; an open book lay across her knees. Anna von Ehrenstreit, the Baltic German mother of my grandmother, surrounded by the children, whom she still had around her in Mariupol. A small, somewhat rustic-looking woman in a simple, dark dress. Her severely combed back hair was probably tied in a knot on the back of her head.

One of the main phantoms from my childhood was a relative of my mother's, who, according to my father, suffered from an incurable mental illness. Even treatment by a famous psychiatrist could not help her. My father was convinced that my mother and I had inherited it. During my entire childhood and youth, I waited for this hereditary madness to break out. Later, long after I had dismissed my father's sinister inheritance theory and asked myself if it did not in fact conceal his own fear of madness, the widespread Russian maniaphobia, which Pushkin had already evoked in one of his poems; later, when I was already grown up and the traumas of my childhood began to engulf me with senseless, absurd fears for which there seemed to be no cure, I occasionally thought that my father was probably right and that my psychic fiasco was rooted in the soil of my ancestors, like couch grass that you could pull at as much as you wanted without ever being able to rip it out, so that I would have no chance of ever freeing myself from the destructive imprint of my childhood.

The allegedly mentally ill relative of my mother could only have been her Aunt Olga, as I now understood. In the book, she was described as mentally disturbed, and had, as I already knew from Konstantin, thrown herself from a window at the age of forty-three. And by the famous psychiatrist who was unable to help her, my father could have meant no one other than Chelpanov, Olga's husband.

Next to a large number of photos of Chelpanov and other Russian philosophers of his era, quite a few pictures of his wife could also be seen in the book. I looked at the apparition of my childhood, which had now become a picture. This relative had actually existed outside of my imagination once; she did not belong to the fictional personnel of my childhood, but had been a human being of flesh and blood, one of my great-aunts, a dark-haired woman with a soft, childlike face, small and decidedly delicate, with large, serious eyes. One of the photos showed her in an extravagant ball dress, with flowers in her voluminous hair, another in an elegant travel suit next to her husband, a third surrounded by her family on the terrace of a dacha which was partially sunk in a thicket of green. The book's author described her as exceptionally intelligent, educated, and soulful. He quoted from the letters that she initially wrote from Mariupol to her fiancé in Moscow, then later from Moscow to her parents in Mariupol. A voice that threw about pet names and Russian diminutives, a type of affectionate sing-song, full of longing for her mother and sisters, full of concern for her brother, Yakov, in distant Siberia. The earlier letters to her fiancé testified to a lack of self-confidence: she urgently advised him to reconsider the marriage; he, of all people, the wonderful, dear man, for whom the doors to the highest academic institutes and the best Parisian salons stood open, deserved another, better wife. She was neither attractive nor endearing, she had been in poor health for a long time, she had not aged well, and often she could not rid herself of dark, refractory thoughts.

Nevertheless, the marriage took place. Olga brought three children into the world and, with the help of a nanny and a housekeeper, she managed a large household which frequently hosted visitors from Moscow's intellectual and cultural elite. She was said to be a loving mother, passionately devoted to her husband, and early on she recognized the political events that would be his undoing. Frequently, she accompanied him abroad, to New York, to Switzerland, to Leipzig to visit the famous German experimental psychologist Wilhelm Wundt with whom her husband worked closely, and several times to the Charité hospital in Berlin. In her final years she was said to have suffered from idée fixe, worrying constantly about her children and her husband. It was said that her thoughts circled incessantly around things and events that she could not explain; she reacted with hypersensitivity to every minor injustice and broke out in tears over trivial matters. Her act of self-defenestration in 1906 was not described in detail, and it was unsubstantiated; it remained an allegation by the author.

Konstantin knew him; he lived in a remote village in southern Ukraine and did not maintain any ties with the outside world. All efforts to come into contact with him and inquire about Olga and the sourcing for his statements about her came to nothing. He did not answer any emails from Konstantin or me.

The longer I thought about the story, the more frightening it became. Did Chelpanov, who supported the theory of inborn traits, see a hereditary mental illness in the psychological instability of his wife? Is it possible that Olga became a victim of his experimental psychology? Did all of us, Olga, my mother, and me, suffer from the Chelpanov disease? Had I now found the author of the idea that had not only possibly encouraged Olga's suicide, but also my mother's? Was it Georgy Chelpanov's notion, taken up by my father, which had been perpetuated for more than an entire century and wound up in my head? Time and again I saw in front of me Olga's small, delicate feet, which minced across a street in Berlin more than one hundred years ago in laced half boots while Georgy Chelpanov visited the Charité hospital. That is how close she had been to me once, in my prehistory, only twenty minutes by foot from my current apartment in Berlin.

Ten years after her death, shortly after the revolution broke out, her husband's star in the scientific heavens burned out, as she had foreseen. He was accused of mysticism, idealism, and anti-Marxism; he lost his professorship at Moscow University; he was barred from the institute he founded, and his books disappeared from libraries. One of his daughters became an artist loyal to the party line who made a name for herself with monumental, heroic sculptures; the second daughter married the French philosopher Brice Parain and went with him to Paris, abroad into the capitalist world, which brought Chelpanov further into disrepute. His son, a Germanist and classicist, contributed to a major German/Russian dictionary which was branded as counter-revolutionary and fascist after publication. The three editors, Chelpanov's son among them, were sentenced to death and shot. Miraculously, Chelpanov himself escaped physical elimination. In the final years of his life, lonely and impoverished, he apparently hung around the entrance to his former institute and asked passersby if they still remembered him. Today, he has been rehabilitated; his books are published once again, and he is written about and researched.

I examined the Ivashchenkos' family photo with the indoor palm over and over. Had my mother been familiar with the original, had she held it in her hand, could her invisible fingerprints be found on the reproduction? The longer I looked at the picture, the more unreal it seemed to me that she came from the world I saw. Nothing, absolutely nothing, of this world could be detected in her. Shouldn't it have at least occasionally popped up, to have shown through, despite all the fearful disavowals regarding her background? How could someone disappear so completely out of their own skin? Or, as a child, had I simply been unable to interpret the signs, had I not seen what I might have recognized instantly today?

I searched for her Baltic German grandmother, but on the internet, I only came upon a relatively uninformative entry from an 1826 register of Austrian nobility: *Zwillach, Jacob, Captain of the First Wallachian Infantry Regiment, was knighted in 1789 as Lord von Ehrenstreit.* Provided that "Wallachian" did not mean a Wallach originating from the geographical territory of Wallachia, but the Principality of Wallachia, it seemed obvious that the ennobled Jacob Zwillach was a relative of my great-grandmother, perhaps her father or grandfather. Possibly, she had even named her eldest son Yakov, my mother's father, after him. Since at that time Romanian Wallachia was a protectorate of the Russian Empire, which also included the Baltic and Ukraine, the Ehrenstreits and the Ivashchenkos in any case moved about in the same country. Anna von Ehrenstreit must have followed Epifan to Mariupol when she was still very young, since according to the church register, she brought her first child, her daughter Olga, into the world when she was only nineteen. Two more children followed in short intervals, Yakov, my mother's father, and his sister Elena. After a break of five years, Valentina, Natalia, and Leonid were born, one after another. If it is true that there is no greater sorrow than that of a mother when she loses a child, then my great-grandmother Anna experienced this greatest of all sorrows twice in her life. When she is fifty-six, her son Leonid died from an epileptic seizure; five years later, her daughter Olga jumped out of a window. Perhaps she was already alone then, abandoned by her husband Epifan. Two years after Olga, she also dies of cancer. Maybe it is some consolation to her that before her death she sees her son Yakov once more, or so we may assume, as he must have returned to Mariupol at this time, following twenty years in exile.

I did not know why I had to keep looking at my great-grandmother, what seemed so familiar to me about her. Eventually the scales fell from my eyes: in a photo from Mariupol that was over one hundred years old, I recognized myself. I was the spitting image of my grandmother; even the way she propped up her elbow on the arm of the sofa and kept the other in her lap, I knew from myself. The genes of my great-grandmother, who was born exactly one hundred years before me, had skipped over two generations and asserted themselves again in me. This also explained why I looked so different from my parents. Maybe this obvious physiological difference had caused my mother to claim I was not her biological child, that in reality I had another mother. She had told me this so often, that even as an adult, I couldn't quite shake the suspicion that this was actually the case. Now, so many decades later, the family photo that showed my great-grandmother dispelled any doubts. I was the great-grandchild of this woman and therefore also my mother's child. I did not know what this evidence meant to me, but while I was looking at my great-grand-mother, a previously unknown feeling stirred in me for the first time in my life, what one might call blood ties. It was something like a deeply felt sense of physical belonging to the human species per se.

While I read the book about Chelpanov, Konstantin had put one of my photo prints from Ukraine in his forum—the one that showed my young mother next to the unknown woman with white hair. One Irina from Kharkiv, who had already been searching for her Italian ancestors for a long time, had also stumbled across Konstantin's forum, and she could not believe her eyes. The photo which she saw there was also glued into her own family album. She had also known the old black and white photo from her childhood, the two women were, as she wrote, "painfully familiar" to her.

There was something fishy going on in my quest. The age-old photo had scarcely made it out of the darkness of my desk drawer when one of my distant relatives turned up, probably the only woman in the world who owned the same family photo and had also looked at it since childhood.

However, unlike me she actually knew who was pictured in the photo. She wrote that the white-haired woman next to my mother was Matilda Josefovna, my mother's mother. I couldn't believe it. The woman with snow-white hair was, after all, much too old to be the mother of my then eighteen-year-old mother. I estimated that she was at least seventy, but Irina's grandmother, who was still alive, made it quite clear that it was Matilda Josefovna, the sister of her Italian grandmother Angelina De Martino.

Irina, who was tied to me by a relationship that I could not understand, told me an unbelievable story: the father of this Matilda, my great-grandfather, Giuseppe De Martino, was descended from a poor family of Neapolitan stonemasons. At the age of twelve, he became a cabin boy, and over the years, he worked his way up to captain. He survived the smallpox, which he caught in Hong Kong, and he was apparently the first Italian to sail all the way around Africa. One day he came to Mariupol on a merchant ship. Here he became acquainted with the daughter of a wealthy Italian merchant, the fourteen-year-old Teresa Pacelli, who fell in love with the handsome captain. One year later, the wedding took place. The now fifteen-year-old Teresa appeared on board the ship with her dolls, and from then on, she accompanied her husband on his travels. In total, she apparently brought sixteen children into the world, of which only seven survived. One of these children was Matilda, my mother's mother. She and her six siblings were raised by relatives in Mariupol, while Teresa, in love with her dolls and her Italian captain, continued to cross the world's oceans. When my Italian great-grandfather finally gave up the seafaring life and settled in Mariupol with his wife, he very quickly grew rich. In those days, Italians who emigrated to Ukraine traded in the renowned Ukrainian wheat, wine, or the inexhaustible coal reserves of the Donets Basin. Giuseppe De Martino chose coal; he exported it all over the world and made millions. The shipowner, whose boats brought the coal to their destinations, was the father of his future son-in-law, my Ukrainian great-grandfather Epifan, who was married to Anna von Ehrenstreit. The two families formed a friendship, and this is how my mother's parents got to know one another: Matilda, the daughter of the Italian coal exporter, and Yakov, the son of the Ukrainian shipowner.

Irina sent a dozen photos of our shared Italian ancestors to my monitor. One showed my Italian great-grandparents when they were still young and evidently on shore leave. The captain and his seafaring wife seemed unprepossessing and bold at the same time, both dressed in black as though for a solemn church visit. Teresa in her black taffeta skirts, which you could hear rustling formally, reminded me of a young Sicilian widow from a Visconti film. Out of the seven children who survived, the only remaining photos were of Matilda and her sister, Angela, a woman with the androgynous beauty of an archangel, who was married to a Greek, the richest man in Mariupol. They lived in a house that was known in the city as the "white dacha," although it was a mansion which didn't resemble a dacha at all. The photo was already from the Soviet period; the Soviet flag fluttered above the Greek columns on the grand balustrade, two nurses in white bonnets stood outside in the park. After the revolution the house was converted into a tuberculosis sanatorium for working people and named after Nadezhda Krupskaya, Lenin's wife.

On some other gold framed photos decorated with vignettes, I could marvel at the three young daughters of my great-aunt Angelina, my mother's cousins. They wore large Russian bows in their flowing hair and were placed on expensive furniture like dolls. I saw them in their Polish nanny's arms, wrapped in furs and muffs, on wintry sleigh rides and in tutus at ballet lessons. Another photo showed an elegant man in a hat and overcoat, a Greek uncle of my mother's, who was also an opera singer, a celebrated tenor at St. Peterburg's Mariinsky Theatre, as Irina explained.

I looked upon the photos of these strangers with astonishment and broke out in silent laughter. As I child, my lies had not been so far off the mark; they were even an understatement. In reality, I was the great-granddaughter of a tycoon, whose coal deals back then were probably a bonanza similar to today's oil trades. My relatives were people who must have lived in the lap of luxury, while the bulk of the population in Ukraine eked out a miserable existence.

But how was it possible that Yakov, my mother's Ukrainian father, who had to pay for his revolutionary ideas with twenty years of exile, married the daughter of a foreign millionaire? Was it only youthful exuberance that led him to join the Bolsheviks, whose political program called for the elimination of his own class? Had he been converted in the camp? Was his return to Mariupol a return to the old well-to-do world, to Matilda, the girlfriend of his youth whom he may have loved already before his exile? Was it a stroke of luck for him that he had been able to marry into a wealthy family, after his own had become impoverished during his years in exile?

Again and again, I scrutinized the photo of my young mother with the old woman, who was apparently Matilda Josefovna De Martino. Although the dates listed in the church register told me that Matilda had given birth to my mother rather late, not until she was forty-three years old, and it stood to reason that when she was deported my mother did not take just any old photos but those that depicted her parents, I found it hard to believe that this white-haired, almost geriatric, woman was supposed to be the mother of an eighteen-year-old. Was it not in fact my mother's Italian grandmother, Teresa Pacelli, the erstwhile seafaring wife, at an advanced age?

Irina had once again confounded all my conceptions of my mother. Was she the child of a woman born at sea, the child of a captain's daughter who grew up with relatives on shore, without a father, but also without a mother, more tolerated than loved, an abandoned, lonely child, who had no real home? Was this woman later able to give her own children something like a sense of security? Suddenly, it seemed that my mother did not first become homeless in Germany, but already in Ukraine, as though she had not fallen out of the nest at some point, but that she never had one because her parents were already homeless. Matilda given away by her parents; Yakov abandoned by his father, the impoverished shipowner who disappeared one day, never to be seen again. And mustn't Yakov in any case have become a homeless man during his twenty years of Siberian exile, a stranger in the world? Were those my mother's parents—two outcasts, two rootless people who found each other? Had it ever existed at all, Ukraine as my mother's cradle? Would I now have to tell her entire story anew?

I was amazed at the reliability of my childhood memories. Once again, something that I had long considered to be a delusion, an inner reality created howsoever, had become a fact. The name De Martino had truly existed in my prehistory; my mother really was the daughter of an Italian woman, and I had not thought up the "coal trader" myself. He also belonged to the personnel of my family background—even if it had to do with an entirely different type of coal trader than is generally associated with this term.

My mother's brother Sergey could also be seen on one of Irina's photos from her great-grandmother Angelina's family. The heavily faded, foxed image was from 1927; he was twelve years old then. Someone had taken it on the shores of the Dnieper, in Kherson, where at that time one of my mother's Italian uncles owned a winery. I looked right into a summer day in 1927, into my mother's childhood, when she was seven. Enchanted, slumbering nature, a boat on the riverbank, a tall, old tree. One could see that the people portrayed in the photo had not taken up their positions randomly, but that everyone stood in an artful relationship to the tree and to each other. In the middle, sitting gracefully in the tree between two forked branches, a young woman whose identity was not known to Irina. Below, at the foot of the tree, three standing girls, Angelina's daughters, my mother's cousins—three beauties who were noticeably older here than in the photos with the vignettes, all three with long thick braids and bright Tolstoy shirts. On a sweeping branch of the tree, a smiling boy with protruding ears. He wore short pants and a sailor's cap, his bare legs dangling in the air.

That, Irina knew, was Sergey, my mother's brother, whose trail Konstantin and I had thus far sought without success. Apparently, in those days, smiling for the camera had not yet been invented, at least not in Ukraine; I was struck by the seriousness of the person depicted in every previous photo that I had seen, including the children, but of all people, my mother's brother smiled. For some reason, it disappointed me. I had thought of him, more than anyone, who had once been so close to my mother, as especially sensitive and melancholy; I had pictured him as the masculine counterpart to my mother. Instead he sat on a tree branch, let his legs dangle in the air and smiled happily into the camera. He came across as a somewhat uncouth, robust boy, full of a zest for life. Even on the surface, I could not detect any similarity between him and my mother. Was I really looking at her brother, or had Irina been misinformed, was this an entirely different boy?

A boat could be seen on the water, quite close to the shore, within it the silhouettes of two people, one of whom held an oar. Was it, so I asked myself, my mother with her sister Lidia? Isn't that really how it was? Why should Sergey have driven to the countryside alone with his cousins? Wasn't the photo most likely from the summer vacation which the children spent together with their Italian uncle on the Dnieper?

I stare at the outlines of the two people in the boat until there are tears in my eyes. I enlarge the photo repeatedly on my monitor, then reduce it again as it becomes blurry after reaching a certain size. I look at it under a magnifying glass and print out different variations, but the two figures in the boat are too small, too distant and too faded; they defy modern technology and keep their secret to themselves, denying me a potential first glimpse of my mother as a child.

Lidia, my mother's older sister, as Irina from Kharkiv wrote, was close friends with her cousin Marusya, the prettiest of the three girls at the foot of the tree. One day, when Lidia and Marusya were both about eighteen years old, they resolved to commit suicide together. The reason for this remains unclear, but Irina thought it could have been caused by the fact that the new system did not offer them any future prospects due to their background. Marusya was not accepted to university, whereupon she tore out her long, black hair, cursed her life, and subsequently fell into a deep depression; that much was known. Perhaps Lidia had a similar experience? In any case she was the driving force behind the plan. The two acquired poison from somewhere and agreed on the day and the exact time when they would both ingest the deadly substance. Marusya stuck to the agreement and died, most likely in terrible agony, but Lidia recoiled from ingesting the poison at the last minute and survived.

It sounded like a horror story, which arose from the Russian affinity for drama; nevertheless, a silent dread stirred within me. Were they all standing in a row: Olga, my mother's aunt, who had thrown herself from a window; Marusya, her cousin, who also died by her own hand; Lidia, her sister, whose courage deserted her in the last moment; and finally, my mother? Was it possible that they had all suffered from the Chelpanov disease? Was suicide a sort of family tradition? Had my then nine-year-old mother understood anything about the tragedy, and how did Lidia live with the fact that she had broken the deadly pact and let her cousin die, thinking it was a shared death? Who was she, my mother's sister, and had the penal camp's Sword of Damocles possibly already hung over her head in those days?

I could have looked online, but somehow to me, the word seemed too intimate to type into the anonymous search engine. I asked Konstantin if he knew a place named Medvezhya Gora. He answered:

> Medvezhya Gora is a train station in Karelia. A long time ago, I was assigned to a position in Petrozavodsk after I passed my preliminary university medical exam. I lived there for a few years, and I once traveled the 160 kilometers to Medvezhya Gora by bicycle, riding through forest all the time. If your aunt had really been exiled to this camp, then there is little likelihood that she died a natural death. The prisoners in this camp had to build the Baltic–White Sea Canal, a roughly 230-kilometer-long waterway intended to connect the Baltic to the White Sea and open the shipping route from Leningrad to the Barents Sea. The prisoners had to cut down thousands of trees; they had almost no modern technology, and practically had to dig the canal by hand. The administrative center of this giant construction site (corrective labor camp) was located in Medvezhya Gora. It was a branch of the notorious Solovki camp, which was located on an archipelago in the White Sea. Earlier, Solovki had been a famous monastery, and in the eighteenth century it became the most feared state prison of the czarist era. Under Soviet rule the prototype for the Gulag Archipelago was established there. No one knows how many people died building the Baltic–White Sea Canal, estimates range from 50,000 to 250,000. Many died right on the job; they sank in the mud and sludge, and they lie buried there to this day.

Enchanted Russian Karelia, with its endless forests and lakes, with its peaceful, hidden, wooden churches—this is where Medvezhya Gora, Bear Mountain, is located. It is an actual place, as a child I had also remembered this name correctly. It was not the first time I thought my mother's sister could not have survived the camp, but now I saw her, driven to death, stamped into the canal bed with all the others who died on this construction site. A 230-kilometer-long canal bed of corpses, among them my aunt . . .

I looked in the atlas. Medvezhya Gora was 2,300 kilometers away from Mariupol. With its fifteen thousand inhabitants, the town lay in an almost immeasurable tract of forest that stretched from the White Sea, a marginal sea of the Arctic Ocean, to Finland. Endless Russian taiga, swamps, wolves, bears, snow more than half the year, polar night, and legions of mosquitoes in the short, warmer period. The totalitarian regime used not only the remote location but also the inhospitable environment for its system of punishment. I tried to picture how long it would take to cover a stretch of 2,300 kilometers at that time. How many days and how many nights did Lidia travel to reach the camp? For the first time I became aware of the full extent of the distances in this vast empire, the entire potential for despondency which this land possessed. Measured in terms of the distance from her hometown Lidia's punishment had been relatively mild; after all, there were Soviet prison camps located much further from Mariupol, ten thousand kilometers or more.

Today Medvezhya Gora is a spa town with well-known mineral springs. Tourists marvel at the spectacle of the northern lights and the white nights; they visit the historic monastery, enclosed by ghostly, eternal walls on the archipelago in the White Sea and one more attraction, described in an online Russian article:

> Once, countless prisoners were killed in the forests of Medvezhya Gora; they had built the Baltic–White Sea Canal and, in the spirit of the time, were known as canal soldiers. A visit to the memorial cemetery produces a strange sensation, a mixture of grief, horror, and helplessness. There are no graves here in the usual sense, only plaques on the trees with photos and biographical data of the dead affixed to them. There are many, many trees, an entire forest. And the forest rustles in the wind, it rustles as though it were speaking to us with the voices of the thousands murdered . . .

Had my mother's sister been a "canal soldier?" Did I have to go and search for a tree in Karelia in order to find her? There, on the trunk of this tree, would I be able to see what I wanted to see so badly, a photo of my mother's sister?

It only became clear to me later, when I checked, that I would not have found Lidia's photo on any of the trees there. The canal was built in the period from 1931 to 1933. Since Germany's offensive against the Soviet Union began in 1941, Matilda, my mother's mother, must have set off to see her daughter shortly before, or already eight years after the completion of the canal. All of this meant that Lidia had survived, or only come to the camp after 1933, when the Karelian trees were already being felled for other purposes. Perhaps she had even settled in her place of exile, as quite a few prisoners did after their sentences were up. Some were forever captivated by the wilderness, others preferred to stay far away from the centers of power, or they had lost contact with home after the long period of exile.

By then, I had exchanged a few hundred emails with Konstantin, sometimes a dozen or more per day. For months already I had been doing nothing other than reading his emails and writing to him as we continued our research together. Despite this, there was still no trace of my mother's siblings. Lidia seemed to have disappeared forever in the turmoil of world history, and we weren't making any progress in our search for Sergey. Konstantin's grand idea to search for him on the popular Russian television program *Wait for Me*, named after a famous Russian war poem by Konstantin Simonov, failed because its editorial staff were overwhelmed. Every day hundreds registered who were looking for relatives, the wait came to more than a year, and the particular story which accompanied it probably had to be even more spectacular than the one we had to offer. With regard to our query at the Central Party Archive, where Sergey, as a former party member, must be registered, we received no answer. Konstantin found the addresses of all the Ivashchenkos currently living in Mariupol; I wrote eighty-four letters, but received only two replies in which a relationship to the sought-after person was denied. The Mariupol registration office, which we wrote to, also replied with silence. We followed a trail that led to a Ukrainian village on the Azov Sea; I corresponded with a youth who maintained that his great-grandparents, who were still alive, had known Sergey, but after this highly promising message and his complaint about the desolate conditions in Ukraine, he once again fell silent. We made inquiries into the inhabitants of a certain Kyiv street because there was a vague indication that Sergey had once lived there; Konstantin even involved a friend, who lived in Kyiv, in the search, but he came back empty handed. Finally, Konstantin wrote to all of the main opera houses in the former Soviet republics and hit the bullseye. The Bolshoi Theater of Belarus in Minsk informed him that Sergey Yakovlevich Ivashchenko was a member of the opera ensemble in the 1950s as a "soloist of the first class." It was known that he was married to a doctor and had a daughter named Evgenia. In 1958, he went from Minsk to the Kazakh State Theater in Alma-Ata. From Alma-Ata, we received only the scant information that he transferred to the Rostov-on-Don State Theater in 1962. From there we heard nothing more.

Since Sergey was born in 1915, we had to assume that he was dead, but nonetheless, we now possessed an important piece of information. He had a daughter, one Evgenia Sergeyevna, who could certainly still be alive. But where should we start with our search? It would have been much more promising if Sergey had had a son. The daughter had probably married and lived under her husband's name, which we did not know. Once again we had reached a dead end.

Because of his service on the front line with the Red Banner ensemble, I had assumed that Sergey was an average talent, but the houses where he was engaged as a first-class soloist proved this to be false. I had a long history with opera. In my youth, when I did not know much about the world beyond the postwar camp in Germany for former forced laborers, I got into the newly reopened national theater in Munich by chance.

It was a performance of *Don Carlos*. I did not quite understand what it was about, but when the aging King Philip began to sing "She never loved me" at night in the Escorial by the light of burnt down candles, I experienced my initiation. I was lonely and sick from hunger, and I had not suspected that this sustenance existed. For the first time in my life, I felt like something was meant for me; for the first time, a piece of my soul reached me from the outside world. The opera, the world of voices, became my first home. I was probably by far the most indefatigable guest in the standing area of the Munich National Theater. My most ardent wish was to be a stone in the building, so I would never have to leave again and not miss a single note of music that was played and sung inside. I heard all the great singers of that time, from Birgit Nilsson to Teresa Stratas, from Fritz Wunderlich to Nicolai Ghiaurov. After every performance I waited, trembling, at the performer's exit, to receive an autograph on the back of my ticket and see my gods up close for a few seconds. Was it possible that my uncle was one of these gods? Could it have been him, who launched into the aria of the Spanish king on the darkened stage back then with his bass, the great lament of the monarch, unloved and exhausted from rule, was it also his voice that had torn me out of my loneliness in a single moment and transformed me forever?

Since, as a general rule, naming someone in the Russian-speaking world did not express a fondness for a name, but a fondness for a certain person, usually for a close relative, there was hardly any doubt that Sergey had named his daughter Evgenia after my mother. Most of all I wanted to run to her and deliver the news: your brother Sergey did not forget you; no, he never stopped loving you. I have proof, just listen—he gave his daughter your name . . .

While Konstantin and I continued our research in the wild blue yonder of cyberspace, my friend Olga visited from Kyiv. Shortly after the collapse of Communism she came to Berlin for the first time from the destitution that Ukraine experienced in those days; she could not believe her eyes when she saw the giant portions of grilled meat which were served to customers in the street side restaurants on the Ku'damm.[10] After that, as a trained civil engineer, she worked as a cleaner in Berlin and sent money to Ukraine so that her grandson did not go hungry. Shortly after the Orange Revolution, she returned to Kyiv, where she once again lived with her ex-husband, a Karaite from Crimea, and her grandson, in their old thirty-six square meter apartment in a prefab concrete building with a view of the sunsets over the Dnieper. Her daughter had long since opted for exile in the Netherlands.

As she did on every visit, Olga also brought me a Kyiv cake this time, an incomparable delicacy of meringue, hazelnuts, and butter cream, which we called a Poroshenko cake after the change of power in Ukraine, since they came from one of the factories owned by the new president. Afterward I always had my Poroshenko stomachache because I could not resist the cake and ate too much of it. This time, Olga was not making a friendly visit; she had come because her older sister Tamara had died in a Jewish retirement home. The funeral had already taken place; Olga wanted to pick up the urn with the ashes and bury it in the graveyard of the Ukrainian village where she had spent her childhood with her sister. Now she arrived from the civil war that had just broken out in Ukraine—on the Maidan, where everything had begun peacefully, there was now shooting.

It was a strange nightmare: the start of my search for my mother coincided with the first seismographic tremors of a fresh military conflict in Ukraine. To me it seemed that the televised images showed the civil war into which my mother was born, as though I was being shown what she had experienced then. The violence would soon reach Mariupol, and, of all things, the first house to burn was the one on the spot where the girls' lycée founded by my great-aunt Valentina had stood. The Ukrainian media wrote about the house "that burned three times." The first time that it went up in flames was during the civil war, when it was still Valentina's lycée. Later, on this exact spot, on 69 Georgievskaya Street, the German occupiers established their employment office; when they withdrew from Mariupol, they set it on fire in order to wipe away the traces of their deportation authority.

This seemed to answer one of my most important questions. According to my hypothesis, Valentina's lycée had probably been rebuilt after the fire, and my mother had taught there when she was young, the niece of the deceased founder. When the German occupiers arrived, they closed the school and set up their employment office in this centrally located building and absorbed the school's staff. Thus my mother became an employee of the German employment office. She had neither selected this position herself, nor had she been chosen; it was an automatic bureaucratic process. In any case, it was far less likely that she had been placed in a job by the German occupiers that, purely by chance, was in the same place as her aunt's former lycée.

Until recently, hardly anyone in Germany had heard of Mariupol; overnight, the civil war put a spotlight on the city. While I was thinking of my mother, the television showed me pictures for the first time of the city where she had lived. Streets, on which she had walked, houses she had known, a small park which may have already existed in those days. And, over and over, the burning house with smoke pouring out of it on 69 Georgievskaya Street, where the Mariupol police headquarters was located at the time of the attack—a central place in my family history, which had suddenly become the focus of attention on German TV news. On one of the plaques affixed to the building, which had defied the flames, it said:

> The German employment office was situated on this place during the occupation from 1941 to 1943. From here, more than sixty thousand Mariupolers were deported to Germany as slave laborers. One out of every ten died in bondage.

Olga's sister Tamara, who had recently died at an advanced age in Berlin, had also been among those who were deported from Ukraine. At twenty, she was deported from Kyiv to Vienna and assigned to work in a cannery. After she returned to Ukraine, she avoided the fate of those who were shot as collaborators and traitors to the fatherland or were sent from one labor camp to the next, but she did belong to the vast majority for whom forced labor in Germany had lifelong consequences. The returnees, who had not successfully resisted deportation by the wartime enemy, were not accepted back into society; most of them led wretched lives on the brink of starvation until their death. Tamara was not allowed to study and could not find work, even the most basic. For many years, she was forced to rely on the support of her parents, who were on the breadline themselves. Eventually, an acquaintance of her parents fell in love with her, a somewhat elderly professor of biochemistry, who asked for her hand in marriage. She did not reciprocate his feelings, but the marriage saved her; from then on at least her physical survival was secured. However, her courageous husband, who was already stigmatized as a Jew, did not go entirely unpunished. For a long time he was the only professor in all of Kyiv who did not receive his own apartment, but was forced to live in a communal apartment with his wife and two children.

I knew Olga's sister only as an entirely unflappable, imperturbable woman. Nothing on earth seemed to move her, her face expressed something like eternal calm. When her husband died in the eighties and her sons emigrated to Germany she followed them—as the mother of Jewish sons she could obtain a residence permit. She spent her final, and still lengthy, stretch as a voluntary returnee to the world where she had once been a slave, as a Harz IV recipient in a high-rise in Berlin's Wedding district.[11] She sat in her one-room apartment watching programs on a Russian channel or kept busy by solving Russian crossword puzzles. She did not seem to hear the German language, and she ignored the foreign country on the other side of the window. By contrast, she described her years in Vienna as the happiest of her life. When she spoke about Vienna, her dull eyes suddenly began to shine, and her pale, waxen cheeks took on a rosy glow. Olga was certain that her sister had fallen in love for the first and last time there, and that her chosen one had been a German. If that was true, then she had taken a big risk. Slavic forced laborers who got involved with Germans were sentenced to death or sent to a concentration camp. If anyone in Ukraine had found out about her love affair with a German, Tamara would also have paid heavily, perhaps with her life. On top of that, her entire family would have had to expect reprisals. Tamara knew this and kept silent her entire life; apparently she had blotted out all the horrors of forced labor from her consciousness and lived in rapturous memories. She was almost ninety when she died, back in the part of the world where she presumably left her soul behind long ago, and she took her secret with her into the grave.

Olga still had to take care of a few formalities related to the handover of the urn, so she stayed for a few weeks. For half the night we listened to opera on YouTube, as we always did when Olga visited. At the start of our friendship almost twenty-five years ago, I had already infected her with my passion for opera. We always listened to the world-famous Russian baritone Dmitri Hvorostovsky, who came from Krasnoyarsk in Siberia. Once he said, "I don't sing to entertain and make you feel good, I sing to shake you up and to hurt you, so that you cry with me." He sang, "*Ah, per sempre io ti perdei,*" and "*Kak molody my byli.*"[12] It was not difficult for him to hurt us with his voice; we sat in front of the screen and cried.

I continued to spend several hours a day on the search for my Uncle Sergey and his daughter Evgenia, my cousin. When I tried my simple trial and error method again one day and asked the Russian Google search engine about a certain Evgenia Sergeyevna Ivashchenko, a random website showed me an address in Kyiv: 26 Krutoy Spusk, Apt. 5. Olga knew the street, which translated as "steep slope." It was located in a prestigious neighborhood in Kyiv's old town, right behind the Maidan.[13] There was a phone number next to the address. When I finally worked up the courage and called, a recorded voice told me in Ukrainian and English that the number no longer existed.

Worrying about relatives had always been a widespread phenomenon on the territory of the former Soviet Union. Constant dangers lurked in its wild and unregulated everyday life; criminality was high. Now that conditions similar to war prevailed in Kyiv, Olga died a thousand deaths when her twenty-three-year-old grandson left the house. She had never allowed him to go onto the Maidan, where he wanted to defend Ukraine's freedom, but now she was so infected by my obsessive quest that she brought him onto my screen via Skype and, after a stern warning, sent him out to the address from the internet.

It took two-and-a-half hours for her grandson to return from his excursion, for Olga it was probably an eternity. He did not meet anyone at the address indicated, and no one responded when he rang at the neighbors.' The custodian told him that an old woman had lived in apartment 5, but that she died and he could not remember her name. Since then, the apartment had already changed hands twice, and it was currently being renovated again.

Prior to her departure, Olga wrapped the urn in two towels and stored it in her suitcase. I brought her to the bus station on the other side of the city. Her sister Tamara, who had spent her happiest days as a forced laborer in a Vienna cannery long ago, returned to Ukraine for a second time—not in a cattle car, but in a comfortable, air-conditioned long-distance bus, this time forever.

Upon arrival in Kyiv after the long bus ride, Olga did not even take the time to get a good night's sleep. She drank two cups of black coffee, which, unimpressed by modern technology, she prepared on a stove plate in a cezve, a long-handled copper pot. Then she lit a cigarette and ran to the metro. Everyone who saw her from behind, or from a distance, took her for a young woman. She was as slender as a deer and, at the age of seventy-two, still climbed the trees at her dacha to harvest fruit.

At apartment 5 on 26 Krutoy Spusk, no one opened the door again this time, but the neighbor was home. She told Olga that the old woman, Evgenia Sergeyevna Ivashchenko, the former neighborhood doctor, had not died at all, but had moved a few years ago. With that, it was more or less clear she was Sergey's daughter. There could be many women named Evgenia Sergeyevna Ivashchenko, but probably only one, who, as the daughter of a doctor, became a doctor herself. Olga nevertheless inquired if the neighbor, by any chance, knew who Evgenia Sergeyevna's father was.

"Of course I know," the woman replied. "He came from Mariupol and was a famous opera singer." She gave Olga her former neighbor's new telephone number.

In Soviet times, people met in their kitchens. Now there were numerous restaurants and cafés in Kyiv, rendering the kitchen superfluous as a socio-cultural space. However, my cousin Evgenia was unable to receive anyone at her home because, as she explained to Olga immediately on the telephone, she had six lodgers in her small two-room apartment. This was unusual even in catastrophically overcrowded Kyiv, where every tiny space was put up for rent.

I knew that doctors were paid poorly in the former Soviet Union. In my mind's eye, an image appeared of an exhausted, careworn, neighborhood doctor who had slaved away her entire life in a shabby, undersupplied district hospital and who now ran a sort of night shelter in her small apartment because she could not live off her pension. An old woman in the squalor of the former Soviet Union.

Olga knew otherwise after meeting with her. She encountered an elegantly dressed woman wearing make-up with an eccentric streak. In her stature and body type she was rather like me, said Olga, who had spent half the night in her crowded apartment, looking for my books and pictures in order to show them to my cousin, who only acknowledged them with a brief glance. Every attempt that Olga undertook to tell something about me, or to find out something from her, was nipped in the bud. Evgenia spoke incessantly about her father, who had apparently been her god. After two hours, patient and gentle Olga had fled from her—even on my screen she still looked worn-out and disheveled, as though she had had a physical altercation with my cousin.

When I phoned Evgenia the next day, I instantly understood what Olga had endured. After at most ten minutes, it was clear to me that I would hardly get a word in, that it would be difficult for me to succeed in asking her the questions I had written down. She greeted me with a piercing scream and immediately talked me into the ground; I wasn't even sure if she actually knew who she was talking to. My only option was to concentrate and try to pull something out that I wanted to know from the river of words flowing into my ear.

My faint hope, that she had still known my mother, was not realized. Evgenia was born in 1943, the exact year my mother left Mariupol forever. It turned out that the Ukrainian youth from the village on the Azov Sea, who disappeared again after a fleeting correspondence with me, was the right lead—his great-grandparents had probably really known Sergey. Evgenia was born in precisely this village during the evacuation—conceived while Sergey was on leave from the front. One day in the same place, when she was three years old, a stranger came into the room and said, "I am your father." And she knew right away that this was true, that this man and no other was her father. From the start, she said repeatedly, they had loved one another "fanatically"—drawing out the second "a" like a long siren.

From her lips I heard about a nanny named Tonya for the first time, who had already lived with my mother's family before the revolution and also stayed with her through all the times and catastrophes after this. This Tonya is said to have recounted that my mother had married an American officer during the war and gone to the United States with him.

I knew the Russian passion for myth-making; I had to take it into account during my search, but here I was astonished by the disregard for historical facts that former Soviet citizens usually knew quite well. Certainly, I had heard of Soviet forced laborers who married American soldiers after their liberation and followed them to the United States, but that had taken place in Germany. It was completely out of the question that during the war an American officer had found himself on Soviet soil, and that my mother could have met him in Mariupol. Even if Tonya had really spread this rumor, it was surprising that my cousin accepted it unquestioningly.

But the news about the nanny closed another gap that yawned in the life of my mother. I had always wondered about what her life was like when the war broke out—her father already dead for four years, her brother on the front, her sister in exile, her mother lost on the way there. I had always wrongly assumed that she was completely alone in this terrible time, because I did not know anyone other than her immediate family members in whose company I could have pictured her. Now I knew that the nanny, Tonya, was probably at her side, a person whom she may have already known before she took her first breath. Tonya had probably heated up the oven when there was fuel, scrounged up something to eat in the ruined city, and run into the bomb shelter with my mother when the air raid warning sounded.

My cousin informed me that Sergey really had named her, his daughter, after my mother. He had adored his little sister, had spoken of her again and again until his death, described her as exceptionally beautiful and intelligent and never stopped waiting to receive a message from her. For the first time in my life, I heard from someone who had loved my mother; she, who I only knew as a pariah. The first loving glance that fell upon her from the outside showed me as never before so clearly and shockingly the extent of the hatred she had been exposed to in Germany. My cousin now had the opportunity to receive the news that her father had waited for so long in vain, but she did not ask me a single question about my mother's true fate. She did not allow me to destroy her illusion of having had an aunt in the land of opportunity. Maybe she even thought that my mother was still alive and that I was calling from the United States.

She knew that Matilda Josefovna De Martino, the grandmother we shared, did not die in the war. However, she never returned to Mariupol from her journey to Medvezhya Gora. My cousin did not know anything about the reasons behind this; she only knew that she last lived in

Voskresensk, a Russian city near Moscow. She died in 1963 at the age of sixty-eight, only seven years after my mother.

If she, my mother, had known what I now knew, then maybe everything would have been different. If she had been able to think about a mother who was alive, then her lot in Germany could have been somewhat easier to endure. Maybe this knowledge would have prevented her from killing herself. Instead, the river may have called to her in the voice of her mother; she may have imagined that she was walking toward her dead mother on the way into the German Regnitz.

My cousin had only seen our grandmother two or three times in her life, but she still remembered the date of her death perfectly. It was the same date as my birthday. On the day I turned eighteen in a provincial German city, my grandmother died in distant Voskresensk, a city whose name means "Sunday" and "resurrection" in Russian. Did she also believe that her daughter was leading a happy life in America?

My cousin described my grandmother as cool, unapproachable, and sarcastic. A tiny, rail-thin old woman with snow-white hair and a long nose who ate only crumbs, like a bird. Everyone was a little bit afraid of her, including Sergey, whose voice she always criticized; it was never good enough. She had only loved one man her entire life: her brother Valentino De Martino. Her daughter Lidia was his child. Incest. Apart from that, my cousin had nothing to say about Lidia, she had never seen her. Sergey never heard from her again after her arrest, and he had also never spoken about her. My cousin thought that Lidia probably died in the prison camp.

Evgenia claimed that Yakov, my mother's father, had taken his own life. He was to be apprehended and forced to make a denunciation, but he avoided this by shooting himself on the evening before his arrest. Supposedly my mother was the one who found the body. Strangely, this sounded familiar to me, as though I had once heard it from my mother. And at the same time I remembered perfectly how she had told me that her father had died of a heart attack. Up to the present day I still felt the rush of horror she experienced when she was taken out of class and immediately understood what had happened. It seemed as though her father had died twice, as though she had experienced this loss two times. In my memory, both versions of his death were accurate. How was that possible? I recalled Yakov's entry in the church register. Didn't the missing entry for the cause of death support the theory that he had killed himself? Was the blank space explained by the fact that the word "suicide" could not appear in a church register?

Most of the time my cousin spoke about her father, Sergey. She said he spoke twelve languages and was the greatest singer of his time, with a typical Italian operatic voice—no one could hold a candle to him. While he was a student in Kyiv he had already made an impression on Stanislaw Kosior, the former Ukrainian head of state, considered to be one of the people chiefly responsible for the famine during the 1930s. When Sergey caught his eye, he had already risen to become a full member of the politburo of the Communist Party of the Soviet Union. He heard Sergey at a concert in the Kyiv Conservatory and promoted his career from then on. Kosior must have been crazy about Sergey because he not only supported him as a singer but also repeatedly invited him into his home. It was a virtually unheard of for a politburo member to grant a mere student access to his private sphere. But soon enough Kosior, like so many others, became a victim of the system that he served. Stalin had him arrested and tortured in order to force him to make some sort of a confession. Because he held out, they brought his daughter and raped her in front of his eyes. Kosior confessed, his daughter jumped out the window, he was shot, and his ashes were thrown into a mass grave in Moscow's Donskoy Cemetery. With that, Sergey's fate was also sealed. He had become a favorite of a man denounced as a public enemy; Kosior's shadow followed him his entire life. Thanks to his extraordinary voice he was booked at major Soviet theaters, according to Evgenia, but real fame only came at Moscow's Bolshoi, and that was closed forever to an erstwhile favorite of Kosior.

I remembered Konstantin's words about Sergey's inexplicable party membership. Now it was clear to me how the camel had passed through the eye of the needle. Only Stanislaw Kosior could have made it happen (probably he only needed to snap his fingers)—perhaps under the condition that Sergey disown his sister, who was in a prison camp? I pictured my uncle as a weak, fearful man, who had made a deal with the authorities and paid for it for the rest of his life. Someone, who needed a strong hand and, for this reason, had chosen a wife whom her daughter described as "Stalin in a skirt" during our telephone conversation.

Evgenia had never been married—this nonsense, in her own words, was not for her. She had lived only for her father, who had apparently inherited his weak heart from his father, Yakov. She became a doctor in order to be able to treat him herself. They had lived a nomadic life, moving from republic to republic, from one city to the next, always there where Sergey had an engagement for a few years. The three of them always lived in temporary accommodation, mostly for several years at a time in a guest room which belonged to the theater. Everywhere, Evgenia had been on the hunt for scarce fruit and vegetables for her father; she had supplied heart medicines from abroad and even eventually allowed herself to be impregnated to give her father the grandchild he longed for, who was now grown up and a married man. She had lived together with him and his wife in the house on Krutoy Spusk, but since she didn't get along with her stepdaughter, they had to trade the big apartment for two small ones.

Sergey suffered a heart attack when he was fifty-two from which he never truly recovered. When he had to give up singing, the family moved to Kyiv, where his lifelong dream of having his own apartment was finally realized. Since he received a miserable pension despite his impressive career as a singer, Sergey was forced to take another job to earn extra money. In his last years, he worked as a guard in an amusement park. "He died on the street," Evgenia said, "One day on the way home from the park, he dropped dead." She was convinced that her father had been murdered: in the park he witnessed a carousel accident that killed several children, and, as a witness, he had been eliminated. Should I believe that? Or could my cousin not bear the thought that her god-like father died an entirely banal death, most likely from a second heart attack, which even she could not have prevented, although she had studied medicine and become a doctor?

My cousin told me more than I could have hoped for, but after a roughly two-hour telephone conversation in which I said almost nothing, I suddenly felt completely empty. I sat in front of the branches of an enlarged version of the family tree, which Konstantin had drawn up for me and hung above my desk—now I could add three branches to it, my cousin, her son and his wife, but I no longer knew what purpose that would serve. I no longer knew what I had been searching for, what all these strangers were to me, what connected me to them. I had felt deprived my entire life because I did not have a family, but that was only because I did not know I was a happy person without this entire burden. The all-consuming grief that had sometimes come over me recently because I would never get to know my Ukrainian-Italian family had transformed itself into dread of this clan. I did not want to hear any more about all the atrocities, all the dark, unrestrained stories of love, hate, and madness, and how, as a consequence, hardly any of my ancestors died a natural death. Everything was mixed up in my head, fiction and falsehood, reality and the delusions of a half-crazy old woman trapped in her own thoughts and her obsession with her father. I had no idea what I could believe and what I could not; I longed to return to the quiet, happy time with the dead, all the beautiful, interesting people on the old black-and-white photos. They had lost their magic for me and acquired the characteristics of my cousin who was alive. She had probably also experienced more terror than could fit into one life; apparently she had never found herself, but hidden behind her role as a daughter. What sort of fate could her son have, who was destined for a life as a grandson?

Evgenia's description of our grandmother Matilda irritated me most of all. Could my mother have cried her eyes out over a cold, aloof, and sarcastic woman? Did the picture which she conveyed to me of her mother owe itself to the transfiguring grief we often feel for something that is lost forever? As a child who had been given away by the captain's wife, Teresa Pacelli, was Matilda later incapable of giving her own children protection and security since she had never experienced this herself?

The sea seemed to be the dominant theme running through my mother's family history. Her Ukrainian grandfather Epifan, the shipowner, had chosen to go by sea when he disappeared forever. Her Italian grandfather, Giuseppe, the captain, spent a large part of his life at sea together with his wife, who brought her dolls aboard the ship but gave away her children in return. Maybe her children Matilda and Valentino were not raised by the same relatives, but separately; maybe the two were distant enough from each other to fall in love one day. Or, had the shared isolation from their parents one day sparked the passion between the two siblings, a passion which had produced Lidia? Was she really the child of incest, of sexual impurity, and therefore an outsider, a family outcast about whom not only her brother Sergey but also her sister, my mother, had been silent? Was all of this connected—the stigma of inbreeding, her suicide pact with her cousin Marusya and the prison camp in which she finally disappeared? Was it like that, or had my thoughts followed the inner currents of my peculiar, monomaniacal cousin who wove incest tales about other people because of her idolatrous love for her father?

If what she said about Lidia was true, if my mother's sister had really died in the prison camp, then my search had come to an end. I could hardly expect to receive more information about my mother from more distantly related potential relatives. My cousin Evgenia had abandoned me in a wasteland, with more questions than I had ever had before, questions for which I would probably never receive an answer. I had lost sight of my mother; she seemed to have disappeared forever in the chasm between fact and fiction, in a flickering void that remained out of reach. Everything that I had found out about her was only material for speculation and hypotheses, material for a fairy tale.

Figure 3. Sergey Yakovlevich Ivashchenko (1915–1984), Evgenia's brother, with his cousins on the bank of the Dnieper, roughly 1927. Author's private archive.

A few days after I called Evgenia, Olga came across her on the Maidan. Although at that time the square was the city's hot spot in the truest sense of the word, Kyiv still had close to three million inhabitants, making it rather unlikely that you would come across someone by chance whom you had just gotten to know a few days earlier. Olga got scared and hid in the crowd, though my cousin probably would not have recognized her again in any case. She had not even looked at her when they ran into each other, instead constantly showing her the dimples from all sides of which her father was so fond and she was so proud. Now she stood a little off to the side and sang, dressed in an elegant indigo blue coat and a large black hat. With a slightly brittle voice and her shining eyes raised to the sky at the edge of the warlike tumult, she sang the Russian version of Massenet's "Elegy," which everyone knew in Ukraine and that her father had certainly once sung as well: "Where have they gone, the days of love, the sweet dreams, the beautiful birdsong . . ."

Still, Evgenia did ask me one question at the end of our phone conversation. She wanted to know if I had ever been to Mariupol. It would have been high time for me to set off on the way there, to see my mother's hometown with my own eyes, but my cousin and I were really not so different. She had barricaded herself off from life behind her father, while I had hidden behind the edge of my desk. For entirely different reasons, I also had something in common with Konstantin. The internet did not only replace the world for him, but for me as well.

I never heard from my cousin again.

It was January on the Schaalsee. Never before had such a long-lasting, icy darkness surrounded me—even in the daytime it hardly became light. I had gotten caught in a kind of polar night, a silence like in space, where at night you only heard the cracking of the ice that covered the lake. Sometimes it was a rumbling, a faint grumbling, which sounded like a railway switchyard. I imagined that, somewhere in the depths of the lake, blocks of ice were colliding and sliding over each another. Only the streetlight in front of my house, the last one in the village, reminded me that I was in the animate world. Though this light also occasionally began to blink, as though it was tired, as though it would fall asleep forever at any moment. The fog gathered in its flickering light like white impenetrable smoke, and once the air was clear, you could see tiny, hard snowflakes floating around, covering the frozen, brown grass like white sawdust. Now, you also often heard the waterfowl screeching. They were trying to preserve openings in the ice by crowding together into small islands on the frozen lake, but over time the warmth of their small bodies had no chance against the ice. The diving holes froze over; the birds' source of food disappeared. Their nightly cries filled me with anxiety, as though I was also threatened with some sort of unavoidable doom.

A marten was living in the engine compartment of my car; he slept there, safe from the cold, and ate his way through essential cables, as was later explained to me at the garage. Apparently, modern martens foraged on plastic and copper; in any case, other than the clicking of the key in the ignition, my car did not make a single sound. Day after day, I resolved to call the ADAC,[14] and day after day, I postponed it. Maybe the persistent darkness made me so lethargic, maybe I did not mind being cut off from the world for a while. My skin felt dry and flaky; I was constantly tired, and I felt an irresistible desire to crawl into a cave with a bear and sleep along with him during his ancient hibernation.

Once, when it was almost morning, I looked up from my computer with alarm. At first I was certain that some sort of catastrophe had struck and that the opposite lake shore was on fire. At second glance what I saw was even more mysterious. It seemed as though a long blood-red piece of tape was stretched straight across the darkness, lining the entire shore on the opposite side. Neither fire nor light looked like this, they both did not have such a sharply delineated edge—as though drawn with a ruler. I asked myself if I had been staring at my screen too long, if I was hallucinating, or if the laws of nature were no longer in force, but minutes later, I glanced into the same stygian darkness as before. Apparently, an unnaturally precise crack in the black clouds had shown the blaze of the heavens behind the darkness.

Meanwhile, I had started working on the book I planned to write about my mother. I wrote with a sense of dedication that I had never experienced before, with a feeling of bliss not at all appropriate to the material, while at the same time, it seemed that I had to dig my way through a mountain whose end I could never reach. I found myself in the dark, in the true sense of the word; I wrote all night and slept through the short felt-gray days in order to rush toward my PC even before I had made tea. Essentially, the family members I had found were the ones who wrote the book. They led me in various, often completely different directions; they became entangled in contradictions and lured me into labyrinths from which I could not escape. There were hardly any visible threads that connected the people to each other; they stood curiously alone in the room, all more or less on their own, all in an only hypothetical relationship to my mother, which was unknown to me.

Konstantin's forum was an inexhaustible source of information. Among other things, it included an archive of the old Mariupol, which sent messages from my mother's former world—describing events that took place when she was between four and sixteen:

> Two thousand five hundred Mariupol workers have assembled for a memorial meeting on the occasion of the death of Vladimir Ilyich Lenin. On April 28, a torch-lit procession of Komsomol members will take place.
>
> The lower part of the city was flooded by a storm tide. One hundred twenty families lost their homes.
>
> The district commission for confiscation resolved to deprive estate owners Khreschtshatnitzkaya, Krasnyansky, Shutenko, and Pasterev of their land usage rights and to exile them from Mariupol.
>
> Of all Mariupol children between the ages of eight and eleven, 25.6 percent do not attend school and are illiterate.
>
> The editorial department of the Azov Proletariat is launching a major lottery in order to gain subscribers. The main prizes are a men's raglan coat, left over fabric, shoes, galoshes, and the collected works of Comrade Lenin.
>
> Volunteers are needed on the right seashore. At least one thousand voluntary assistants are required for the construction of the Azov steel plant. Militant participation in this voluntary initiative is a question of honor for each of us.
>
> A Palace of Culture will be built for the Ilyich Iron and Steel Works, and cultural centers will be established at the harbor and at Azov Steel.

Additional plans call for the construction of new holiday homes and the expansion of the local sanatorium.

The start of the political trial of Mariupol party schoolteachers begins. They are accused of having founded a Trotskyist, bourgeois-nationalist group.

At a meeting of the Mariupol women's shock workers, bonuses of 150, 200, and 250 roubles were awarded. In addition, every delegate received a small cask of marinated sprats.

The Workers' Cinema has acquired a sound system and will show a sound movie, from February 10 to 12, for the first time in our city. It is a film adaptation of the novel *Mother* by Maxim Gorky.

How might it have looked then, my mother's native city? It probably had little in common with the sunny southerly city on the sea, which had supplanted my wintry image when I read the newspaper article about the soccer match in Mariupol. My image of the city changed once again. Even before the revolution, Mariupol had been an industrial city, and in Soviet times, industrialization was promoted forcefully as shock workers set world records in labor productivity. The smoke-belching chimneys of the great factories towered above the city; poisonous emissions covered the blue summer sky and descended on the streets and the people day and night. Torgovaya Ulitsa was there, with numerous stands and kiosks that didn't have much to offer after the revolution: a bit of curd, meat, a few tomatoes and potatoes from private gardens—unaffordable for the majority of the hungry population. Fontanaya Ulitsa with the well where people had still drawn water for themselves and their livestock up to the turn of the century; Gretscheskaya Ulitsa, where my mother's cousins may have lived before they were driven out of their palace; Italyanskaya Ulitsa, where the house of my Italian great-grandparents probably stood. Horse-drawn carts rumbled over broken cobblestone; then in 1933, when my mother was thirteen, the first streetcar, a single one which traveled in both directions on a single track.

The wilderness began immediately behind the center. There were no more paved roads, only a labyrinthine network of paths and trails created by pedestrians. Small houses with tiny gardens stuck to each other, intertwined, little stone houses, wooden huts, mud huts, barracks, pavilions, shacks, sheds; someone lived everywhere, three-and-a-half square meters per city resident. No sewer system, dirt, garbage, stench, poverty. Epidemics, typhus, malaria. Homeless children who lost their parents in the turmoil of the civil war roamed about, searched for rubbish, and stole, sleeping during the winter in the curbside tar boilers where construction workers stirred hot tar in the daytime for road construction.

And the sea, the Azov, the shallowest in the world, as though it was made just for my mother, who could not swim . . . did she splash about in it, did she go to the shore frequently? With other girls, with boys? What sort of bathing suit did she wear? Did people have such things at that time, or did they swim in their clothes, in their underwear? Despite everything, didn't my mother have wonderful, carefree moments in her daily life, something like the exuberance of youth? Was she crazy about poetry, the latest hits, or boys? Did she go to the skating rink in winter, where you could rent skates and where young people moved across the ice to the sounds of an orchestra which played there? Did she go to plays, concerts, and dances in the Palace of Culture? Did she like one of the many admirers that she probably had? Or did she secretly love the one who did not want her? Did she dream about him and write him letters that she never sent? Or was my father her first love? Had she actually ever loved him?

While I got lost in ideas and hypotheses and searched in articles about the old Mariupol for elements and fragments of my mother's life, which consisted more of gaps than anything clearly discernible, Konstantin continued to look for her sister, Lidia. He had already followed countless leads in vain, and when the notification eventually arrived from the memorial site of the former camp at Medvezhya Gora that they had no record of a prisoner with my aunt's name, I lost hope. But Konstantin would not have been Konstantin if he had given up. He pressed on, and one day, he came across a list of victims of the Soviet Union, 1923 to 1953. In this thirty-year period alone, more than forty million victims were listed. The name Ivashchenko was found on the list thirty-nine times, Lidia Yakovlevna Ivashchenko among them.

The email address of a man named Alfred Kramer was listed on the same webpage; he lived in Odessa and offered professional help in the search for victims. Konstantin found an entry on the internet about him—he was an ethnic German, a member of various committees in Odessa, who was involved in city politics in a not entirely transparent way. We wrote to him, and already the next day, he informed Konstantin that he had looked in the state victims archive in Odessa and found the file of the person we were seeking. The client in Germany should transfer two hundred euros to him by Western Union, and then she would receive a digital version of the file within a few days.

Konstantin advised me not to transfer anything for the time being; first we needed proof that it was really my aunt's file. When he asked the Odessite for evidence, he notified us that the victim's place of birth was listed as Warsaw. Konstantin thanked him for his efforts, and we began to think about another approach. But a few hours later, an additional detail was presented to us from the archive: the victim's mother was a certain Matilda Josefovna Ivashchenko, born De Martino.

I transferred money to Ukraine for the first time in my life and began to wait. Owing to my impatience, I checked my mailbox twenty times a day. We had really found her, the untraceable, mysterious Lidia, the name De Martino cleared away any doubts. Although Lidia's foreign birth in Poland created new mysteries, Konstantin had once again shone a light into the darkness. In 1911, the year my aunt was born, not only Ukraine but also part of Poland belonged to the Russian Empire. Accordingly,

Lidia was not born abroad—though the question remained why she had been born so far from Mariupol. Immediately the thought arose that the remote birthplace supported the idea that she had been conceived incestuously. I did not know what sort of sense it made, but I imagined that Matilda had fled to Warsaw in order to give birth to the child of her forbidden love, far from her social circle. At the same time I told myself I was crazy, since I continued to elaborate upon the delusions of my deranged and garrulous cousin.

More than two weeks had passed since I transferred the money. Alfred Kramer confirmed that he received it, but I had heard nothing from him since. I was almost certain that I had been taken in by a fraudster. It was impossible that someone had free access to a state victims' archive and that he could then make a private business out of sending copies of files to clients in foreign countries about whom nothing more was known than an email address. But I was thinking with my German brain again. Alfred Kramer, so Konstantin assumed, gave part of the money that he received from his clients to an employee at the archive, allowing him to access and copy the corresponding files—standard practice in this part of the world, but again and again these Eastern European ways transcended my limited Western understanding. However, time passed, and nothing else arrived from Odessa. When I inquired, I was told to be patient; it was explained to me that the file was in unexpectedly poor condition and that a lot of work was required to sort its five hundred faded pages and put them in the right order. I caught a gentle hint of further demands for money, but already two or three days later, sixteen consecutive emails arrived in my mailbox, a dangerously large amount of data in individual ZIP files. Indeed, it must have been an enormous amount of work to sort every single partially disintegrated sheet and put them in a machine and scan them. I was ashamed over my mistrust. The two hundred euros, which I had transferred, and which the ethnic German may have had to split with a second person, were a laughable sum for the amount of work done—aside from the fact that what I had received was priceless.

The first page of the file consisted of a badly cut, crumpled piece of brown wrapping paper with the mug shots of five women and two men glued to it. They had been photographed in such a way that they appeared to be dangerous criminals. Only a single photo out of the total of eight defendants was missing: Lidia's. It had quite clearly been removed, a blank space between the other pictures under which only her name could still be seen. I was so disappointed that I almost cried.

A flood of interrogation transcripts, decisions, orders, decrees, the arrest warrant, the search warrant, the indictment, and still more interrogation transcripts followed. The smell of mold from the eighty-year-old paper seemed to waft from my screen out of a basement archive in Odessa where thousands of victims' files waited to be exhumed.

Lidia's file showed that she was really born in Warsaw and that she lived there with her parents until the age of five. After the family returned to Mariupol, she lodged with my Italian great-grandparents. There, Lidia spent the years before she began her studies in Odessa.

I always drew a blank when I tried to imagine the sort of home where my mother grew up in Mariupol; now it seemed certain to me that she had also lived in the house of her Italian grandparents. Considering the wealth that Giuseppe De Martino had accumulated with his coal business, it must have been a grand and luxurious house, though by the time my mother was born it had undoubtedly already been seized by the state. It was probably crammed with strangers, the dispossessed enemies of the people had presumably only been left with a nook in their former house. It is quite possible that my mother grew up among people who hated her, for whom those like her were fair game, who now owned not only the house, but also her parent's furniture, dishes, and carpets, who maybe even wore their clothes, and spit in the soup of the former blue bloods and members of the property-owning class in the communal kitchen. They probably could have murdered them with impunity at any moment.

From her file, I learned that after Lidia completed her literary studies in Odessa she returned to Mariupol and worked for a short time at the *Azov Proletariat* newspaper, which I had first encountered in the Azov's Greeks archive. On November 5, 1933, when she was just twenty-two years old, she was arrested. She was accused of belonging to an anti-Soviet association called the Group for the Liberation of the Proletariat and charged with subversive, counterrevolutionary activities. The goal of the association, which was allegedly founded in Odessa in 1931 and had established cells in various Ukrainian cities, apparently consisted of overthrowing Soviet power because, in the eyes of group's leaders, it had betrayed socialism and established a form state capitalism hostile to the working class. The group's members, all literature students, were to establish literary societies in as many Ukrainian factories as possible and then gradually enlighten the workers and win their support for a counterrevolution. The group's conspiratorial meetings, so I read, took place in the members' apartments, including a number of times at Lidia's; she was living with one of her father's sisters in Odessa, her Aunt Elena, the elegant woman in the brocade dress, whom I knew from the family photo with the indoor palm and whose name I now found once again in her niece Lidia's court records.

What had it been like when she was arrested on November 5, 1933, a twenty-two-year-old, from my current perspective, practically still a child? When had they come? At their preferred time, at night or early in the morning, when everyone was still asleep, when they caught their victim drowsy and defenseless? Had my thirteen-year-old mother also been awakened by the inexorable knocking at the door, feared by millions back then, night after night? Had they known, or at least sensed, that Lidia's arrest was imminent, or had it come as a complete surprise? Had my mother witnessed how the house had been searched, how her sister had been put in handcuffs and led away? I had to think of Anna Akhmatova's "Requiem":

They took you away at dawn,
And I followed, as though behind a corpse,
In the dark room the children wept,
The candle guttered by the icon stand.[15]

Prior to her sentencing, Lidia spent half a year in pre-trial detention in the prisons of Mariupol, Odessa, and Donetsk, about half the time in basement cells. The interrogation reports, at close to three hundred pages, were a farce according to Konstantin. In those times, statements by the accused were forged, manipulated and extorted via threats and the use of force. And—since people were shot merely for telling a joke—statements were certainly made in circumstances of mortal fear. It was not uncommon for interrogators to rape female defendants; they were tortured or subjected to so-called conveyor belt interrogations where acute sleep deprivation soon made it impossible for them to know what they were saying. But this didn't make any difference, since for the most part, the interrogation reports of the accused were either dictated or invented by the interrogator, who was under pressure from above and required to produce a satisfactory result for his superior. The truth was of no interest to anyone. The sole purpose was to fulfill the daily quota for the machinery of destruction, to satisfy Stalin's insatiable demand for human sacrifice.

Indeed, Lidia's statements were nothing like actual speech, much less that of someone speaking with mortal fear. The contents of all the reports consisted of the same prepared, clichéd phrases. Apparently Lidia had betrayed all of her comrades; she named names and addresses, described their backgrounds and activities within the group, and sketched their personalities in detail. With mind-numbing monotony and in an absurdly epic breadth, the same ideological and political discussions of the group were reproduced, their shared reading enumerated, the rehearsal of conspiratorial and seditious behavior was described, and repeatedly the ten points of the group's written political manifesto were cited. Entirely out of context, Lidia declared that she had rejected her aristocratic origins long ago and that she condemned her grandfather, Giuseppe De Martino (the large-scale exporter of Donbas coal), as an exploiter of the Ukrainian people. Her parents, she assured, had never owned anything and were merely subletters in their former family home. That was the only place in the report that seemed authentic to me; it may have been Lidia's desperate attempt to pull her head out of the noose by distancing herself from her origins. All of the reports ended with one and the same confession, which may have been formulated by a well-meaning interrogator:

> Long before today, I already recognized what great harm I and my like-minded colleagues caused the Soviet people through our counterrevolutionary activities. I acted out of political naivete and ignorance under the influence of our leader, Bella Glaser, who made a strong impression on me with her exceptional education and her charisma and enticed me into incorrect thoughts and actions. With a pure heart, I put everything in the report for the Soviet dictatorship of the proletariat that I know about "the Group for the Liberation of the Proletariat." I am aware that my guilt under Soviet law consists not only of my false convictions and activities within the group, but also because I have concealed everything. I am guilty in every sense, but I hope that, through my faithful, candid statements, I can atone for a portion of my guilt and that in the future I will be allowed to carry out honest work for my Soviet fatherland.

Times had changed dramatically since the fall of the last czar, but the methods used to punish renegades stayed the same. All of the accused members of the group were sentenced to three years in a penal colony "beyond the borders of Ukraine." The sentence was inexplicably mild considering the fact that the case dealt with subversive conspirators who wanted to overthrow the system. Only Bella Glaser was not able to survive. The ringleader, who continued her political activities in a Siberian prison camp, was arrested again and sentenced to death by firing squad. I examined her mug shot: a young, unmistakably intellectual woman wearing a beret and round Trotsky glasses, who was, according to her file, Jewish. Ten years later, she would probably have been murdered by the German Nazis if the Soviet secret police had not done it already.

If Lidia was really an anti-Soviet activist, if the Group for the Liberation of the Proletariat had even existed, or if it was invented by the secret police as a pretext to punish people like Lidia for their family background—although she was the sister of a man mercifully allowed to join the party by Stanislaw Kosior and the daughter of an Old Bolshevik, who had paid for his convictions with twenty years of exile—there was no answer to all that. But if Lidia had really dared to oppose Stalin's dictatorship, then she must have been a very different person from my mother. It appeared as though the sisters had been virtual antipodes. Lidia, strong, brave, maybe almost reckless; my mother, it seemed certain, had already been over-sensitive, timid, and defenseless as a child. At least Lidia had been a well-fed and well-looked after child; my mother had never known anything other than hunger and fear. Maybe that is what constituted the crucial difference between them.

From the file it emerged that Lidia did not die; that, contrary to my Kyiv-based cousin's assumption, she survived banishment. Among the papers I found an application for rehabilitation which she filed fifty-five years after the end of her sentence, in 1992, after the collapse of the Soviet Union. She was eighty-one years old at the time. The request was granted after a short processing period. For her three years in the camp Lidia received a compensation payment of 115,425 rubles. Konstantin calculated that at that time you could buy about 500 bread rolls with this money; it came to less than half a roll for each day in the camp. In addition, post–Soviet era inflation had reached its peak by then; the currency declined so rapidly that Lidia's laughable compensation was probably worthless a few days later.

The request for rehabilitation was written by hand; small, slanted letters, surprisingly graceful and even for an eighty-one-year-old. The address was at the top of the page: when the application was made in 1992, Lidia lived in Klimovsk, a small city fifty kilometers from Moscow. I put the address into Google Maps and rubbed my eyes in surprise as I was shown not only the street but also a satellite photo of Lidia's house. I had made it all the way to my mother's sister's windows, up to the front door through which Lidia once went in and out. A typical Soviet construction from the 1950s: very imposing, painted matte pink, winter gardens, balconies, no sign of Eastern European dilapidation. On the other side of the street a small birch forest could be seen, an oasis of calm in the middle of the city, right next to a supermarket where Lidia presumably went shopping. I did not know which windows had belonged to her apartment, but I knew that I saw them. A wondrous technology that allowed me to peer into the most remote corners of the earth from my desk showed me the house where my mother's sister had lived at least until her eighty-first year. I felt a burning regret. I had been in Moscow so often as a translator, for the first time in 1972, when Lidia was only sixty-one years old. No abyss, no eternity separated me from my mother's past in Ukraine; I was only a stone's throw away. If Lidia had already lived in Klimovsk at that time, I could have reached her in an hour by train.

Now I also knew that Lidia's term in exile had already been over for five years when Matilda made her way to Medvezhya Gora to visit her daughter shortly before the start of the war. What tied Lidia to this remote place after she was released? Did she marry a man who lived there? What lay between the plank bed in Medvezhya Gora and the urban 1950s apartment with central heating and hot water near Moscow? Had Lidia actually ever returned to Mariupol after her arrest, or had she never seen the city again afterward? Did she have a family, descendants whom I could search for? The fact that her maiden name was listed in her rehabilitation request indicated that she did not (it was solely thanks to this document that I was able to find her). I saw one of those old Russian women in front of me, born in the czarist era, who had survived the revolution, the Gulag, the war, and all the catastrophes that followed in her country; tiny old women whom hunger had taught to always keep a piece of bread stored in the cupboard and who looked like saints, like white paper, almost like air. Their bodies had defied so many deaths that they seemed immortal. Lidia would be one hundred and two years old now, and I thought it not out of the question that she was still alive.

As I could now easily calculate, my mother was only eight or nine years old when Lidia went to Odessa to study. And that was already the final farewell. After she finished her studies, Lidia did in fact return to Mariupol once, but not for long. She was arrested in 1933 when my mother was thirteen years old. In Germany, she may not have had any particularly vivid memories of her sister, especially since they may have only spoken about her behind closed doors after the arrest. As a counter-revolutionary, she had become a danger for everyone who knew her, relatives most of all. Presumably my mother had already stopped speaking about her sister in Ukraine and continued this in Germany—out of an ingrained fear over which reason has no control.

Now I nearly knew more about my mother's siblings than I did about her. Among other things, I knew that Sergey had studied singing and that Lidia had studied literature. This filled me with the feeling that an almost mystical bond existed between us. I must have been related to them since across all the chasms of our different eras and worlds I also felt most at home in the same places—in Lidia's world of literature and in Sergey's world of music. But what did I share with my mother? I racked my brain over what major she had chosen, but every time the memory seemed within my grasp it slipped away. I only knew that my mother graduated with distinction; at least my father had often mentioned that with pride, although the mental illness which my father believed she suffered from could not be compatible with what he understood as intellectual achievement.

If my mother had really worked as a teacher at her aunt Valentina's former lycée, then she must have studied subjects that would have prepared her to go into teaching. Maybe she had studied German philology, the German language, in which she had already been initiated by her father, the son of the Baltic German Anna von Ehrenstreit? Could it be that she had acquired her remarkably good language skills in Germany in such a short time, or is it not more likely that she brought them with her from Ukraine? She had always been able to speak the language in Germany, unlike my father, who was like almost everyone else in the camps. Despite her profound sense of inferiority, in a foreign country she was superior to my father because she could understand and make herself understood, and interpret the signals around her much better; the country remained a closed book for him his entire life. In Germany my parents' public roles were reversed. In government offices and all the other important places of the German-speaking world, my father was deaf and dumb, dependent upon her. And a man like him probably could not forgive a woman for something like that; he probably also hated my mother for it.

The fact that my mother was still very young before the war did not mean she hadn't already earned her teaching degree. In those days in the Soviet Union enjoying your time in college was out of the question. Being allowed to study was a privilege that had to be earned through diligence and achievement, with the goal of participating in the establishment of socialism as soon as possible. At twenty, or twenty-one, my mother could certainly have already been standing in front of a class and teaching.

Much of the information, which I had puzzled over and sought along labyrinthine paths, probably could have been taken from the papers stored in our basement when we lived on the edge of a provincial German city in an enclave for former forced laborers, the final stop in my mother's journey. The papers that she brought with her from Ukraine, including diplomas which presumably never interested anyone in Germany, lay in a tin box with the relief of a German castle on the cover. I had often examined the pages in the basement, reeking of mold and covered with

Cyrillic letters—I could even make out individual words since my mother had already taught me the Russian alphabet before I started going to the German school—but one day, when I was about eight years old, I decided that we didn't need these old papers anymore, at least I didn't need them anymore. When I was once again sent into the basement to get coal I committed one of the worst crimes of my childhood. I took the box of papers and dropped it in the dumpster that stood under the stairs in the basement. I did not want there to be any evidence of the family background I so hated; I wanted it to disappear forever. Later, after my mother's death, my father searched for the papers and naturally did not suspect that they had landed on a garbage dump and probably long since decomposed. He thought someone had stolen them from our basement, perhaps one of the Soviet spies that he believed surrounded him at all times.

Konstantin and I began our search for Lidia's potential descendants. Since most people in the former Soviet Union owned their own apartments and moved much less often than in the mobile western world, Konstantin was certain that there were people living in the house in Klimovsk who had still known Lidia, presumably even relatives who had inherited her apartment and moved in after she died. Konstantin advised me to send a letter to the address written on Lidia's rehabilitation request. I was supposed to write Lidia's name on the envelope and add "or relatives/neighbors." In addition, we sent an email to the Klimovsk city administration to request information about my aunt and her descendants, in case she had any. This attempt did not seem very promising to me. There must also be a minimum level of data protection in Russia; the authorities could not be permitted to provide information about their citizens to total strangers, especially a completely unknown petitioner from abroad without any documentation to prove she was a relative. In any case, we had already written to various authorities a number of times and never received an answer; all the information we possessed had been obtained by other means. But I did as Konstantin advised, especially since I had nothing to lose, and again one of the obligatory miracles took place to which I had almost grown accustomed during this quest. After just a few days, I received an email from the Klimovsk registry office. I read:

> Dear Natalia,
> Regarding the inquiry which you sent over the internet to the municipal authorities, we can share the following with you: the records of the Klimovsk registry office show that Lidia Yakovlevna Ivashchenko died on August, 22, 2001. Her daughter Elena Yurevna Ivashchenko died on October 10, 2001. At present Lidia's grandson Kirill Grigorievich Zimov lives in the apartment at 5 Roschtschinskaya Street. Unfortunately, we do not have any more information.
> Sincerely yours,
> Svetlana Likhacheva
> Director of the Registry Office

The last sentence confused me most of all. What additional information could be added to the findings I had already received in the email? What could have been "more" than the address of Lidia's grandson? If at that moment, someone had asked me the question that was so often posed about the essence of the Russian soul, without any hesitation I would have named Svetlana Likhacheva from the Klimovsk registry office as an example. She had not acted as a civil servant, but as a human being, and had handed me, a foreigner from Germany, the key to Lidia's life and maybe the key to my mother's life along with it.

The date of Lidia's death written in the email from Klimovsk indicated that she lived for another ten years after her request for rehabilitation; thus, she lived to the age of ninety-one. A mere twelve years ago, I could have met her in the matte pink building across from the small birch forest in Klimovsk. She had lived fifty-five years longer than her sister, my mother. She had probably seen her for the last time on the day she was arrested. Could she even still remember her when she died almost seventy years later? Presumably she had gotten married after all; at any rate, she had had a daughter, my cousin Elena, who was also already dead.

After I forwarded the email from the Klimovsk registry office to Konstantin, things moved very quickly. He found a Kirill Grigorievich Zimov right away on Odnoklassniki, a social network popular in Russia. This man lived in Klimovsk, and he was forty-one years old. Both points indicated that it was Lidia's grandson. Konstantin left him a message with my email address and sent me his photo from the social network. I was shocked. During my quest I had gotten used to the fact that my relatives were good-looking, educated people; now I had apparently arrived at the opposite end of the spectrum. I peered into the dull, apathetic face of a man who looked like a giant, bloated baby. Apparently he was one of those members of the Russian proletariat whom Lidia, his grandmother, had once wanted to liberate. He sat on a shabby sofa with a greasy carpet in the stereotypical Russian baroque design behind him—one of those post-Soviet dwellings where the roommate's name is usually alcohol.

If it had been the first photo that I had seen of my mother's family, I would not have been surprised in the least: it would only have confirmed my expectations. Compared to the world that my mother inhabited in Germany, the photo exuded something of the homeliness, the middle-class security, that seemed so desirable to me as a child. But how could I reconcile this man's appearance with that of all the others, whose photos I had seen before? Was this the deplorable remnant of the family?

Only now, when I read the email from the Klimovsk registry office word for word for the fourth or fifth time, did I notice one strange detail. Lidia died on August 22, 2001, and her daughter Elena died on October 10 of the same year, or just seven weeks later. What could that mean? It was not difficult to picture a geriatric mother whose will to live is extinguished by the death of a child, but why did the daughter die right after her ninety-one-year-old mother? Had she, presumably also an older woman, suffered from a grave illness and been unable to cope with the death of her mother? In any case, it was almost inconceivable that no connection existed between the two deaths.

In the meantime I had grown wary, so I asked myself if some new family disaster was hidden behind it, particularly since I discovered another irritating detail in the email from the registry office. I had something rare in common with Kirill Zimov, who, if I understood correctly, was my second cousin. Our mothers both died on October 10, though their deaths took place fifty-five years apart. I could not resist the thought that this was no chance coincidence, that it was all connected in some spooky way, that somewhere in the fog I would discover that my family history had taken another sinister turn.

I still held out faint hope that the photo from the social network was not Lidia's grandson at all, that it was only someone with the same name, but the good fortune which had accompanied me on this quest continued. Once again, I had found a relative. My laptop announced that an email had arrived from Kirill Zimov. I read:

> Hello Natalia!
> I received a message that your mother was my grandmother's sister and that you wanted me to send you an email. I know that my grandmother had a brother and sister, and I know that their names were Sergey and Evgenia. I don't know anything about Sergey except that he was an opera singer; my grandmother had a record of his singing which she often played for me. About your mother, Evgenia, I heard that she married an American officer and emigrated to the United States. My grandmother Lidia spent a long time looking for her, but without success. In those days there was no internet.
>
> My grandmother had two children; Elena, my mother, and Igor, my uncle. My mother is dead and my uncle lives in Miass, but unfortunately

I don't have his address. I live with my wife and two children in my grandmother's old apartment. I am attaching a few photos.
Yours truly,
Kirill Zimov

I opened the attachment. There she was . . . Lidia, who had been missing for so long and presumed dead, whose name I not so long ago assumed had been written on a small memorial plaque on a tree in Karelia. She did not look a lot like my mother, but she seemed strangely familiar—as though I was looking at the picture I had formed of her out of the void. A serious, sensitive, and proud woman with a very direct, searching gaze; you could not say for certain whether it expressed aggression or fear. A gaze through which she seemed to be measuring herself against an unseen figure standing opposite; under no circumstances would she be the first to lower her eyes. Short, curly locks and a simple summer dress with a white collar. I could not guess Lidia's age in this photo, whether it was from her time in the camp or afterward, but if Medvezhya Gora was already behind her, she had survived the attempt to break her completely unscathed.

In the second photo, I saw a completely different woman. I estimated that she was about fifty; she looked grim, hard, inscrutable, like an impregnable fortress, a sphinx. Here, it seemed to me, you could see a survivor of the machinery of destruction, ground down further and worn out from the times that followed, the long demoralizing years of daily life in the Soviet Union. In this photo, she projected something of that species, *Homo sovieticus*, which her grandson seemed to embody. Here, he could be seen next to his grandmother at the age of about three, a chubby, serious child who seemed to be made of white marshmallow. You could already clearly see the outline of his future bulk.

A third photo showed Lidia as an old woman. A tiny, extremely delicate old lady with a full head of snow-white hair; everything hard and embittered had once again fallen away, and the young Lidia radiated through the wrinkled skin. She sat upright in an armchair, impeccably dressed and coiffed, with a string of pearls around her neck and her thin, stockinged legs positioned in front of her, meticulously ladylike.

Kirill wrote that after her divorce she lived alone for more than thirty years and that she was able to look after herself until her death. She was very agile and disciplined right to the end, exercising daily and always eating her meals at the same time. She worked as a teacher of Russian language and literature until she was almost seventy, and remained completely mentally alert. In July, 2001, she fell down in her apartment and broke her hip. She died of heart failure in the hospital a short while later.

Regarding her time in the camp, Kirill only knew that she was employed as a teacher in a penal colony for juvenile and young offenders and that this was probably the only reason she was able to survive. She had gotten married in Medvezhya Gora, and her son Igor, who was born in the camp, must be about seventy-five now. Kirill had not been in touch with him for a long time, but he knew that he lived beyond the Urals in the Siberian city of Miass.

Kirill never knew his great-grandmother Matilda, who died five years before he was born. But he still remembered very well how, as a child, he traveled with his grandmother Lidia by train from Klimovsk to Voskresensk to put a homemade wooden cross on his great-grandmother's grave. I instantly pictured the scene: an older woman and a small boy transporting a wooden cross by train and carrying it to the cemetery in Voskresensk. They had probably taken the wood for the cross from the forest earlier, maybe from the birch grove that could be seen from the satellite photo of Lidia's house. An amateurishly nailed together Russian Orthodox cross with the traditional slanted third bar that now stood in the cemetery in Voskresensk, a city whose name meant both Sunday and resurrection. Surely a small plate with the name Matilda De Martino or Matilda Ivashchenko affixed to the cross, an enamel medallion with a photo, as was customary in Russia.

I found some comfort in the thought of Matilda's grave. I could place her somewhere now, unlike my mother. I now knew that she was not torn apart by a German bomb during the war, but that she died a natural death at the age of eighty-six and had lain in the Voskresensk cemetery ever since under a wooden cross with her name on it made by her daughter.

By then, Kirill had also received the letter I sent him by regular mail. The letter carrier had known Lidia, and remembered that Kirill was her grandson. That too was a Russian miracle, though Konstantin and I did not need it any more thanks to Svetlana Likhacheva from the Klimovsk registry office.

I asked Kirill about Sergey's record, which Lidia supposedly played for him as a child. In reality, this could not have happened since my cousin Evgenia, who worshiped her father's every note, had complained that there was not a single recording of his voice. Konstantin had also already moved heaven and earth to dig up a recording, but despite the fact that Sergey had been engaged at the most important theaters of the former Soviet Union, it was as though he had been purged from the annals of Soviet opera history. Kirill continued to insist that he remembered his voice perfectly and that he knew the record had a dark blue label with gold lettering. It must have gotten lost when the apartment was cleaned out after Lidia's death, and it probably landed in the garbage dump by mistake.

Actually, Kirill wasn't such a bad guy. I couldn't reconcile his emails with his photo; it may have just been a very unflattering shot. He worked as a programmer, wrote flawless Russian, and remained unfailingly polite, which did not support my conclusion that he had fallen victim to alcohol, Russia's national drug. He sent me many photos of his children (a boy and a girl, both pre-school age) whom he seemed to love and on whose proper upbringing he placed great value. I saw both children in the kitchen finger painting and blowing out candles on a birthday cake.

His matter-of-fact manner and sense of propriety were a bit strange. He answered all of my questions thoroughly, but never showed any emotion. Only once, when he tore a photo of his mother while taking it out of an album to scan it, did he get so upset that the extent of his rage irritated me and made me feel guilty.

The only thing he had told me about his mother so far was that her marriage had not lasted long—his parents got divorced when he was two years old. His father was still alive, and he saw him frequently. When I asked him warily why his mother died so young, he wrote:

> I was raised differently than other children in Russia. My mother and my grandmother did not want to have anything to do with Soviet society and gave me an entirely false picture of the Russian people and my contemporaries. They considered the other children in my neighborhood to be primitive and debased. I was kept away from them and lived in the virtual world of mathematics, for which I had a special talent even as a child. Anyone who is raised like that can never start a family and have children. I only succeeded because I was able to pass through the Russian school of life as a seaman in the navy. You asked me about the reason for my mother's early death. The reason is that I murdered her. I was found not criminally liable and put in a mental institution for four years.

It was late at night. The ice was no longer cracking; it was now swimming in fragile islands on the lake, but at night, there was still the same seemingly endless darkness. I stared at the email in front of me and asked myself if Kirill Zimov was making a fool of me. Certainly, I knew that there were murderers in the world, even those who had killed their own mothers, but was it possible that I, of all people, was related to one of them? I, who had not been related to anyone for my entire life? I cursed myself for having begun this quest. What had I gotten myself into? Why was I doing this to myself? My thoughts rushed to Konstantin, but at this hour, he had already long since fallen asleep, seeing as it was two hours later in Cherepovets. Also, none of my friends were still awake; I could not call anyone. Slowly, I understood; the apathetic, dull gaze in the photo, Kirill's stereotypical courtesy and lack of emotion, the use of the word "correct" when he referred to raising his children, his disproportionate anger over the torn photo of his mother. Since I knew the date of her death, it was easy for me to calculate that Kirill Zimov was thirty years old when he murdered her. Did he become capable of committing this murder after going through what he called the Russian school of life in the navy, considered to be the most brutal branch of the Russian military? Doubtless he was already mentally ill before being committed to the psychiatric hospital, and it is certain that he was not offered any psychotherapy in the Russian clinic, but treated with drugs prior to being released as a zombie. Maybe he was also under heavy medication now, to me he seemed like a ticking time bomb. I was horrified when I thought of his wife and two small children. Who was this woman, who had entered into marriage with such a man? Wasn't she worried about her children and herself?

The motive that first occurred to me was the apartment: the permanent, catastrophic housing shortage in Russia which often held entire extended families captive in a tiny space for their entire lives and drove many people insane. Even Mikhail Bulgakov in his novel *The Master and Margarita* wrote that Muscovites are human beings just like everyone else, no better and no worse, only the housing shortage has ruined them. Had Lidia's grandson also been ruined by the housing crisis? Did he kill his mother in a dispute over the apartment which became available after Lidia's death? Was this the reason why mother and daughter died almost simultaneously? In any case, the evidence seemed to suggest that as long as she was alive Lidia had held her grandson in check. Her death must have set him free.

For some reason I was certain that Kirill had strangled his mother. I saw her before me, my cousin Elena, with the giant baby's massive paws around her neck. In one photo that Kirill sent me she was an imposing woman with a powerful presence and an intense sensuality—in contrast to her decidedly delicate mother, Lidia. Maybe she put up fierce resistance, maybe it had been a long death struggle. And all of this happened on the same date as my mother's death—the niece and aunt both died violent deaths on October 10, one as a result of an external act of violence, the other through violence against herself.

I thought of Svetlana Likhacheva from the Klimovsk registry office. Now I understood the sentence in which she informed me that she did not have any *more* information. She wrote that sentence precisely because she did. After all, registry offices did not only issue marriage certificates but also birth and death certificates, and Svetlana Likhacheva would have known about the murder not only as an employee of the registry office but also as a resident of Klimovsk. Mothers were sacred in Russia, and news about a matricide would get around in no time in a relatively small city. Maybe Svetlana Likhacheva's extraordinary helpfulness was due to her sympathy for me and my ignorance; maybe she knew what I would find at Lidia's old address.

I asked myself why Kirill had confessed to me, a distant relative who appeared out of nowhere, to whom he was not obligated to say anything under any circumstances. Was it because he had a guilty conscience, or shamelessness because he did not feel guilty at all? Was he taught to deal openly with his crime? Could that be a part of the code of conduct that his Russian schools of life had taught him, first the Russian navy and then the Russian mental hospital? And who was Lidia, the sister of my mother, whom I had spent so much time trying to find, who had allied with her daughter to control a child because she did not want him to become a Soviet man? Was she raised with a rigid class consciousness and taught to look down on Soviet people? Did the nobility's disdain for ordinary people lurk behind the family's liberalism and their commitment to the community? Did Lidia succeed in clinging to her class consciousness during some seventy years of Soviet rule, or was she, on the contrary, one of the defeated? Had she, without having noticed it herself, become part of the totalitarian system by taking possession of her grandson together with her daughter, isolating him and breaking him down, just as the system had once seized, isolated, and broken her? And, after he had gone through the

Russian school of life in the navy and become a Soviet man after all, had he done away with the nobility a second time by murdering his mother, a representative of that obsolete social class whose unfortunate remnant he was as well? Why did he have to do that in order to be able to marry and have children? What had happened between him and his mother?

I spoke silently with Konstantin. I knew that he rushed to open his inbox every day after he got up. Sometimes he even answered me before he had to go to work, which at this time of year meant heading out into the bitter cold. I clicked "forward" on Kirill's email and sent it to Konstantin with the comment that now we had really landed in a crime thriller, which is what we jokingly called our quest.

I stared into the blackness outside the window, which only reflected the light of my desk lamp, and asked myself what sort of family my mother really came from. And what did all of this have to do with me, the Soviet and post-Soviet fiasco, the never ending Russian *fatum*, the inability to wake up from a collective nightmare, imprisoned between subservience and anarchy, between patient suffering and violence, this entire unenlightened, gloomy world, this family history of helplessness, dispossession, despotism and death, this disastrous Russia—the eternal *mater dolorosa* who embraced her children so mercilessly. As a girl I had instinctively done exactly the right thing by running away and escaping from my origins without suspecting what I was really a part of. Now more than ever, I was overcome with the feeling that my rebellion was useless, that for me there was no salvation, that I was rooted in a poisonous and foul ground out of which even a matricide had emerged.

At this unusual hour, my notebook gave out the quiet signal that a new message had arrived. It came from the Azov's Greeks. Konstantin had once written to me that during the course of our long exchange he had learned to read my mind. Now he must have read it in his sleep and gotten up again. He did not go back to bed that night, we emailed each other until morning. In his eyes, Kirill was an unfortunate, pitiable person, a fallen man whom I had found in order to extend my hand to him. But Konstantin overestimated me. I did not possess his humanity, his all-encompassing Ukrainian-Greek soul; I dreaded Kirill, even from a great distance. "I am not giving up hope that at the end we will still find someone you can embrace," Konstantin wrote me in his last email that morning. He had already been dreaming about this for a while: When we have found them all we will meet in Mariupol and celebrate with a feast. I did not know if I still wanted to find anyone, but to meet Konstantin in Mariupol and embrace him—what a thought!

I had begun to fear my findings, and the good fortune that followed me so persistently during my investigation. But now I naturally couldn't simply forget that apparently I had a cousin somewhere in Siberia who, in case he was still alive, was possibly the most important witness in my family history. His sister's killer, of all people, had led me to him. From Kirill Zimov, I knew that this Igor was born in the Medvezhya Gora prison camp, in other words between 1931 and 1933, so that it was entirely possible that he had still gotten to know my mother, even if he was just a small boy at that time.

Before we began to look for him, Konstantin achieved the impossible—a stroke of genius. Kirill was right, an album that included my uncle Sergey's voice really did exist. Konstantin found it on the internet, a 1956 recording of the opera *Chornomortsi* by Mykola Lyssenko.[16] It was a recording by the National Symphony Orchestra of Ukraine, with Sergey Yakovlevich Ivashchenko singing the bass part. Konstantin sent me the recording in advance on my computer.

I heard my uncle's voice on an electronic recording with perfect sound quality, allowing me to forget what a distant time and place it came from. After the first notes, I was already hypnotized. For decades, ever since my first visit to the opera in Munich, I had searched for such voices and now I had found one of them in my own family, one of those singers I always thought did not sing at all, but simply breathed. Or cried.

I looked at the summertime photo in front of me of the lively adolescent with a sailor's cap on his head sitting barefoot on a branch by the

Dnieper. There was nothing to indicate what would later emerge from this boy's throat: a voluminous base with a timbre, which, as is always the case with great singers, seemed to come not from the throat, but from another place that was not quite of this world. Sergey was forty-one years old in 1956 when the record was made; it was the exact same year my mother died. I tried to add her light soprano to his bass, to imagine what it had sounded like when they sang together. It seemed like a hallucination to me, that her brother's voice was now here in my room, that I heard it while I looked at my wall, my furniture, and the maple tree outside the window, knowing that my mother used to hear this exact same voice, that it was a part of her life in Mariupol.

I now saw my cousin Evgenia in a new light. If you had a father with a voice like that, you were almost inevitably lost. I was no longer surprised that she had sacrificed her life for him, that until today he had remained the center of her existence. People shield themselves from beauty in order not to lose themselves and abandon the rules of life. Evgenia could not protect herself; her defense was unsuccessful, and for this, she probably paid a high price.

I kept clicking the file with Sergey's voice; I did not know what was stronger, the joy over what had been found, or the pain over what I had missed out on. There was a long period during which I could have also met Sergey in Ukraine if I had known about him. Two years before his death I had driven with my former boyfriend in our own car to Moscow (which was still unusual at that time) to visit our Russian friends, and on the way back we drove across Ukraine. I had eaten ice cream on the Maidan in Kyiv, and as we wandered among the steep, old alleys we may have walked past Sergey's house. I had missed him; thirty years ago he dropped dead in the street on his way home from a park where he worked as a security guard. But his voice lived on, I had found it, it was here in my computer, and I could listen to it whenever I wanted. Of all the miracles that had occurred during my quest, this one struck me as the most incredible.

On Odnoklassniki, where Konstantin had already discovered Kirill Zimov, he now found a thirteen-year-old from Miass who had the same family name as Lidia's son, a Siberian teenager who wore a zany red cap and an expensive-looking watch on his wrist in his profile photo. It was quickly established that he was Igor's grandson. He even still remembered that his great-grandmother was named Lidia Ivashchenko. Now everything depended on whether this thirteen-year-old could act as a liaison between his grandfather and me, or whether the old man merely got on his nerves. But he turned out to be very cooperative and intelligent. Just a few days later, he sent me a message with a telephone number. His grandfather, he wrote, was speechless after hearing the news and waiting impatiently for me to call.

By then, I had gotten my car repaired after it had been chewed up by the marten, so I packed up my things that same day and drove back to Berlin (I could have called Siberia on my mobile phone, but that would have cost a fortune and probably been an acoustic disaster because of the distance). There, for the first time in my life, I dialed a phone number in Siberia. The number that the thirteen-year-old sent me seemed to be correct, at least I could hear it ringing, and shortly thereafter someone picked up the receiver. The male voice on the other end shook noticeably when it asked whether we should address each other with the formal or informal "you."[17] "We searched for your mother for a long time," my cousin said, "we waited a long time for a sign of life." My voice also shook suspiciously while I searched for words with which to begin the conversation.

As I now learned, Kirill Zimov had not only murdered his mother, but also destroyed her brother's life. After Igor's aging mother died thirteen years ago, followed shortly thereafter by his sister Elena, who was murdered by her son, he suffered a stroke from which he never recovered. Now he was seventy-eight years old and almost totally dependent on his wife, whose mobility was also severely limited after battling cancer.

As a trained geodesist, he had last worked as the director of a large building materials company in Miass, where he had lived for the past sixty years. He had two children, three grandchildren, and one great-grandchild. His son and daughter had become successful entrepreneurs in the new Russia; the family did not seem to lack anything. Thanks to the satellite camera I could take a look at the modern high-rise where he lived with his wife—by Siberian standards probably the last word in luxury. From his large balcony, he could see out onto the foothills of the Urals and observe the enormous temperature fluctuations—in a few minutes the mercury rose or fell in front of his eyes by fifteen degrees.

Unfortunately, Igor had never known my mother. He had never been to Mariupol, and my mother had never been to Medvezhya Gora. Moreover, it very soon became clear to me that he was not the witness I had hoped to find. As a child of the camps, he had learned his lesson early and, like so many of his fellow citizens, had chosen internal emigration. He lived according to the motto of the famous three monkeys, who closed their eyes, ears, and mouth. Either he truly knew nothing about his family background, or keeping silent about it had become part of his character. He never mentioned Stalin and Hitler, but only referred to them as "the two mustaches," and he also expunged the name of his nephew Kirill from his vocabulary. My questions about him fell on deaf ears.

Once, while Igor was on one of his short walks, I spoke with his wife Lyubov, who told me that Kirill had gotten up at night and gone over to his mother's room and suffocated her with a pillow. Afterward, he went into the kitchen, scraped a jar of mayonnaise clean, and went back to sleep. Lyubov said that Kirill's mother had loved her husband more than anything, and that after he abandoned her, she poured all of her love into her son. Supposedly, she idolized and completely spoiled him. She considered him to be a prodigy because of his gift for mathematics, and she promoted the idea that he was a genius. But over the years, he became increasingly despotic, and, having grown into a giant, he began to threaten his mother more and more; on several occasions, she fled to her brother in Miass. On one occasion he destroyed all of her furnishings because he was of the opinion that she had been alive for far too long and that it was finally time for her to exit in order to make room for the youth. That certainly wasn't the whole story that could be told about my cousin Elena and her son Kirill, but maybe I also didn't want to hear all of it.

From the few words that Igor said about his mother, I understood that Lidia was a gruff, unapproachable person, evidently reticent like him. He could not remember if she had ever embraced or caressed him. Igor thought the idea that she was the product of an incestuous relationship between her mother Matilda and her uncle Valentino was nonsense, a delusion of his cousin Evgenia, with whom he had not been in contact in decades.

He had lived under the same roof with his grandmother Matilda for a long time after she moved in with them in Medvezhya Gora. During the war, the family was evacuated to Kazakhstan, where they struggled to survive for five years, until Igor's father obtained a position as a chief engineer in Voskresensk. Matilda never returned to Mariupol, but stayed with them until her death. At the end she was apparently almost deaf and usually spoke only with her eyes; most of the time she could be seen sitting at the kitchen table playing solitaire. From what Igor said, I could conclude that she had also been an unfriendly, harsh, and unapproachable woman, matching the description that Sergey's daughter Evgenia had provided.

Why had my mother portrayed her as a maternal, Madonna-like woman, whose kindheartedness knew no bounds? Was it possible that Matilda had a special relationship to my mother, to her last child, who had been born so late? Was it possible that this gentle, defenseless girl absorbed all of the love that Matilda had not otherwise shown to anyone? Was my mother the only one who had known Matilda as the soulful, gentle woman she described?

Igor, who as a child had never felt loved by his mother or grandmother, left home at sixteen with a light heart to study in Moscow, and after he took his exams, he was assigned to a position as a land surveyor in Siberia. There, so he told me, he began to drink uncontrollably. If it weren't for Lyubov, he would have fallen into a roadside ditch at some point and never gotten up again.

In response to my questions about our uncle Sergey, he either could, or would, not say anything; he only mentioned that he had seen him once in a performance of *Ruslan and Lyudmila* in Alma-Ata. He was still a child then and he was afraid of his uncle's thunderous voice. In passing, he mentioned that Sergey had been a lead singer in Germany after the war. A fictional scenario instantly played out in my mind's eye: my mother and her brother meet by chance on German territory. He is a soldier in the Red Army assigned to entertain soldiers with arias from Russian operas; she is a former forced laborer who worked for the war-time enemy. Would the siblings have embraced, or would they have faced each other as adversaries, irreconcilable to the end? What would it have meant for my mother if she had known that her brother was also in Germany, maybe right nearby? Would her life have taken a different turn if she had known what I now knew—is it even possible that she would have taken advantage of the opportunity and moved back with him to Ukraine, especially since it must have become clear to her in the meantime that she had no future in Germany?

Once again I received family photos, this time from Igor via his son's computer: his children and grandchildren on vacation in Finland, Italy, and the United States; his son's large and impressive house in Miass, set on a large plot of land with shaggy pine trees and equipped with a Siberian sauna; photos of family celebrations with dozens of guests and tables groaning with food and drink in an atmosphere of Russian pomp.

Among Igor's old family photos, I was surprised to find not only the picture of my mother in a headscarf when she was young but also the one where she had written "grandfather and two acquaintances" on the back. Only here there were not two but three acquaintances. In all the years I had owned the print, I had never noticed that it had been cropped. In Igor's photo, Elena could also be seen next to Natalia and Valentina, my mother's third aunt whom I already knew from the family photo with the indoor palm. *Lumière Odessa* was written on the border of the fully intact photograph in ornate lettering, arranged perpendicularly. Now I could reconstruct the context in which the photo had been taken. From Lidia's case file, I knew that her aunt Elena had lived in Odessa. Yakov, my mother's father, had driven there with his sisters Valentina and Natalia to visit Elena. On this occasion, the four siblings went to the studio *Lumière* to have their picture taken. I saw my mother's father with three of his four sisters. Only Olga was missing, she was living with her husband in Moscow unless by that time she had already ended her life. But why had Elena been cut out of my mother's photo? Konstantin explained that after the revolution countless people disappeared from photos. They removed themselves or were removed by others because they had become a danger to those with whom they had been captured together on celluloid. Was it the case that not only Lidia but also her aunt Elena, posed a political risk? Or was Elena eliminated because of a private, family feud?

I clicked on another photo and saw Sergey as an adult for the first time. In one of the pictures, he wore a Red Army uniform and the Order of the Red Star, a very young man then, all spruced up with a soft, still almost childlike face. In the next photo he might have been twenty years older, a very masculine, imposing man with dark, curly hair, a strong chin, and my mother's melancholy eyes. Publicity photos depict him as Prince Gremin in *Eugene Onegin*, as Count Tomsky in *The Queen of Spades*, the title role in *Boris Godunov*, as the Great Prince of Kyiv in *Ruslan and Lyudmila* and as Mephistopheles in Gounod's *Faust.* Sergey was, as now became clear, not only an exceptionally gifted singer, but also a great actor. In every photo, he was somebody else; he must have had many more faces than these few pictures could show. He exuded a frightening power, something demonic, oscillating and impossible to pin down.

As I now noticed, one of the attached picture files was labeled, "The children of Matilda Josefovna De Martino and Yakov Epifanovich Ivashchenko: Lidia, Sergey, and Evgenia." My heart skipped a beat. I opened the file and did not understand what I saw. I recognized Lidia right away, who could have been eighteen here; the roughly thirteen-year-old boy was undoubtedly Sergey, but where was Evgenia, my mother? Between the siblings there was only an unknown little girl with a giant Russian ribbon in her hair, the kind that always look like small propellers on top of children's heads. Slowly, in stages, I grasped that exactly this unknown girl was my mother. At first glance, the distance had been too great from my memory of the adult woman to this child, although my mother's features could easily be recognized on this small face—her eyes, her forehead, and her chin. She must have been about eight years old; she wore an expensive-looking white lace dress, and her black hair was styled in a precision-cut page boy with short bangs.

It was nowhere near what I had imagined she looked like. So dressed up, so delicate, a child from a good family. No trace of her parents' poverty. They had probably dressed her up in the last things they had and sent her to the hairdresser's before the trip to the photographer's. While her siblings looked into the camera, she looked through it. Absent, shrouded eyes, already as a child the embodiment of melancholy. Without question my mother, and yet also a strange child whom I could not approach. So delicate and fragile that I would not have dared to touch her, to take her into my arms. A tiny princess wrapped in white lace from the planet of incurable sadness. I didn't know if my knowledge of her fate put it into my mind, or if at this young age, it was already apparent that she was doomed, that it would be impossible for her to withstand the horrors of her time. It was hard to believe that this transparent, lucid creature nevertheless lived for thirty-six years, years of an era in which everything was against her and aimed at her destruction from the start. Presumably, the photo from Lidia's estate reached her son in Siberia and from there my screen in Berlin. My tiny, lost mother, whom they fished out of Germany's Regnitz about thirty years later—in my search I had penetrated almost all the way to her origins, I probably couldn't find anything more from her than this childhood photo.

The final photo sent from Miass showed the house where my mother grew up, the house of my Italian great-grandparents, Teresa and Giuseppe De Martino. Igor's son had driven with his wife to Mariupol a few years ago to walk in the footsteps of his ancestors, and he had photographed the severely dilapidated building. In Soviet times, when my mother lived in Mariupol, the street was named Ulitsa Lenina, since then it had had gotten its old name back. You could read it in white lettering on a dark blue sign that was attached to the gate—a street named after Saint Nikolai, the miracle-worker, the patron saint of travelers, prisoners, and orphans, Nikolaevskaya Ulitsa.

The house consisted of two wings which extended around the back to form a hidden courtyard. In the photo, you could only see the two front sides which faced the street and were connected by an archway. The old edifice was a portrait of post-Soviet melancholy and neglect. You could literally smell the decay, the urine, the garbage, the dry rot in the walls. Crumbling stone, eaten away by time and industrial pollution, from which it was only possible to guess how the house had once looked, close to a hundred years ago when my mother was born. With a bit of imagination, you could still recognize the ornate window moldings, the elaborately woven, wrought-iron ornamentation, the charm of the flower-shaped dormer windows, now overgrown with grass and brushwood, reminding me of storks' nests. The weathered archway between the two wings was made out of gray stones that appeared to be loosely layered atop one another and seemed as though they could collapse at any moment. A rusty gutter, cables hanging off an ancient antenna on a roof of porous tile. Two incomplete coats of paint, one blue, the other pink.

Seeing the house conjured up images of my mother's life in Mariupol. I saw her as a little girl playing in the inner courtyard behind the archway, frolicking about with other children and her brother Sergey. I heard the nanny Tonya calling after her; I saw her walking through the then intact archway with a schoolbag on her back. All of her journeys must have gone through this archway, and they must have begun on this street. The broken cobblestones, partially overgrown with weeds, that were pictured in the photo may have been from that time. Assuming that

Nikolaevskaya Ulitsa was located in the Italian district in those days, my mother may have sometimes visited her cousins in the neighboring Greek district, and she may have often heard Greek spoken alongside Ukrainian, Russian, and Italian. The Italian language was still present in the city today; at least the area around Nikolaevskaya Ulitsa was teeming with Italian restaurants (as I saw on the satellite photo), though that was more likely a manifestation of the new era than a remnant of the past. No place on earth had ever been more distant and unimaginable to me than the one now in front of my eyes on the screen.

The phone calls between me and my cousin Igor had a strange quality, since our possible topics of conversation were limited. Igor was not only reticent, but, like most Russians, also a person who always pored over the great, shared grief and buried the individual within himself. Moreover, the Russian code of conduct forbid questions that would touch upon something unpleasant, and it was not customary to talk about your private problems. For all intents and purposes, Igor and I never spoke about anything. We had no common themes; we had lived our lives in different worlds, but I felt that there was a deep and sensitive soul hidden in this lonely old man who did not want to speak, or could not. Gradually something like a gentle love developed between us.

Igor always waited impatiently for me to call and worried the one time when I didn't check in for three or four days in a row, and I worried as well; I was afraid that the thin thread of Igor's life would suddenly snap now that I had found him. In the intervals between our phone calls, I thought about him, and I sensed that the reverse was also true.

In Russian your cousin is called your *dvoyurodny brat*, or second brother, but usually you drop the "second" and simply say "brother." "What is my brother doing?" I asked Igor's wife when she picked up the phone. I tried it out, uttering a word that was entirely new to me, brother; it was inconceivable I had a brother, and for him, I was a sister—"what is he doing right now?" I asked myself several times a day. And yet Igor was much more than a brother to me. Although he almost never spoke about our family, he was the living link between me and my ancestors, the Ukrainian-Italian clan which in the meantime I had cursed so often; he personified that clan, and there were moments in which it seemed to me that he was going to tell me something about my mother. On the other hand, he seemed to have found something in me of the sister Elena whom he had lost and whose death by her son's hand had shaken him so badly that his inner light only flickered weakly. It was some comfort that this condition had persisted for more than ten years, a chronic flickering, that might still drag on for a long time. I could not replace Igor's sister for him, but sometimes, I sensed that not only was he a gift for me, but that I was the same for him, an unexpected new connection to the world, from which he had already shut himself off.

What Konstantin had wished for me had come true. At long last, I had found someone I could embrace, this nearly eighty-year-old, gravely ill, and reticent man in Siberia, with whom the strands of my life converged. My search had come to an end; there was nothing more for me to find. I could hardly believe it, but I had tracked them all down, my mother's entire family, not only the dead but also those who were still alive. I could not hope to receive any additional information about my mother from more distant relatives. Igor was the final station in my quest, which began with a whimsical game on the internet one summer night on the lake. And yet there was still something else waiting for me.

When Igor and his wife moved into the comfortable high-rise with an elevator after his stroke, he kept his apartment on the fourth floor of an old building just in case. Now the older of his two grandchildren in Miass had announced his plans to marry. He did not face the same fate as most newlyweds in Russia, who had to take shelter in their parents' cramped two-room apartments—there was plenty of room in his father's house. But he wanted to live apart from his parents. When they were clearing out his grandfather's old apartment, where he intended to move with his wife after the wedding, they found two notebooks on top of a cabinet under layers of flaky dust. It turned out that they were Lidia's journals. Igor had no idea how they could have ended up on top of this cabinet, and they had almost been thrown out together with the old furniture.

Igor could not read the notebooks; his eyes weren't good enough anymore. Maybe he did not even want to read them? And as someone who grew up in the Soviet Union, he was still accustomed to the ban on making copies. He could not imagine that now, even in Russia, you could simply walk into a copy shop and make as many copies as you wanted of any document, so he allowed his son to send me the valuable notebooks by mail. With a constant, inner trembling, I thought of the long and dangerous journey being made by the records of the witness I might finally have found. It seemed to me as though the notebooks had only been waiting for me to appear during all those years when they lay under a growing layer of dust, as though Lidia had put them on top of her son's cabinet just for me.

Time passed, and my fears were confirmed: the shipment did not arrive. Every day I waited for the mail; my mailbox on the ground floor of the house was always stuffed full of advertisements and other junk mail, but the package from Siberia was still missing. Had the notebooks fallen victim to censorship, had they been confiscated? Or had they gotten stuck on one leg of the journey and disappeared? I thought of a book I had once translated where coeds worked part time as mail carriers during the semester break. They took the heavy mail bags from the post office, dumped the contents in the nearest garbage bin, and took the rest of the day off. Had the crown jewels of my quest met a similar fate?

Eventually it turned out that Russia's shambolic economy was not to blame for the package's failure to arrive, but that the cause lay elsewhere. Deutsche Post had sent the notebooks to my address on the Schaalsee despite the fact that I had not filled out a form to have my mail forwarded. When I arrived there on a stormy April day, the damp envelope with the taped-over Berlin address fell out of the mailbox and into my hands. It had probably already been sitting there for weeks, exposed to the elements in the lonely metal box on the side of the house.

I carried my bags quickly into the cold house and ripped open the envelope, in a rush, as if the voice of my mother's sister could still be lost at the last moment. The notebooks were a bit damp, but undamaged, one green, the other brown, both roughly in A5 format, the uneven pages sewn together, as though they had not been produced by machine, but by hand. They were not diaries, but something like a memoir which Lidia had written when she was eighty, ten years before her death. The checkered pages were covered with the tiny, slanted handwriting that was already familiar to me from the rehabilitation request, surprisingly even for an eighty-year-old and written as though in a single spurt, almost without any corrections.

A poem from Georgy Ivanov was on the first page:

Russia is happiness. Russia is light.
Or, perhaps, there is no Russia at all.

And the sunset did not burn down over the Neva,
And Pushkin did not die on the snow,

And there is no Petersburg, no Kremlin—
Only snow and snow and snow, fields and fields . . .

Snow and snow and snow . . . And the night is long,
And the snow will never melt.

Snow and snow and snow . . . And the night is dark,
And it will never end.

Russia is silence. Russia is dust.
Or, perhaps, Russia is only fear.

A noose, a bullet, the frozen dark
And music that drives you mad.

A noose, a bullet, a forced-labor dawn
Over that for which there is no name in the world.[18]

I wrapped myself in a wool blanket and sat in the big armchair by the window that looked out onto the stormy, slate-gray lake and began to read. It began with a quote from the Book of Deuteronomy, "To me belongeth vengeance, and recompense." I swallowed. I waited breathlessly for the first mention of my mother. It's true that Lidia reported on her birth, but beyond that, she was hardly mentioned in the memoir. I had to satisfy myself by looking for my mother between the lines, in her former milieu, which her sister had seen with her own eyes and now showed me up close.

PART TWO

Aunt Lidia's Journals

My mother's father Yakov, who was sentenced to twenty years in exile for his revolutionary ideas, is allowed to spend the final years of his banishment under surveillance in Warsaw, at the edge of the former Russian Empire. In 1911, his daughter Lidia is born there.

As I already suspected, Matilda De Martino is not Yakov's first wife. Lidia spends her early childhood together with her step-brother Andrey, a product of her father's marriage in his place of exile, who is awestruck in Warsaw where he sees a city for the first time.

Yakov earns a modest salary as a history teacher at a Warsaw high school, but he is married to a woman who, thanks to the vast fortune of her Italian parents, is very well off. They reside in a spacious apartment in the heart of the old town, where they employ a Polish cook, a Russian nanny, and an English tutor, Miss Wigmore. Yakov calls her Miss "Hello and Goodbye" because she wears a hat with two identically small visors on the front and the back. As a small child, Lidia already speaks all three languages, mixing them up constantly, while her father speaks French as well, the language of the Russian nobility, and German, which he learned from his Baltic German mother, Anna von Ehrenstreit. Matilda is an extremely gifted musician; she plays Chopin and Mozart on the expensive grand piano which stands in the apartment. Polish intellectuals, musicians, and poets are frequent guests. Yakov is permitted to travel around Sweden and England, where he secretly meets with activists from the revolutionary worker's movements that are based there. This does not prevent him from living in grand style in Warsaw and vacationing with his family in Poland's elegant Lazienki health resort. It is a luxurious exile that ends when the Germans march into Warsaw in 1915. Yakov is allowed to return to Mariupol, a free man after twenty years. Shortly after, they return to their old hometown, Sergey, my mother's brother, is born.

During this time, Mariupol is a multicultural city. Ukrainians, Russians, Greeks, Italians, French, Germans, Turks, Poles, many are Jews. The city lies on a hill, from every location you can see the Azov, which is known for its abundant fish stocks. When the enormous schools of sturgeon and pike perch swim past, the water seems to boil.

The fishermen live all the way down on the beach, a bit above them up the hill are the workers, mostly longshoremen. Wooden huts, earthen huts, shacks and sheds, in which people live crowded together in deep poverty. There is no plumbing, no electricity; people have to draw water from a well with buckets. Muddy ground, stench, and mosquitoes. The hungry children play in the dirt; the fathers drink. Malaria, cholera, and typhus rage. At night, they burn pine chips in the huts.

The shacks and kiosks of the penniless Jews are on a third layer above the sea. Here you can find the coveted matches, shoelaces, shaving brushes, petroleum, rusty nails, used books, melons, corncobs, millet, rock salt, phylacteries—everything conceivable and inconceivable. And children here everywhere as well, half-naked, dirty, and hungry, the boys with payot on their temples.

Figure 4. Siblings Sergey, Evgenia, and Lidia, roughly 1928. Author's private archive.

Two iron and steel works, built by the French, stand a bit outside the center, behind the harbor with its ships and loading cranes. The people who work here, and live in their own settlement, are a bit better off than the longshoremen. Their brick homes have water and electricity, and at least their salaries allow them to afford enough to eat. The plants' smokestacks spew their filth out toward the city day and night; the sirens that mark the end of every shift replace clocks for the people of Mariupol.

Yakov lives with his family in the "upper city," which is reserved for the middle and upper classes until the revolution. Here there are restaurants and bars, a club *Soleil*, hotels named *Continental* and *Imperial*; there are Greek tavernas and Italian trattorias, theater, a large bazaar, and expensive stores, a multitude of Russian Orthodox churches, a cathedral, synagogues, a Roman Catholic church built by one of the Italian inhabitants, and a Polish church. Droshkies drive through the streets, lottery tickets, and fish pierogi are sold; gypsy women read palms, and on Sundays, a brass band plays in the park.

Matilda's father Giuseppe De Martino, the wealthy Italian businessman, allowed his daughter and her family to use a wing of his house on Nikolaevskaya Ulitsa, one of the stateliest homes in the entire city. The only property that is more luxurious is the "White Dacha," where Matilda's sister Angelina lives with her Greek husband and their children. The most glamorous balls and garden parties in Mariupol are held in the White Dacha; they host concerts and charity raffles. Matilda, on the other hand, lives with her parents and gives piano lessons; Yakov, who holds a law degree, is only able to find a job as a paralegal. After their return he immediately resumes his former political activities, once again conspiring with the Bolsheviks, the outlawed faction of the Russian Social Democratic Labor Party. How it is possible that a staunch Bolshevik like Yakov married the daughter of a tycoon and, as I now learn, even lives together with his family under the same roof as his father-in-law, a class enemy—about this Lidia writes nothing. As it turns out, this is not the only gap in her memoir.

Teresa Pacelli, Matilda's wealthy mother, looks down on her stepson and his roots in Ukraine's impoverished nobility. She turns up her nose at Yakov's family because they don't have any servants other than the nanny, Tonya, and they eat meals with only three or four courses. In Warsaw, her daughter apparently received a generous allowance; now, back at home, she is forced to give piano lessons in order to earn money.

On the whole, the house of my Italian great-grandparents Teresa and Giuseppe appears to have been a refuge for impoverished relations. Other than Yakov's family, the lodgers also include Uncle Federico, one of Matilda's brothers, who helps his father run his businesses and occupies a modest suite. In addition there is the "little granny" from the Pacelli family and the "big granny" from the Amoretti family. The big granny owes her nickname to her imposing size and her magnificent braid, which falls all the way to her knees. She had been married to a Russian aristocrat who lost his entire fortune at the roulette wheel and eventually died of tuberculosis. Since then, the penniless big granny, who was widowed at an early age, has been living in her sister Teresa's house. The little granny experienced a similar fate. She really was very small and delicate, her face was captivatingly beautiful, but her body was disfigured by a hunchback. Her father, who owned a number of vineyards, ensured that she received an excellent education; she spoke several languages and stood out for her witty conversation and her refined manners. She became lady-in-waiting to the czar's mother, Maria Feodorovna. After some time, she married her off to a very good-looking, but dirt-poor officer, who could not accept that he had a hunchback for a wife. He squandered her entire dowry and disappeared, never to be seen again. And thus one day, the little granny turned up once again in Mariupol. She had not been able to cope with her disaster and had gone a bit crazy. She answers questions in monosyllables, at most. Usually, she says: "I don't know, I know absolutely nothing." Most of the time she never speaks.

The part of the house where the owners, Lidia and Sergey's grandparents, live, is like a museum where you can gaze at objects from all over the world. Silk from China, carpets from India, carved ivory figures from Africa, valuable mosaics and chests from Persia, frightening masks from Ceylon, huge seashells in which you can hear the roar of distant oceans, Arabian tapestries, porcelain figures from Japan, crystal bowls from Venice, and much else, which Teresa and Giuseppe brought back from their journeys at sea. There are fruit baskets and vases with fresh flowers on the tables; in the salon, where they receive guests, dance, and play music, there is a framed portrait of the czar's family amid a gallery of Italian family portraits including a cardinal in a red robe and an Italian ambassador in Portugal. Giuseppe's father is also portrayed, the Neapolitan stone mason, a man with giant shoulders, a bald head and a monocle in his eye. The inlaid parquet floor, slippery as ice, becomes a skating rink for Lidia on which she secretly slides. She is especially fascinated by a pair of pier glasses which stand across from each other in one of the rooms. When she stands in front of one of the mirrors, her image is reflected in the second mirror and then thrown back to the first again, and on and on, so that she sees herself reflected endlessly.

Her grandparents' household includes two chambermaids, a cook, a laundress, the caretaker, a coachman, and a chauffeur. Only the chambermaids have the right to address the master and mistress directly, all the others may only contact them through the chambermaids. Once Lidia looks into the kitchen where the servants are sitting and chatting while they eat lunch. At her glance they fall silent. "How can I help you, madam?" one of the chambermaids asks. Someone whispers, "Who here is a madam? She lives on her grandparents' charity, after all." Lidia is mortified. "My father works," she says defiantly. The cook offers her a handful of sunflower seeds; Lidia runs off.

Out in the courtyard, where my mother will also later play, you can hear the voices and sounds from the adjacent barrel maker's, which stands behind a wall of dark cypress trees on the neighboring property. It is the workshop of the Jewish Bronstein family, but in those days, no one knows that a member of this family will later come to call himself Leo Trotsky and that his cousin will play a significant role in Lidia's life. The smell of lilac and wild rosebush wafts through the air, grapevines climb up the facade of the house. The stables are located in the back of the courtyard; the coachman feeds and brushes the three horses every day. There are two carriages in the carriage house, one for daily use and another for special occasions, as well as a large sleigh for the winter. A garage has been built onto the carriage house. At that time, there are two automobiles in all of Mariupol, one of them belongs to Lidia's grandfather Giuseppe.

Lidia is still a little bit afraid of her mother Matilda, even though she never punishes or even reprimands her. She merely looks at her continually with her half-severe, half-mocking eyes, so that Lidia never really knows if she disapproves of her behavior or if she is simply making fun of her. It never occurred to her to seek warmth, tenderness, or protection from her mother. She receives all of this from her Ukrainian nanny, Tonya, who hugs her and makes her laugh. From her Lidia learns Ukrainian, which her parents consider to be a primitive Russian dialect, but which will later save her.

Lidia is often alone. Her mother has a lot of piano students, whom you can hear practicing scales and études all day. Her father is either in his law office or attending the Bolshevik's secret meetings, he never has time. Sergey is still too young to play with Lidia, and her stepbrother Andrey is already grown up. Soon he will follow in his father's footsteps and fight in the civil war—he is killed a few days after it starts.

Lidia is jealous of the other children, whose mothers read them fairy tales. Her own mother never does. Perhaps this contributes to the fact that she teaches herself to read at the age of five, without any help. Later she cannot remember how she managed to do it. She runs her fingers over the lines, studying letter by letter, until she gradually figures out the meaning of the individual rows of letters. She is completely exhilarated, and she reads and reads. After finishing the fairy tales, she takes books from her parents' library. By the age of six or seven, she has already read Dostoevsky's *Netochka Nezvanova*, Ivan Krylov's *Fables*, and Leskov's *Tale of the Cross-Eyed Lefty from Tula and the Steel Flea*. She dives into the adult world, entirely convinced that she understands every word written in the books.

In Warsaw, when Lidia was three years old, her mother had already started to give her piano lessons. Lidia hates practicing scales and fingering, but she composes. She doesn't have to do very much, one chord follows another; she simply has to follow the notes that she hears in her head. It is exactly like reading; only at the piano she does not read with her eyes but her ears. At the piano, the letters are notes, which connect to form words and sentences. Once her mother pokes her head through the door. "Why are you playing such a difficult piece?" she asks. "You aren't ready for that yet." She has no grasp of her daughter's abilities.

In the evening, after the day's work is done, Grandfather Giuseppe often gathers the family together. His sons and daughters, who were born at sea and then given away, stop by, with Eleonora, a pianist who lives in

Petrograd, visiting occasionally as well. They eat, drink, and converse; the main topic is almost always politics and the looming inferno of the revolution. In between, someone sits at the Jakob Becker grand piano and plays. At some point the grandfather says, "Come, Matilda, sing us something." Lidia's mother has an unusually beautiful, dark, and warm voice, between a contralto and a tenor, with which she sings Neapolitan songs, arias, and romances from Tchaikovsky and Rubinstein. Her brother Valentino usually accompanies her.

Nothing clicks in my memory when I read about my grandmother's singing. Yet it is impossible that my mother told me nothing about it, since her own singing must have come from her mother and, undoubtedly, from her brother Sergey. She sang constantly, if she wasn't crying or lost in one of her eerie silences. She sang when she was washing the dishes, when she was sweeping, and when she stood in front of the mirror to put up her hair. We all sang, together, almost every day, and I played the accordion. I even got up at night and played in my sleep with the music stand in front of me, but with my eyes closed. As a child my father had been a choirboy in the Russian church in his hometown, then he became choirmaster, and after working as a forced laborer in Germany, his voice is what allowed us to survive. At first he sang for the American occupiers who wanted to hear Russian songs and paid him in kind; later he earned money as a member of a Cossack choir. Perhaps my parents already sang together in Mariupol, maybe my mother fell in love with the harmony of their voices. In any case, they had this in common, beautiful voices and a love for singing which was also passed on to me and my sister, who later studied music and became an opera singer. She followed in the footsteps of her uncle Sergey, though she had no idea that he even existed. In Germany, I was always the best singer in my class; my voice was my only claim to fame, the lone positive attribute of the Russian whom I embodied. And when we sang at home, my mother, my father, my sister, and me, when our voices merged, then we belonged together, forming a family, a *we*, that otherwise did not exist.

Lidia writes that her mother, ordinarily so cool, has a singing voice that is full of warmth, magic, and tenderness. Matilda's singing is the greatest joy of Lidia's childhood. Although she does not read her any fairy tales, after Tonya puts the children to bed, she comes into the room again to say goodnight. Before leaving, she sits in an armchair by the window and starts to softly sing Russian and Italian lullabies, "*Spi mladenets, moy prekrasny, bayushki bayu . . .*" and "*Ninna nanna, ninna oh, questo bimbo a chi lo do . . .*" For Lidia this means security and home, her mother's dark and mysterious voice which allows her to fall asleep happily at the end of every day.

Every morning, her mother tries to disentangle the impenetrable black mess on Lidia's head. She works with a variety of combs and brushes to bring order to the unruly head of hair. "You are our little witch," she jokes, without suspecting how seriously her daughter takes these words. After reading fairy tales, Lidia knows that witches can fly, and she is secretly convinced that she can too. She is the only girl who joins the neighborhood boys in running across the roofs of the densely packed houses on the street, jumping from one to the next. Sometimes the tiles slip out from underneath their feet; the boys scream, but Lidia has no fear. She leaps with the knowledge that nothing can happen, that the laws of physics do not apply to her.

One day when she is climbing alone on the roof, she takes a step into the air. She is lucky. She does not fall onto the cobblestones but lands on a sandpile on the street directly beneath her. Her career as a witch ends with severe contusions and a concussion.

In the summer, Matilda's brother Valentino frequently sends a horse-drawn carriage to pick up Matilda and the children and bring them to his dacha outside Mariupol. The dacha lies on a hill surrounded by an enormous garden, and from the rooftop terrace, you can look down on the sparkling blue sea, the sandy white beach, and the ships in the harbor. A fountain burbles in the courtyard, two stone lions guard the front steps. The garden, which extends all the way down to the sea, is maintained by a gardener named Erich Klarfeld, whom Valentino brought specially from Germany, and who lives in a small house on the property. Footpaths crisscross the entire garden: there is a shaded path where it is always cool because the sun's rays cannot penetrate the leafy green roof as well as a sunny path where deck chairs are placed between rose bushes for sunbathers, who treat themselves for various winter ailments. Other paths are lined with fruits trees and berry bushes, still others lead through small, artfully arranged seas of flowers with glowing colors, which change every season. A small stone stairway leads down to the beach and the changing cabins. When guests come in the evenings, the garden is lit by colorful garlands of light; Italian red wine, Crimean sparkling wine, and homemade ice cream are served.

This is the place where Lidia spends the happiest days of her childhood. Uncle Valentino plays dominoes with her and lets her ride on his back; her mother acts as though transformed in his presence, becoming lively and approachable. Although her brother has personnel for everything, she picks berries herself and cooks jam in the summer kitchen. In the evenings, Valentino turns on the gramophone, plays records, and dances with Matilda on the terrace. Abruptly, Lidia adds that her father never set foot in his brother-in-law's dacha. The sentence hangs in the air without any explanation, but if there is a hint of a love affair between Matilda and her brother in Lidia's writings, then it is here.

In winter, Lidia loves to go on outings in the sleigh; she likes this even more than the automobile. When there is snow on the ground, she wants nothing more than to climb into the sleigh every day and fly through the white spray, wrapped in her fur, the snorting horses in front, and the bells jangling on their harnesses. Once, when Lidia has the nerve to ask her grandmother to take her on an extra trip, she looks at her granddaughter condescendingly, "Do you have horses, by any chance? Do you have a coachman? You have nothing, you are parasites."

Lidia is beside herself. She knows that fleas and bugs are parasites. She storms into her father's room even though it is forbidden to disturb him while he is working, and this time she even forgets to knock. "Papa, grandmother said that we are parasites. Is this true?" she asks, breathless. Her father takes off his glasses and looks at her with his solemn gray eyes, "Yes, daughter, it's true," he says. "We live in an unjust society. But that will soon change. After the revolution, there won't be any rich or any poor anymore, and then we won't be parasites."

From that point on, Lidia waits impatiently for the revolution. And she does not have to wait long. A few weeks later, it is time. It begins joyfully, without any drama. In the streets, you can see people smiling, singing new, unfamiliar songs, and waving red banners. Lidia's parents also celebrate together with her grandparents and the other relatives. They sing the "Marseillaise," and make a toast with champagne. To freedom! The portrait of the czar's family in the parlor is taken down. They are happy that the new, democratic era has finally arrived.

While I read, I ask myself how this was possible. Were her grandparents naïve? Didn't they know what awaited them? Did they not even remotely grasp the political goals backed by their son-in-law, who wanted to eliminate people just like them?

In just a few days, the shooting starts. People arm themselves with stones and throw them through windows. An angry mob also tries to storm the wealthy De Martino's house. The caretaker still supports his masters and manages to calm the people's rage for one last time before the beginning of the looting, the anarchy, the terror, and the constant fear. Various political forces and gangs fight for control of Mariupol; sometimes one, then another, seizes power. People hide in basements or burrows to save themselves from the shooting in the street. The latest victors make themselves known by raising a banner atop the bank. The czarist flag represents the White Guard, the red flag the Bolsheviks, the yellow and blue flag Symon Petliura's nationalists, and the black flag Nestor Makhno's anarchists. During the five years of civil war, power changes hands seventeen times in Mariupol. The most dangerous conquerors are those who manage without a flag. With them, you have to prepare for especially brutal attacks and robberies.

Everything has changed in the house of my still unborn mother. Matilda stays behind with her two children while her husband Yakov and stepson Andrey fight for the Bolsheviks in the civil war. Little by little, all the servants also disappear, though not before taking whatever they can carry off. Once Lidia opens the bathroom door just as the cook, Daria, wraps her grandmother's washbowl in a silk bathrobe and drops it into a large basket. "But that belongs to grandmother!" Lidia cries, aghast. The cook: "We are living under communism now. What is yours is also mine." Lidia thinks for a moment and adds, "But what is mine is not yours."

One night Lidia watches her grandfather and his son Federico through a crack in the door as they sit under a lamp at the table piled high with gold coins. They make small stacks of coins and roll them up in newspaper. "Now they are going to get the hell out of here, your high-class relatives, the capitalist gang!" one of the chambermaids who is still living there hisses at Lidia as she walks past. The next day the grandparents and Uncle Federico really are gone, apparently forever. In any case, Lidia never mentions them again, leaving another gap in the narrative. At least I am now aware that my mother never got to know my Italian grandparents, that they were no longer around when she was born. Maybe they were murdered or sent to a camp, or maybe they escaped with their gold.

Uninvited guests now arrive almost every day at the aristocratic house on Nikolaevskaya Ulitsa; they walk around and take a look, searching for something. One evening, two armed men turn up and start to tear out the telephone line from the wall in the hallway with their bayonets. "Why are you doing that?" Matilda inquires and asks the men to show her their papers. One of them puts his fist in front of her face: "Here is the document." Then he points to his revolver: "And here is the argument."

New organizations are founded constantly. Once there is a sort of demonstration on the main street. A dozen young women and men run across it stark naked, with only a red banner across their shoulders: "No More Shame!" Onlookers laugh and jeer at them. Meanwhile, Lidia and Sergey collect bullets and cartridges in the street and play Reds vs. Whites. Lidia's friend Masha says, "I can't play with you anymore. Your mother is a White, mine is a Red."

The only servant remaining in the house is the chauffeur. One day he invites Lidia to go for a drive with him in grandfather's automobile. She is excited; it has been a long time since she has driven in a car. She climbs into the back seat of the cabriolet dressed just as she is, in a light summer dress and barefoot. The chauffeur races the vehicle at high speed across the city streets, and soon they arrive at Uncle Valentino's dacha. The chauffeur stops at the gardener's house and gets out without saying a word, leaving Lidia alone. What is he up to? Has he taken his former employer's granddaughter hostage? Is he negotiating over Valentino's fortune with the gardener? The dacha looks abandoned, the shutters are closed, there are weeds growing in the cracks between the cobblestones—there is no trace of Uncle Valentino. Lidia wanders around; it is already becoming dark, and she is starting to freeze. Finally she crawls into a pile of sunflower seeds, still warm from the heat of the sun. She grows tired and falls asleep. Eventually she is awakened by the light of a flashlight that the chauffeur shines in her face. "It's time to go, madame," he says. Then he sneers and corrects himself, "Of course I mean, former madame." He drives Lidia home, lets her get out, and roars off in grandfather's car, never to return. When Lidia walks through the door, dirty, barefoot, and shivering from the cold, Tonya lets out a cry of relief. Lidia's mother and the nanny had spent hours looking for her and thought she had disappeared forever in the tumult of nighttime Mariupol.

One morning Lidia is awakened by loud noises. She jumps out of bed and, still in her nightgown, runs over to the salon, where the commotion is coming from. There she sees a stranger in a sort of leather top hat, a black field tunic, riding breeches, and boots. Empty sheaths and a grenade dangle from his belt. He waves a sword around; it describes circles in the air and makes a frightening whistling sound. Occasionally the blade falls on one of the armchairs, and you can hear how the upholstery bursts with a soft pop. Lidia spots her mother and Tonya, who have fearfully squeezed themselves into a corner. The man yells, "I demand that you bring me a pair of pants right away. And they had better be black. If not you are all dead." Matilda assures him that they do not have any black pants, that everything has already been taken from them, but he does not believe them and becomes increasingly enraged. Suddenly the servants' door opens quietly, and the little granny appears in the salon. She is dressed respectably, and her hair is properly coiffed, as always. "What's going on here?" she asks politely. "What can we do for you, sir?" For a moment, the burglar is speechless; then he repeats his demand for a pair of black pants, though not as loud this time. "Excellent, young man," the little granny replies. "Please contact a clothing store." After uttering these words, she gives him a friendly nod and disappears once again, just as quietly and inconspicuously as she appeared. Matilda has gone pale, she begs the armed man for mercy: "Pardon me, she is an old woman who is not really all there anymore . . . "—"But so elegant," he replies, bewildered. "So elegant . . . " He looks around hesitatingly and quickly snatches a bronze candle holder that is still standing on a console in the ransacked salon and storms off.

On another occasion, two drunks break in and demand alcohol. They find one last bottle of brandy in the kitchen, drink all of it, and then decide to prepare fried eggs. They place a Venetian crystal bowl over the flame and beat the eggs in it. Of course, the bowl shatters with a loud crash. The drunkards double over with laughter and shout over and over again: "Death to the bourgeoisie! Death to the bourgeoisie!"

For a long time, people have been coming and going through the house at will; the former owners no longer have any say in the matter. The secretary of Semyon Budyonny, the leader of the Red Cavalry, moves into Grandfather Giuseppe's old office temporarily, a stroke of luck for the residents since his presence protects them from robberies, at least for a short time. Once some sort of general moves in with his lover, another time it is the wife of an intelligence officer, who takes the remaining clocks and mirrors with her when she disappears again.

When Tonya goes to church on Sundays, she meets people wearing clothes that belong to Lidia's parents and grandparents. Once she sees a girl in the white Arctic fox fur coat that Lidia always wore on sleigh rides. But in the meantime, the sleigh is also gone; the carriage house is empty. The carriages, the horses, and the sleigh were all stolen by Nestor Makhno's Black Army.

One day people from some sort of committee appear in order to confiscate the "remains of bourgeois property" in a completely legal manner. Tonya has sensibly stored all of the most essential items in a large chest, and she explains to the gentlemen that its contents are her personal property. They cannot take anything away from her, a member of the proletariat. While they inspect the rooms and put everything they can grab into giant sacks, Tonya keeps shouting, "No, I want that; I am also entitled to some of the people's property!" The furniture and the carpets are loaded onto horse-drawn carts, along with Lidia's beloved pier glasses. The chandeliers are torn from the ceiling, and the curtains are ripped from the windows. Finally, the grand piano is also carried out. The music, Lidia writes, disappears from the house forever.

Once when Lidia and Tonya are out in the city in their never-ending hunt for food, they come across the former business club, now renamed "The Workers' Palace," as indicated on a plywood panel at the entrance. Tonya bravely enters the building, taking Lidia by the hand. A marble staircase with a red carpet leads to the upper floor. There are men in boots, leather jackets, and caps everywhere; they peer into luxuriously appointed rooms through open doors. Lidia is astonished when she looks into one of them and recognizes her grandfather's rococo desk and her grandmother's makeup table. "Oh my!" Tonya whispers, "your grandma's and grandpa's furniture." They see the black grand piano on which Lidia once played and composed in an empty hall where shards of glass from a broken window lie on the parquet floor. It is being used as a sort of bar top, piled high with empty bottles, dirty glasses, and ashtrays overflowing with cigarette butts. Each visitor to the new Workers' Palace receives a free pierogi in the canteen. Lidia gulps hers down right there, but prudent Tonya quickly slips two more into her purse. Later they hear that a Chekist took a liking to the valuable Jakob Becker grand piano. He has it delivered to his house, where he presents it as a gift to his wife so that she can learn to play.

Although almost no one owns anything anymore, the looting continues. Matilda decides to temporarily seek refuge on the adjacent, Russian side of the Azov Sea with her children and her pregnant sister Eleonora, who fled to Mariupol from the shooting in Petrograd. She is still convinced everything that is going on is only a bad dream that will be over again at any moment. In the throng at the harbor, they manage to get hold of four places on a dilapidated old ship, overcrowded with other people who also want to escape. At night they sail into a hurricane. The small, rusty ship is at the mercy of the waves; it groans and creaks, as though it is going to break apart at any moment. Matilda holds onto the edge of the sink and groans; Lidia feels as though she is hanging upside down in the air. Someone shouts, "Help! I can't take it anymore, throw me into the sea!" Later they find out that it was Giannina Sanguinetti, a relative of the De Martinos, who was beside herself with fear and seasickness.

Their arrival in Yeysk is like a dream—the early morning sun shining through the mist over a glassy, peaceful sea and a quiet sandy white beach. There is nothing to remind them of the furor from the forces of nature in the previous night. They enjoy an almost two-month-long vacation from the civil war, which has not yet arrived in this area. An old, cozy guesthouse where you can have a modest meal every day; a Jewish baker and the smell of fresh bagels. Grapes and peaches are for sale at the market—Lidia has already forgotten that such things exist. They spend all day at the beach, swimming and sunbathing. Gradually everyone gains a bit of weight and starts to look like their former selves. Then Matilda's sister Eleonora gives birth to a baby girl in the local hospital. She only has a thumb and a little finger on her tiny hands, the three fingers in between are missing—the child of a pianist, born with mutilated hands. It must have been the result of the daily anxiety and terror that Eleonora endured during her pregnancy.

For a long time, the journey back over the calm, bright, blue sea remains the last moment of happiness for those who return home. Everything that caused them to flee Mariupol has only just begun. On the way back from the port, they experience a nightmarish scene: coffins are being carried across the main street from which suffocated screams and knocking resound. The White Guards have trapped the Red Commissars inside to show the people what awaits them if they collaborate with the Reds.

The gun battles in the city have gotten worse. Mariupol has once again fallen into the hands of Nestor Makhno. Raiding parties from his Black Army tear across the streets in *tachankas*, their heavily armed horse-drawn wagons. Everyone closes their shutters and hides in order to avoid being murdered.

One evening Matilda and Tonya are standing at the window and whispering to each other. The power is out again; the flickering of a kerosene lamp is the only light in the room. Shots are heard in the distance. "Pray, children, so that no bad people come here," Matilda says. Icons have been attached to the headboards of the two beds—Lidia has Holy Martyr Lidia and Sergey, Venerable Sergius from Radonezh. Every night before they go to sleep, the siblings kneel and say prayers with folded hands. Lidia has gotten used to the nightly ritual and has come to see God as a sort of family friend. Sometimes she asks him for advice. On this night she also kneels down, and, with tears in her eyes, asks him to protect them from the bad people. She finishes by crossing herself and crawls confidently into bed, feeling that she has done her duty.

Shortly thereafter someone tries to break down the front door. It is made of solid oak, but it is clear that it will soon give way under the powerful blows. Matilda opens the door. Two men in civilian dress burst in armed with shotguns, bayonets, and pistols. Cursing wildly, they surround Matilda and demand money, gold, and diamonds. Matilda insists that she doesn't have anything anymore, that everything has already been taken, but of course, they don't believe her. The men turn the entire house upside down; in the basement they tear open cans of preserves with their bayonets because they think there are valuables inside. They become more and more angry since they can't find anything. "Sleep, children, sleep," one of them says finally and orders Matilda to stand against the wall. Then he points his pistol at her. Matilda doesn't say anything, she doesn't scream, she doesn't resist. She merely wraps herself silently in a woolen cloth, stands against the wall, and looks off over the men's heads into the distance.

Suddenly loud footsteps are heard. "Hands up!" someone yells. Again strangers burst in; this time in uniform. They disarm the burglars and push them out into the courtyard. They hear screams and shots. Later it transpires that Tonya managed to steal into the kitchen and climb out the window in order to get help from the Reds.

That night Mother's hair turned white, Lidia writes, thus solving one mystery. It explains why there was a white-haired woman in the photo of my mother taken when she was still a child. Matilda already had white hair when she gave birth to my mother at forty-three. A white-haired woman who gives birth to a child, who breastfeeds an infant. She probably had black hair before, like my mother and all the Italians in the family, but my mother had never known her otherwise, with hair that had aged twenty or thirty years in a single night. In the morning, Lidia also discovers a few gray strands in the part on her four-year-old brother's head, and a white streak in her own hair. The sign of mortal fear, which they all carry from now on, after a night in which Lidia lost her faith in God.

One day, in the summer of 1919, Lidia and Sergey's father Yakov turns up unexpectedly. He had secretly abandoned the front line in the ongoing civil war and stays only one night. But the visit has profound consequences: Matilda becomes pregnant. So there it was, the beginning of my mother's existence. It was probably a hot July night, stolen from the civil war, in a ransacked and ruined house in Mariupol's upper city. A fifty-five -year-old man and a forty-two-year-old woman, whose hair turned snow white overnight from horror, conceive a child in a moment of careless abandon; in such times, neither of them could have wanted another baby. Presumably they are ravenous for each other; maybe they think that they are holding each other for the last time. Yakov's son Andrey has already died in the civil war, and he, Yakov, will depart the next morning, leaving his wife and two children alone once again to fight for a Bolshevik victory that should finally bring peace. Two children, and after this night a third, an imposition, a disaster for Matilda who feels she is too old for another pregnancy and has no idea how she can provide for an additional child.

The church register indicates that my mother was baptized on April 30, 1920, in the Cathedral of Saint Charalampos, the largest and most beautiful church in Mariupol. Soon this house of worship will also disappear forever from the face of the earth; it will be ransacked and then demolished, just like most of the other churches. My mother's godmother is Aunt Eleonora, who gave birth to the child with the tiny, mutilated hands in Yeysk; her godfather is a man named Paul Haag, an honorary citizen of Mariupol. A German like Erich Klarfeld, Uncle Valentino's gardener. Maybe the family had an affinity for Germans, perhaps via my mother's father, who was the son of the Baltic German Anna von Ehrenstreit? But how did Paul Haag end up in a Ukrainian city on the Azov Sea? What sort of special services had he rendered that he was awarded an honorary citizenship? And what connected him so closely to my mother's parents that they chose him, a German, as her godfather?

I found his name on a list of victims on a Russian-language website. He was arrested as an enemy of the people in 1937 and sentenced by a troika. Three letters are written after the judgement, "VMN." From Konstantin I learn that this is the abbreviation for *vysshaya mera nakazaniya*, or the maximum sentence. As a rule, troika courts do not last longer than five minutes; the verdict is carried out on the spot. Maybe the German Paul Haag didn't even understand the situation he was in. He was arrested and shortly thereafter a bullet bored through his brain.

I notice that he died in the same year as my mother's father. Does this point to a connection? Was it possible that Paul Haag had been expected to denounce Yakov? Had he been left with the choice of becoming a traitor or ending his life since he knew that the secret police would find the ways and means to make him talk? Was it possible that he and Paul Haag were old comrades, fellow travelers who had been combined in a joint case? Or had they shot my then seventeen-year-old mother's godfather at that time simply because he was German, since in those days all foreigners were generally suspected of being spies, having become enemies solely due to their background?

Actually, Lidia writes, my mother's baptism should have taken place one day earlier. However, they are forced to spend that day in the basement because of the constant shooting outside. It is impossible to leave the house because bullets are raining down in the courtyard. Prior to the baptism in the church, Lidia comments succinctly, her little sister receives a baptism by fire.

As I already surmised, the world into which my mother is born is extremely cramped. It is the time of the so-called compressions. Lidia thought that you could only compress air or hay, but lo and behold, people can be compressed as well. At first the propertied class was relieved of their furniture and other possessions, then their real estate was seized. Her grandparents' former house is gradually packed with more and more people. No one in the entire residence has a place of their own; the occupants are a single body whose limbs are engaged in a constant battle for a few centimeters more room. Lidia still remembers a few of them.

There is a Georgian officer in traditional Circassian attire who carries a sword and a pistol on his belt and lives together with his wife and several children. He has a wound from the civil war and suffers from a tic: at short intervals he twists his head upward and makes barking sounds.

There is a Chekist with his family. He is rarely seen; he "works" at night and sleeps during the day. His daughter is Lidia's age and lets it be known at every opportunity that Lidia belongs to "yesterday's" people, the kind her father shot in the civil war. Usually the mother follows right behind the daughter and reprimands her: "That one there belongs to the wrong crowd. A bourgeois left over by mistake."

There is a Jewish family, the Aronovs. Three girls dressed up like dolls, until the long-awaited male heir is finally born. Fully in keeping with the spirit of the time his parents name him Kin—the abbreviation for Communist International. Others name their children "Tractor," "Energy," "Locomotive," or "Trolen"—a combination of the first syllables of Trotsky and Lenin.

And there is the Wajner family with their six children. Lev and Clara, the two eldest, are Chekists, always dressed in leather with pistols in their belts. Chaim and Etka, the middle pair, catch tuberculosis shortly after their arrival and die. Rachel and Maim run around outside in the courtyard and call Lidia and Sergey "decadent, foppish intellectuals." Lidia parries: "And you are primitive and stupid proletarians."

These, and all the other new occupants behave quite impudently. If the plumbing happens to be working in the kitchen, they pound on the door late into the night until someone opens it for them so that they can get water. Matilda counts the buckets since she receives the water bill. However, the water supply to the house is soon shut off permanently, and everyone has to go outside to the pump and collect it in buckets. When the power is cut once again, the new residents are convinced that the bourgeois former owners have shut it off to harm the working class. In the beginning, Matilda still tries to keep the toilet clean, but it is a hopeless undertaking. After a short time, it becomes so dirty and gives off such an infernal stench that it has to be nailed shut.

Lidia says nothing about her father's return from the civil war, merely touching on the fact as such. Maybe she is in a rush because she is afraid she will not live long enough to tell her story to the end; perhaps, at eighty, she can only vaguely recall events that happened so long ago. It had been fifty-eight years since her arrest; the last time she saw her father. He died while she was in exile. "We were wrong," he said after Lidia was taken into custody. "We never wanted any of this. I did not fight in order to lose my daughter."

My mother Evgenia sees her father for the first time after his return. It is possible that he picks up his little daughter, who was born while he was away, and that she begins to cry since she is afraid of the stranger. That is how it could have been, the first meeting between my mother and her father.

As a reward for fighting in the civil war, Yakov is given a position as an examining magistrate by the victorious Bolsheviks. The salary he receives would have been just enough to feed the family until recently, but in a period of hyperinflation, it is not worth much anymore. "Money is falling" is a popular dictum at the time. No one knows where the money is falling from, or where it lands; there has never been so much and so little at the same time. When Yakov receives his salary, he takes it straight to the market and purchases food, since it may already be worthless the following day. Sometimes his salary is also paid in kind. Everyone exchanges all that they have for food; as an examining magistrate, Yakov constantly handles cases involving extortionate deals. A man, who has already exchanged all his possessions for food, sells the hut he lives in for ten blintzes.

Fortunately, there is the Azov Sea. Its abundant fish stocks save many people from starvation. People wade in up to their knees and hold pillowcases in the water. Nevertheless, even the Azov Sea's stocks are not inexhaustible, eventually this food source also begins to run out. On the Sundays that her father has off, he takes his fishing pole to the harbor, and if he is lucky, he returns in the evening with a few scrawny gobies.

Once Tonya scrounges up the remains of some oleiferous fruit. Together with Matilda, she pushes the thick pomace through a meat grinder to make small cakes, which they fry in castor oil. It does more harm than good as they all get sick and regurgitate the pulpy mass without digesting any of it.

Sergey helps feed the family by shooting crows with his slingshot, and Tonya puts them in a soup. The crow's meat is so tough that they have to chew on it for a long time before swallowing it in clumps.

When her father brings home a sack of gingerbread cookies he received once in lieu of his salary, they turn out to be moldy on one side. But no one pays any attention to such trifles. Tonya steams the rock-hard cookies in a pan or turns them into porridge.

Many people eat dogs and cats. After all the dogs and cats have been eaten, some turn to cannibalism. There are stories of women who use food to lure children into their homes before killing them and turning them into roasts and mincemeat. When Matilda comes home from the market and slices the jellied meat that she bought into pieces, she finds a child's ear. It is brought to the police, but they can't catch the culprit. There is talk of a woman who killed her baby and cooked it in a soup, which she served to her other three children. Then she went outside and hanged herself in the shed.

One evening there is a quiet knocking at the door. Lidia opens it. A strange and mysterious creature stands in front of her. It has an extremely bloated torso and two naked legs, as thin as broomsticks. Its skin is a bright, almost flame-like orange, and its stomach is so taut it seems a tap would be enough to pop the abdominal wall and send a flood of water onto the floor. In a hoarse, barely audible voice the creature asks for Tonya. She rushes up to her, lets out a scream, and starts to cry. It is her sister, Marfa, standing before her. In the kitchen Tonya undresses her, bathes her, and burns her lice-infested clothes in the oven. Lidia hears the words "forced collectivization" for the first time. The activist brigades took everything from the farmers in her village, down to the last egg, the final piece of grain. A sack of pumpkin seeds was the only thing they missed. After a few months, when the pumpkins they had planted ripened, all of the villagers acquired the orange hue that could now be seen on Marfa; it is the color of pumpkin flesh, which became the only and final source of food for the dying people. Marfa's entire family is starving; she is the only one that somehow managed to reach her sister Tonya in Mariupol.

After a combined effort restores some of her strength, Tonya puts her up with a relative who lives in a mud hut in the lower city. He lost a leg in the civil war, but views this as a stroke of luck. "Now they no longer have any use for me," he says. "I saved my head by getting my leg shot off."

Then comes the summer when the entire harvest dries up. The trees in Mariupol wither, and the asphalt melts underfoot. There is no more water, the plumbing breaks down; more and more people die of cholera and typhus, corpses lie in the streets. It often takes days until they are thrown onto horse-drawn carts and taken away. The scorching hot city is filled with the smell of putrefaction.

They have to walk to the bottom of the hill in order to draw water from the fountains. Tonya goes in front, a yoke across her shoulders with two buckets attached and two more in her hands—no one can imagine where she gets the strength. Matilda, still weak from childbirth, can only carry two small buckets. Lidia and Sergey make up the end of the procession—Lidia with a large jug and Sergey with a small one. Their father doesn't join them; he has to work, if only to earn the daily bread ration. A neighbor looks after my mother, little Evgenia. Many people are underway with containers, trudging along with what little energy they have left under the scorching hot sun.

They have to wait a long time at the fountains; the water only flows in a thin trickle from the hillside. No one stands, everyone drops to the ground as soon as they reach the destination, forming a prostrate line that struggles to push itself forward. Lidia notices a man stretched out on the grass. He is not moving, and there is a swarm of green flies over his face. He is either dead, or about to die. Tonya crosses herself and looks away, while Lidia has since become so inured to the sight of corpses that she is hardly moved.

After drawing the water, they make the journey home, one hour uphill with the heavy containers. At least the sun is finally setting, and it gets a bit cooler. At home Lidia's mother cuts the daily ration of 200 grams of bread that her father receives into six pieces. In addition, everyone gets a cup of boiled water and half a green tomato.

Meanwhile, Mariupol has been entirely destroyed by the civil war. In 1922, not a single factory is still running, and the shops are yawningly empty. Bands of marauders continue to roam through the city, and every day there are new reports of cannibalism. No one in my mother's family has the strength to stand; everyone lies in bed apathetically. Lidia's father Yakov is too weak to go to work; as a result, the family loses their tiny bread ration. The entire library, that was once in the house, has long since been exchanged for food. Lidia reads the few remaining books over and over again until she no longer has the strength to hold them. It is also likely that no one has enough energy to take my mother out of her little bed and change her diapers. What did she look like when she was two or three years old? Like the children in countries where there are famines today, tiny skeletons with distended bellies and huge empty eyes?

They are saved at the last minute by the Americans. An organization called ARA sends ships full of food to Mariupol and sets up an aid distribution center in the city.[1] After a thorough examination, my mother's family is also categorized as eligible for the aid. All those who have the same good fortune and are still able to drag themselves to the food distribution point receive a plate of creamed corn, a portion of cornmeal porridge, and a cup of hot cocoa every day from then on. In addition, they receive a piece of tasteless, light, white bread.

When the New Economic Policy (NEP) is introduced at Trotsky's instigation, the temporary liberalization of agriculture and trade improves the supply situation almost overnight. After a short time, almost everything is back in the shops, street trading flourishes, restaurants re-open their long-closed doors, and there are even concerts at the spas along the shore again.

Lidia gets her strength back, but her health, which has long been poor, is so badly affected by the famine that she suffers one serious illness after another. The family used to have their own family doctor, a quiet old man who auscultated the sick, tapped their chests, and examined their throats and eyes. At the end of every visit, Matilda offered him a cup of mocha and a slice of sponge cake and handed him an envelope with the payment. Now, no one has a family doctor anymore; they are all assigned to the polyclinic in their district. One day Lidia has a high fever and a bad headache. A plump blond arrives, takes a quick look at her, and promptly issues a diagnosis: "Classic meningitis. There is no cure." Her mother is silent; she seeks out the old doctor. In the meantime, Lidia has gotten so sick that she is unable to speak or open her eyes. Light as a feather, she already hovers over the bed. But she can hear what the doctor says: "You will probably have to say goodbye to your daughter, Matilda Josefovna, she has almost no chance." Lidia cannot speak; she lacks the strength, but in that moment, she decides that she will not die under any circumstances, if only out of defiance. And then her body sinks back down onto the bed.

When she wakes up one morning, she experiences an insurmountable craving for chocolate. She never asks for anything because she knows how poor her parents are, but this time she can't resist. She starts to cry and beg. Matilda buys 100 grams of "cornflower" brand chocolate candies and gives Lidia half of one every day, a candy cut straight down the middle. And little by little, she really does recover, but then she contracts malaria. Once again her condition is life-threatening, until her father manages to get hold of some quinine. It takes effect immediately, but causes hearing loss that will remain with her for the rest of her life. After malaria, she gets the Spanish flu, which already killed her aunt Valentina, and when she survives this she is diagnosed with tuberculosis.

A city appears in her memoir that I have already come across during my quest: Kherson. It is where the photo was taken of little Sergey sitting in a tree on the Dnieper. Now I learn that the uncle who owned a vineyard there, which had not yet been confiscated, was named Antonio. The family probably visited this refuge many times. As a child, my mother probably ran barefoot through the grass and bathed in the Dnieper, but if they had tried to teach her how to swim, she never learned. In any case, Lidia spends an entire summer at the vineyard. The fresh air, the good food, and the peaceful location perform a small miracle: in autumn, she returns fully recovered to Mariupol.

She is now twelve years old and has yet to see a school from the inside. Matilda is still convinced that the new government is merely a nightmare that could end at any moment, and since school attendance is not yet mandatory, she adamantly keeps Lidia away and teaches her herself. Lidia's subjects include math, French, Russian literature, history, geography, embroidery, and religion. Her mother also teaches her how to set the table for a six-course meal, how to curtsy, how to dance a *Pas de Gras* and a *Pas de Patineur*—things that Lidia will most definitely not need to know in her later life. She is never urged to do any housework. Matilda still envisions a future for her daughter in which it is not appropriate for people of her status to hold a broom, and it is highly likely that she raised my mother exactly the same way, for a future with servants. She passed on to her daughters what she had learned; she absolutely refused to accept that the world she came from had disappeared forever. Tonya did all the menial work around the house, so that when she married my father, my mother had truly never touched a broom before. I don't know how she was able to work as a forced laborer in Germany with her decidedly unpractical hands, but it was probably quite simple, a few basic movements that she had to repeat from morning until evening at a conveyor belt. The disaster of her incompetence did not begin until later, after she was freed, when she had to prepare soup for the first time, heat up a stove, or sew on a button.

Matilda's private lessons don't go smoothly. She doesn't need to teach Lidia how to read, she has already mastered that, but teaching her how to write turns into a power struggle between mother and daughter. Not only is Lidia unaccustomed to the standard hand movements of everyday life but also she is left-handed. Matilda does not accept this. She sees her daughter's left-handedness as an aberration, which can be traced back to her stubborn and rebellious nature. As soon as Lidia grasps the pen with her left hand, she is rapped on the finger with a ruler. Lidia cries, flails her arms wildly, and secretly throws the pens, for which her mother has scrimped and saved, into the oven. The drama increases when she learns embroidery since her right hand is totally incapable of the fine motor skills it requires.

Eventually Lidia refuses to participate in the lessons, and Matilda, who is powerless in the face of her daughter's obstinacy, sends her to a private tutor. From now on, Lidia goes to Sofia Vasilievna, who teaches a group of children in her apartment. By then, it has once again become possible to go out on the street without having to worry about suddenly being caught up in a firefight. The time of political power struggles and anarchy is over; the order that Generalissimo Stalin, the father of nations, will soon create for his thirty-year reign is already hanging in the air.

Sofia Vasilievna and her husband have thus far been spared from robberies and confiscations; they still live alone in a large apartment filled with comfortable furniture in an old prerevolutionary building. It is also cold; the children sit at a large living room table in their overcoats. Sofia Vasilievna wears a vest made of newspaper. Lidia's stomach grumbles, but she is happy. Learning with the other children frees her from her isolation; for the first time in her life, she feels like a social being, belonging to a small, conspiratorial community of outsiders. And Sofia Vasilievna allows her to write with her left hand; she understands that Lidia can't do it any other way, that her hand will not conform to the norm. But her happiness does not last long. After just a few weeks, Sofia Vasilievna and her husband are arrested as enemies of the people and exiled to a distant province.

From that point on, Lidia insists on going to school just like everybody else. Her mother does not want to allow it, but when Lidia goes on a hunger strike and doesn't eat anything for more than a week, Matilda, who knows how inflexible her daughter can be, becomes frightened and gives in. Tonya sews a schoolbag for Lidia out of canvas, and instead of ink, which is not available, she receives a small bottle of potassium permanganate along with two notebooks that Tonya made out of grandfather's old accounting records.

In the Soviet school, there are no classes anymore, only groups. The word "class" is reserved to define social strata. French as a foreign language has been eliminated; it is considered bourgeois. Grammar is also no longer taught; it is considered an unnecessary burden. History class is now called, "the History of the Revolutionary Movement."

Lidia is immediately made to feel the disastrous consequences of her upbringing. The pupils are required to keep the classroom clean themselves, sweeping and wiping. They have to wash the windows and seal them in winter by stuffing newspaper into the cracks to block the draft. They also have to heat up the potbelly stove in the classroom and search for fuel together outside in the street. Lidia is doubly handicapped—first because of her lack of experience with such things and second because she is left-handed, constantly in conflict with the right-handed world. Soon they insult her at school, not only as bourgeois and decadent but also as slow and handicapped. The teachers forbid her from writing with her left hand; through dogged effort, she forces herself to write with her right hand but always receives the lowest mark on her essays because she "scribbles," and her limitless imagination is not appreciated.

She is also ashamed that she doesn't have any textbooks; her parents can't afford them. Lidia does the homework for two twin sisters with limited academic abilities, and in exchange, they share their books with her. Sometimes they also give her a piece of their sandwiches. She cannot resist, as she is always hungry, but afterward she is ashamed.

Slava Bronstein is also in her group, the son of the neighbor who owns the cooperage. They used to play together in the courtyard, but now Slava doesn't want to have anything to do with her anymore since she is from a family of "enemies of the people." Constantly, he announces: "My uncle is the most important person in the party and in the entire Soviet Union. His name is Lev Davidovich Bronstein." Everyone knows that Trotsky is concealed behind this name, the most important man in the country after Lenin. Slava is envied and feared. But soon Bronstein, alias Trotsky, is declared to be a "Jewish traitor" and a "fascist lackey" and toppled. "Slava," the children in the school now shout, "your uncle was expelled from the party. Be careful that your family doesn't get it too." Contemptuously Slava retorts, "We have nothing to do with this character. Our name is Bronstein, and he is called Trotsky."

For Lidia, school is a traumatic experience. It is here that she experiences the full extent of her status as a misfit; she remains an outsider until the end, an enemy, a rare bird. Her original sin is that she has the wrong background; it is her indelible stigma, and I slowly understand what that says about my mother. I had always imagined that she was deeply rooted in the Ukrainian world, connected to it with all of her nerve fibers, but since she came from the same family as her sister, she must have been an outcast as well. Her life as a foreigner in Germany presumably was not something new for her, but a continuation of what she had always known. I had had a false impression of her all along. She had not been uprooted but had been rootless from the start, a displaced person from the day she was born.

After graduation, Lidia stands in line for weeks at the employment office, though she also has no prospects here due to her origins. She is not welcome anywhere in the new society; they treat her like a criminal who has no right to exist everywhere. For half a year she scrapes by working as a private tutor, for which she receives free lunch. Then she comes to a decision that will have far-reaching consequences: she wants to go to Odessa and study literature. Although she knows that people of her background are also not well-liked at the new universities—most places are reserved for the children of workers and peasants—she at least wants to give it a try. Naturally she has no chance of winning a scholarship or

Figure 5. Lidia Ivashchenko (1911–2001), Evgenia's sister, roughly 1935. Author's private archive.

getting into a dormitory, but two of her aunts, Elena and Natalia, live in Odessa and are willing to take her under their wing for the duration of her studies even though they are penniless.

Lidia's parents are stunned. They are still on the breadline and had set their hopes on the income Lidia would bring home after receiving her diploma. In addition, they are worried about their daughter, who wants to go so far from home in such uncertain times. Lidia has a guilty conscience because she is leaving her parents and siblings behind in hunger and misery, but for her the thought of staying in Mariupol is the same as dying. An "advantageous marriage," as her mother imagines, is completely out of the question for Lidia. She sells almost all her possessions at the market, cuts off her braid, buys a train ticket to Odessa and sets off.

It turns into a merry adventure. Lidia has to transfer many times, and she completes part of the journey on the roof of a train. She is young and has her entire life ahead of her, despite everything. By then she understands that she has to hide her background, that the truth will not get her far. As she rides into the wind on the roof of the train, she invents a model working-class biography for herself.

My mother is eight years old when Lidia leaves home. Was it difficult for her to say goodbye to her older sister? Will she miss her? How should I picture her life during that time? Does she also receive private lessons from her mother, or is she sent to school from the start? Is she shunned completely like Lidia, or is she able to arouse her classmates' sympathy despite her background since she is friendlier and more flexible than her sister? Where will she study in the future, as there are no universities in Mariupol? Will she also receive accommodation from her aunts in Odessa? Or perhaps her brother Sergey will take her to Kyiv, where he is studying in the conservatory and has a powerful patron?

In any case, I am able to calculate that her student years coincide with the blackest period of the Soviet Union, the time of the so-called Great Terror, when the purges reach their height. According to estimates made by historians, the leviathan devours between three and twenty million people, or even more—widely divergent figures with a great divide between them. My mother must have taken a big risk by pursuing higher education. Instead of going into hiding like many others with her background did, she exposed herself. I don't know what drove her, of all people; I only know one thing for certain: she was hungry the entire time. Right up to her final years in Germany, hunger is the one constant in her life. Maybe it is also hunger, among other things, that drives her into the hands of the German occupiers during the war, the hope that she will get more to eat in Germany. I remember the fearful look of desire in her eyes whenever she ate—always as though they might take her meal away from her at any moment, as though she was doing something forbidden. She had to keep eating to stave off starvation, but it seemed as though her body was unable to digest the food, thus remaining famished. No matter how much she ate, her body remained emaciated and childlike.

Lidia is allowed to stay with her aunt Elena in Odessa; the costs of her upkeep are shared with her other aunt. She has breakfast and dinner at Elena's, and she goes to Natalia's for lunch. Since it is necessary to pass an entrance exam in order to gain admittance to a university in the Soviet Union, the main issue now is whether Lidia will even be allowed to take it. Her only hope is Elena's husband, an artist who also holds a lectureship at the university. However, he married into the nobility and belongs to the "decadent intelligentsia," meaning that he is on shaky ground in the hallowed halls of the new educational system. Still he somehow manages to push his niece's application through.

Since the new Soviet citizen must be well-rounded, the university applicants are grilled about their knowledge of all the classic subjects. This creates a dilemma for the professors because the children of the workers and peasants, who must be granted the majority of places at the university, barely possess the necessary prerequisites needed to pass the difficult exams. But if the professors admit too many students from the educated class, it can cost them not only their professorships but also their heads. However, most of the workers' and peasants' children receive a recommendation from the trade union or collective farm party committee, which exempts them from the entrance exam.

For Lidia, mathematics is the biggest hurdle; she does not understand any of it. She cannot do much more than add two plus two. But she is incredibly lucky. When she stands in front at the lectern and stares blankly at the assignments that the professor has written on the board with chalk, he is suddenly called out of the room. Another candidate, a math whiz, jumps up from his seat and scribbles the solutions on the board at lightning speed. When the professor returns, he doesn't suspect a thing—he nods contentedly, Lidia has passed. She returns the favor by writing an essay for her savior during the Ukrainian exam, since he doesn't know the language at all. Both have taken a major risk. If they had been exposed, they would not only have been dismissed from the university immediately, but probably also have been charged with sabotage.

In physics and chemistry, Lidia also profits from her Ukrainian language skills, for which she has her nanny Tonya to thank. Most of the professors can only speak Russian, which has been discredited and declared to be the language of a chauvinistic great power after the revolution in Ukraine. Aunt Elena's husband advises Lidia to use the situation to her advantage, and she plays her part in the comedy perfectly. During the entrance exams for physics and chemistry, she looks impudently into the eyes of the old professor and claims to only speak Ukrainian. The poor man struggles to ask the exam questions in Ukrainian, and Lidia tells him some nonsense that he naturally cannot understand. After ten minutes, he dismisses her with a top score, so terrified that he is bathed in sweat.

The literature, history, and geography exams do not present any problems for Lidia. "If you came from the working class," they tell her at the end, "we could give you a place at our university right away." But without knowing why, Lidia is convinced they will accept her anyway; at first she doesn't allow any other thought to enter her mind. And lo and behold, a few days later she finds her name on a notice on the registrar's office door. It is an announcement with the names of all the accepted students.

For Lidia, the university is a sacred place. Here, all the world's knowledge can be found; here, the testimonies of human history are stored. Every day when she enters the foyer, the first thing she sees is a huge sculpture in the balustrade: Atlas carrying a globe with a clock inside on his shoulder. Seeing the clock always reminds her of her father, who also once studied here. When he entered the building as a young student, the golden hands told the time for him as well.

In the Soviet era, strict discipline prevails at the universities, with fixed schedules and required courses. The study of literature also includes history, psychology, German philology, linguistics, and military studies. The professor of history, a tall, haggard man with a long nose, starts every lecture with a quote from the Chronicle of Nestor: "The Polans lived on the Pripyat, the Drevlians on the Desna." He speaks with such familiarity over events from the distant past, it is as though he experienced them himself. A very lively and witty man, but after a short time, he stops appearing at the lectures. It is rumored that he has been arrested, but then one day, he is back again. He sticks his long nose into the syllabus and begins his lecture with the quote about the Polans and the Drevlians once again. Shortly thereafter, he disappears again, this time forever. He is replaced by a young, self-righteous type with a fat, rosy face. For him, history consists only of class struggles, the people are always the driving force who are held back by a hegemon; all rulers and military leaders are merely products of their epoch. It is very easy to adopt this historical perspective, no one ever asks for a chronology; the lecturer probably doesn't know it himself. The students have to speak up as much as possible, or else they receive a bad mark for passivity. After the lecturer has listened to them attentively, he issues a judgement on almost everyone: deviationist, Menshevik, Trotskyist, czarist, and so on.

The psychology professor explains to the students that "psyche" means "soul," but that in reality, the soul does not exist. At birth, a human is a blank sheet of paper, which society then inscribes with its signs. After he has paid this tribute to the times, he holds a very intelligent and original lecture. Sometimes he suddenly looks fearsome and points to the ominous teachings of Sigmund Freud, Josef Breuer, and others, whom he duly condemns as idealists and mystics. Nor does he spare Georgy Chelpanov, Lidia's uncle. He diligently enumerates the titles of the books that spread false and harmful teachings, to the delight of the more intelligent students, who subsequently run right to the library in order to check them out.

The professor of linguistics speaks more than a dozen languages, but his favorite is not Ukrainian but Persian. This alone incurs the wrath of the student party cell. His claim that Ukrainian is not a separate language, but a dialect of Russian, triggers a veritable storm of indignation. Patriotic activists hiss and rail at him, but they have no convincing points. Eventually they write a complaint, and they would have loved to have chased him out from the university, but he is a member of many foreign societies, belongs to Britain's Royal Society, and corresponds with numerous scholars from all over the world. He is too much for these tiny, spiteful ankle-biters. Someone suggests that he leave the country, but he refuses. Unperturbed, he puts up with the constant attacks and explains over and over, "I have not read Lenin. I don't have the time." Once Lidia has the good fortune to stand next to him in a line of people waiting for bread. Discretely she slips her ration into his bag.

Professor Bachmann, an energetic, humorous man, teaches German language and literature. In his class, Lidia learns German so well that even decades later she can read Goethe and E.T.A. Hoffmann almost without a dictionary. Once, many years after completing her studies, she walks across the grounds of her prison camp to fetch petroleum for her lamp. The prisoner in a quilt jacket and ragged bomber hat spends a long time examining her ration card, asks who she is and slowly pours the petroleum. "Don't you recognize me?" he asks finally. Lidia really does not recognize him. He laughs sadly. And then she realizes Professor Bachmann is standing in front of her. As a teacher, he had been too good to hold onto his job at the university.

The military instructor is straight out of central casting: a brawny man with rough features. "Stand up!" he roars every time he comes through the door. A student who lost both his legs in the civil war, and can only move about with difficulty on crutches, remains seated. "What nerve!" the instructor roars. "You are showing disdain for military discipline. Stand up at once!"—"I beg your pardon, Comrade Instructor," a student representative says shyly. "He is an invalid."—"Quiet. Stand up at once!" The invalid attempts to pull himself up by his crutches, but he falls back on the bench. Someone shouts, shocked; the crutches fall to the ground with a crash. After a moment of painful silence, the instructor notices the hostility of the masses and reverses course. "You may remain seated, Comrade."

In the military skills course, the students must learn how to march, crawl through mud, and shoot. Lidia is only five feet tall; she is swallowed up by the uniform they have forced her into. Her military overcoat nearly touches the ground and with every step she loses the boots that she has put on over her shoes. She is extremely nearsighted and has no strength in her right hand. She is such a poor shot that on one occasion she almost hits the instructor. His face turns pale with rage, then bright red. "Attention! Hand over the gun! Dismissed!" With that, Lidia's military career is finished; from then on, she is excused from practical training. Inexplicably, the instructor still gives her a B for her efforts.

Again and again, heated discussions break out over which language should be used in the lectures, Russian or Ukrainian. Ukrainian is favored by the majority of students, the party, and the leadership of the Ukrainian writers' union. All things Russian are demonized in tirades, which last for hours on end. A large post hangs in the entryway: "Speaking Russian on university property is prohibited." All sorts of languages are spoken—German, Yiddish, English, French, Greek, and Italian—but Russian, which everyone speaks and understands, is banned.

The topics that are presented in the literature seminars speak for themselves. For three to four hours, they discuss whether Pushkin and Gogol were small or mid-sized estate holders. Students are required to count the conjunctions in Griboyedov's comedy, *Woe from Wit*, because, it is claimed, you can deduce his worldview from their total number. Lidia receives an assignment to write about the "agricultural aspects" of Tolstoy's *Anna Karenina*.

Students are urged to go into factories and create literary salons to scout for talent under the slogan, "Shock Workers in Literature." When a worker exceeds the norm, they are told that a literary talent lies dormant within him, which must be encouraged. Some of Lidia's classmates earn quite a bit this way. They pick out a "writer" in a factory, ghostwrite something for him, and publish it under his name. They split the royalties, and both sides are satisfied.

The shock workers are exposed to literature, and the literature students are introduced to factory work. Lidia is assigned to work in a jute mill with the goal of developing her into a "well-rounded socialist." She gets up at five thirty in the morning before being shaken in the streetcar for close to an hour. Sometimes, together with her classmates, she sleeps standing up during the ride. They hand over their passes at the entrance to the factory, drop by the foreman's office, and head for the storeroom. There they sink into the piles of jute and sleep for another two to three hours until the party activists wake them up with admonitions and threats.

The students are required to experience every aspect of jute production while they are assigned to the factory. The initial stage is the most dreadful. Lidia must unroll a giant, dusty bale of jute, smooth it out and throw the sheet on the conveyor belt with all her might. It is a job for a big, strong man, not a very slight woman weakened by hunger. Lidia is reprimanded constantly. She stands in a giant cloud of dust, constantly coughing and unable to breathe properly. As she tries to unroll one bale, the next one is already being brought up. Afterward, it takes her almost half a year to cough up all the jute dust.

After two weeks at the conveyor belt, she is transferred to the spinning works, a room with a long row of spinning machines, which make a deafening noise. Since she is nearsighted, Lidia cannot see the broken strands and constantly grabs at the wrong ones. The supervisor scolds her, and the management begins to take notice. The situation is ominous. A woman with pampered hands that are not used to work and not suited to it—what could be worse in a workers' state?

The third stage, the weaving room, is her salvation. Here, primitive, manually operated looms are used to make sack cloth. A thick strand that Lidia can easily see, she recognizes breaks immediately and adroitly untangles strands that have become entwined. She learns how to tie knots and is soon able to use the loom without any difficulty. The supervisor begins to praise her and allows her to work on her own more often. At the end of the second week, she is already a shock worker. As a reward, she receives an extra spoonful of porridge and a cabbage pierogi in the canteen. One day the manager approaches her and says, "You are a clever girl! What do you really learn at the university? Literature? You are only making life difficult for yourself. Literature won't put food on the table. Stay here with us. We will give you a place in the hostel; you will receive an excellent salary as well as the additional weekly food ration for shock workers. You will belong to the working class instead of these scrawny intellectuals." Later, Lidia often recalls the manager's words. She would have been spared a great deal in life if she had followed his advice.

Eventually, she befriends a few of her classmates. Names from Lidia's file reappear in her journal: Anna Bokal, Sarah Bortman, Anna Edelstein, Lev Poznanski, and especially Bella Glaser, who makes a powerful impression on her—the daughter of a Russian Jew who emigrated to the United States and recently returned. Bella's mother divorced and fled with her from the world of "cursed capitalism" to the Communist paradise. But Bella still has some American glamor about her. She wears silk stockings and stylish shoes with metal buckles, owns a flapper dress and a purple fur. A charismatic young woman with an unusual education, a razor-sharp, analytical mind, and a powerful independent streak. Little by little, she gives Lidia to understand that she thinks the Soviet Union is everything but a worker's paradise. In her eyes it is a corrupt party oligarchy that has betrayed the workers. She says things that others do not even dare to think. Carefully, she initiates Lidia into the activities of the "Group for the Liberation of the Proletariat," which she founded, and plays an active role in the underground. Over time Lidia becomes her coconspirator, meeting regularly with her and the other members. It is the only place where she can speak freely and express her thoughts openly. For this reason alone, the group becomes a necessity for her. Lidia is often afraid that she will no longer be able to withstand the pressure to conform and perform a permanent masquerade, that she will do or say something that could have a profound impact on her life. The group is a sort of refuge, a hideout, a respite from the omnipresent eye of the surveillance machine.

Campaigns to combat illiteracy are continually underway. Students must pay a tribute for the privilege of being allowed to study, and thus Lidia is selected to teach the workers in a shoe factory how to read and write. The factory employs two hundred people in total, and nine are selected for the course according to some mysterious principle. A classroom is set up within the factory and adorned with a portrait of Lenin and a red flag.

On the first day, Lidia notices that all the shoemakers can already read and write. She is confused and looks at them helplessly. Then the senior student makes a naive suggestion: "To ensure that we are following the rules, we should complete the planned program, Comrade Teacher." And so it transpires that the shoemakers spend three months writing dictations after work as fast as they can, and as illegibly as possible, with many grammar and spelling mistakes that Lidia assiduously corrects in red ink. After the dictation, Lidia reads to them from novels and books of poetry, or she tells one of her own stories, which she has always been able to dream up with ease. The shoemakers listen, riveted.

At the end of the course, a brash woman dressed in military attire and a red kerchief arrives to evaluate the students' progress. They show her the notebooks, filled with corrections, and when they read the newspaper aloud, they stutter and deliberately get stuck. The party representative is very pleased with the students and their teacher. She expresses the hope that the workers will soon be able to read newspapers and discuss the contents afterward. Then she departs.

As a reward for participating in this farce, Lidia is given a subscription to the opera as well as a voucher that allows her to travel to Crimea with the shoemakers for four days. They visit Yalta, Alupka, Alushta, and Sebastopol. Lidia finally gets enough to eat in the hotels, and she enjoys having her own room and swimming in the ocean. She is courted vigorously by her students. In order not to hurt their feelings, she gives them to understand that she has already given her heart away, though she loves them all. This appears to satisfy them.

Upon her return, she is paid nine rubles per student, and the grateful shoemakers give her two pairs of well-made high-heeled summer shoes to remember them by. With the money and the new shoes, she makes her way to Mariupol for her first vacation, where she is immediately confronted with her family's misery once again. Her parents and siblings are starving. Her father Yakov earns next to nothing; he has become an invalid and is almost blind. Her mother Matilda has to read the court records aloud to him and do his written work. Tonya has found a position at a textile factory, but she continues to help Matilda around the house and even supports her financially. My ten-year-old mother Evgenia goes to school; Sergey, now fifteen, works for the campaign, "Church Gold for the Hungry." He, though also half-starved, helps to strip the churches and synagogues in the city of everything valuable—gold, silver, diamonds, rubies, and other gemstones—and delivers it to a collection point. For this, he receives a small bread ration every day.

Lidia realizes that no one had been waiting for her at home, that here she is just an extra mouth to feed. She would gladly help her family if she only knew how. Most of all she would like to return to Odessa right away, but then she receives a message from her aunts explaining that their circumstances have changed. Elena's son has gotten married and now her daughter-in-law is also living in the cramped apartment—there is no room for Lidia anymore. Natalia has taken in the sixteen-year-old son of a friend who was arrested together with her husband, and now it is no longer possible for her to contribute to Lidia's upkeep either.

It is a tremendous blow to Lidia. She sinks into resignation for a few days before turning defiant. Boldly, she resolves to return to Odessa anyway. If she is standing in front of Aunt Elena's door, she will not simply turn her away and render her homeless, Lidia imagines. And her calculation is correct. Elena lets her in and even offers her a bowl of soup after the long train journey. She is forced to spend the night on a pull-out sleeper chair, but at least she is back in Odessa.

The following day she immediately dashes off to look for work. It is pouring rain, and she is soaked to the skin, but once again she is in luck. She gets a job at a distribution point for food coupons. She sits at a dark counter all day, checks IDs, and tears off coupons for people who stand in a never-ending line. Her wages are so abysmal that she cannot afford to buy enough food to eat, let alone give Aunt Elena something for allowing her to stay in the apartment.

Bella Glaser steps in to help her. She is close to the director of the university library and arranges a job there for Lidia. From then on, once the lectures are over, she has to lug books from five in the afternoon until ten at night—carrying them from the stacks to the circulation desk and from the book return back to the stacks. The work is exhausting, but Lidia earns a bit more than before, and she feels at home in the library. After a short night in the sleeper chair, she often rushes off to the university in the morning and arrives too early. She doesn't have a clock, but she must not arrive late under any circumstances. Sometimes, if it is still locked, she falls back to sleep on the steps in front of the entrance.

Everyday life is becoming more and more depressing, and the future looks increasingly bleak. People are cramped together, yet everyone thinks only of themselves—they are consumed by their own struggle for survival. There is nothing in the stores besides unsweetened jam made from prunes. On a good day, the menu in the cafeteria consists of a soup that is nothing more than a runny grain porridge and a main course of somewhat thicker grain mush. On a bad day, there is cabbage soup followed by steamed cabbage. For the most part Lidia skips breakfast entirely, though at the university buffet she sometimes buys a soy meatball which can be chewed for a long time as it has the consistency of hard rubber.

In the spring, the students are sent to nearby villages where they promote the establishment of collective farms and once again combat illiteracy. At so-called "meetings," Lidia is required to cant hollow phrases in front of the farmers about the well-rounded Soviet citizen and their bright future in the collective farms. The year is 1932; it is the beginning of the Biblical famine known as the Holodomor. Until recently, Ukraine, blessed with fertile black soil, was considered the breadbasket of Europe. Now it is turning into a morgue. *Holod* is the Ukrainian word for hunger, *mor* comes from *moritj*—to wear down, to torture. Stalin's grand experiment in collectivization, which will also later be recorded in world history as a genocide against the Ukrainian people.

Although it is sowing time, the fields lie fallow. Seizing the land has brought the entire Ukrainian agricultural sector to a standstill. Farmers who have been driven off their property roam about, living on the wet ground, mainly women with their sick, emaciated children. Men who refused to allow their property to be collectivized were taken to camps or murdered. The famine has wiped out entire regions. There is no one left to bury the dead. They rot where they die. Madness and cannibalism are rife.

Upon their return from the countryside, the students boast of their triumphs, how many farmers they were able to persuade to join collectives and how many uprisings they were able to put down. Lidia's report is composed in the Communist's rhetorical style; as she writes, it contains many pointless figures and quotes from Stalin's speeches. "Young lady, you could amount to something yet," the head of the executive committee says good-heartedly. "You just need a bit of polishing."

One day Uncle Valentino turns up in Odessa. Lidia last saw him when she was a child, quite some time before her grandfather's former chauffeur took her along on the mysterious excursion to see the German gardener and then disappeared with the automobile. She never forgot the image of the abandoned dacha, already marked by signs of dilapidation, and she cannot believe her eyes when Valentino, whom she held for dead, is suddenly standing in front of Elena's door. He says nothing about where he has been all this time, but apparently he succeeded in salvaging some of his fortune since he can afford to stay in a hotel. He tells her about his brother Antonio from Kherson, on whose vineyard Lidia once recuperated from TB. In the meantime, his property has been expropriated, and he has been sent to Siberia with his wife and daughter. There, the daughter, who suffers from bone tuberculosis, has no chance of survival. Valentino wants to try to help the family escape to Odessa, and then cross the Black Sea to Romania together with them.

While he is in the city, Valentino invites Lidia out to eat several times and buys her a few urgently needed articles of clothing. It is like a dream or a fairy tale. The happy times that she spent as a child at his dacha together with her mother strike her as the experiences of someone she read about in a novel.

After a few weeks Valentino's brother, Antonio, and his family really do arrive in Odessa after travelling along a dangerous and secret route. Valentino bought their freedom for an astronomical amount and is hiding them in a fisherman's hut in the harbor. A cutter is supposed to take the fugitives to Romania on a moonless night. Lidia says goodbye to Valentino, hugging him with the bitter certainty that she will never see him again; only her mother knows for sure whether it is her uncle or her father. Later she hears that he and his brother Antonio, together with his family, were able to travel to France via Romania, where they became winemakers once again.

As a parting gift, Valentino gave Lidia six heavy silver spoons engraved with the De Martino monogram. These spoons feed her for half a year. Every month she exchanges one at the Torgsin, a store for "trading with foreigners," although no one does business with foreigners there anymore. The Iron Curtain has long since shut out the rest of the world, and the word "foreigner" has become a curse. Now Odessites are exchanging their remaining possessions, a last piece of jewelry, an old dinner service.

In the middle of the Holodomor, this store has everything that was on offer in the time of Czar Nicholas II: oranges, chocolate, ham, coffee, caviar. With the money that Lidia receives for one silver spoon, she buys a month's supply of grain, oil, and dried vegetables. At home she prepares soup or kasha from this in Elena's kitchen.

Tracing paper sold in stationary stores turns out to be an unexpected source of income. By chance she and Aunt Natalia find out that one layer is made of batiste. They soak and then boil the paper until the batiste peels off. After it has been dried and ironed, the batiste is sewn into wonderful underwear that can be sold at the market or exchanged for food. Of course Aunt Natalia does not own a sewing machine, so they sit up half the night stitching under a lamp in the kitchen. The only problem is that they cannot purchase large quantities of tracing paper on a regular basis as this could arouse suspicion. Aunt Natalia's daughter, Anechka, eventually provides a solution. She works in a library and discovers a large number of drawings on tracing paper in the archive. Since the India ink cannot be cooked out of the batiste despite all their efforts, the undershirts, panties, and bras sewn by Lidia and her aunt from then on contain the mysterious, fragmented patterns of technical drawings. Despite this, there is huge demand for their "collection" on the black market, though they have to be careful because the police are everywhere. They are lucky and never get caught.

Lidia frequently brings in additional income thanks to the forced Ukrainization of the Odessites. For a sizeable fee, she is contracted to translate factory regulations and labor brochures from Russian into Ukrainian; on another occasion, she is hired to test the Ukrainian language skills of the city's postal workers. She gives them a dictation exercise, and the examinees, who can only speak Russian and understand at best half of what she says, submit results that are riddled with errors. Lidia has to give all of them a mark of "unsatisfactory," after which they are all forced to take Ukrainian language lessons. Thanks to her nanny, Lidia speaks such perfect Ukrainian that everyone takes her for a native speaker. This not only helps her to gain urgently needed income but also gives her the essential proletarian air that is necessary for survival.

Nonetheless, in her final year, an attempt is made to expel her from the university. Without explanation, she is suddenly assessed huge tuition fees. It is clear to everyone that she cannot pay them. As she is about to drop out, she comes up with the only, and final, trump card she can play. At bottom, it is fraud, since her father has long since renounced the Soviet State, but Lidia leaves no stone unturned and obtains the court ruling under which he was sentenced to twenty years exile for participating in the anti-czarist revolutionary worker's movement. She submits the document with a corresponding note in the president's office, and when she passes by the bulletin board in the foyer the following day, she finds her name included on the list of the university's best students. She no longer has to pay tuition.

She writes her thesis in three days, following the principle that at the end of the day you can put just about anything down on paper. She compares the Ukrainian writer Mykhailo Kotsiubynsky to Maxim Gorky, and puts forward the fantastic theory that Gorky's work is strongly influenced by him. Her tutor is astonished; he has never heard the theory before. He is also amazed that she wrote her thesis in Russian, but she explains that it is only thanks to her education at the university that she knows the language well, as she first learned it here. She receives a top mark for coming up with this nonsense. Her diploma states that she has now qualified as a lecturer in literature, though in order to be diplomatic, it does not state whether Russian or Ukrainian is meant.

Her job at the university library, where she had most recently worked as the head of the reading room, ends in scandal. After her request for three weeks' vacation is denied, she stops coming to work. When she returns in three weeks' time, she finds an announcement on the door: "The shirker L. Y. Ivashchenko is strictly prohibited from entering the library." But this does not matter to her anymore, her time in Odessa is up in any case.

For the graduation party, her kindly Aunt Natalia sews a dress in trendy electric blue and a white bolero made of batiste extracted from the tracing paper. To go with the outfit, Lidia wears a pair of elegant shoes she received from the cobblers. The party and Comrade Stalin treat the graduates to a *frikadeller* with potatoes, along with a sweet roll and a cup of tea for dessert. Lidia notices that she is obviously not the only one who posed as a Ukrainian ingénue from the countryside. When the fun starts and the dancing and drinking begin, most forget that they must speak Ukrainian and slip merrily into Russian.

Lidia returns to Mariupol. Making it possible for her brother and sister to get an education and supporting her parents are what she now sees as her main duties. She has no plans for the future, and does not think about a real career or starting a family. Survival remains the only goal.

She is taken on as an editor and translator at the *Azov Proletariat*. The salary is reasonable, and there is also a free lunch in the cafeteria. In the evenings, after the newspaper deadline has passed, she works as an instructor once again, teaching reading and writing to the workers in a steel plant. The two salaries allow the family to obtain more or less enough to eat, and her parents seem to revive a bit.

Once, when she has only been at the paper for a few weeks, a story comes in just before deadline that is supposed to appear in a prominent place in the next day's edition. A closed party meeting is scheduled for six o'clock the following day in the library pavilion of the Park of Culture; attendance is mandatory. Lidia translates the basic text into Ukrainian and gives it to the printers. The next morning a storm erupts: the tired and frightened party activists assemble at six in the morning in the park (missing the meeting could have gotten them killed) and are surprised that the chairman doesn't show up. It emerges that the meeting is scheduled for six o'clock in the evening, instead of six in the morning. They can't figure out whether the author of the announcement made a mistake or if Lidia simply mistranslated it, but now the long-smoldering animosity toward her explodes. Lidia is attacked openly and harassed; she is put under observation and asked trick questions. Suddenly they are interested in what sort of books she reads. Surprisingly, a colleague latches onto her, accompanying her home every evening and interrogating her about her life. Lidia is lonely and is not opposed to chatting.

When she finally receives a telegram from Odessa with the message, "Nina has fallen ill, get a vaccination," it becomes clear to her that she is in serious trouble. Bella's codename is Nina, and "sick" obviously means that she has been arrested. Lidia will later remember perfectly that she walked home from the editorial office for the last time on November 9, 1933, accompanied by her charming colleague. The still and mild air, the flowers still blooming in the garden—for a long time it is the last completely normal evening in her life.

She teaches a lesson at the steel plant on the following day as usual. The workers are tired; they have been slaving away all day, but they pay close attention. After about half an hour, the door opens quietly, and the director of the instructional department motions her outside. Lidia apologizes to the students and departs. Two men in civilian dress stand in front of the door and ask her to follow them. She wants to inform her students first and grab her briefcase, but the men say it is not necessary. On the street in the pale light of a lantern, they show her some sort of paper with a stamp on it. The she hears a voice as sharp as a knife, "You are under arrest!"

She is driven home in an NKVD vehicle.[2] Only now, in the short drive to her apartment, does she remember the incriminating material that is lying in a drawer at home: Bella's manifesto, scrawled on cigarette paper. It describes the party as a gang that is hostile to workers and calls for a new revolution against the terror of state capitalism. In addition, there are a number of letters from Bella in which she openly encourages Lidia to gain access to the workers of Mariupol by founding literature clubs in the city's factories where she can agitate. Even the warning telegram from Odessa failed to remind Lidia about this incriminating evidence. She cannot understand how she could have been so careless.

During the search Lidia manages to whisper to her mother that she is going to be taken away. The entire apartment is dismantled, every crack is searched, and naturally Bella's letters are also found together with the manifesto, which Lidia had rolled up and hidden in a book between the spine and the book block. At around midnight she is taken to the NKVD headquarters. Was there a final glance, a parting word between her and my mother? The sisters will never see each other again. When Lidia writes down her story at age eighty, my mother has been only a memory for almost six decades, faded perhaps beyond recognition in her recollection.

The grilling at the station lasts until morning, then Lidia is allowed to sleep on the sofa in the interrogation room for a few hours. She is awakened by a man in a uniform who orders her to follow him. She puts on her coat and takes the parcel that her brother Sergey has brought. As he stood in front of her, he cursed her as a traitor to the fatherland, a renegade, and an egotist who has brought ruin to the entire family. Presumably, it is the last meeting between the siblings. Later, in the memoirs written after Sergey's death, Lidia says she could not forgive him for a long time—it was only later that she understood he was forced to distance himself from her. This was the only way to protect the family, and himself, from further harm.

Outside, Lidia is forced into a prison van and brought to Donetsk, to the main regional prison, where her head is shaved and she is put in isolation in a basement cell. The light shines day and night; the cell is equipped with an iron bed and a latrine. In the first few weeks, she is interrogated daily and asked the same questions over and over. Then the interrogations are suddenly broken off; it appears as though she has been forgotten in her dungeon. Although the rats and cockroaches torment her, she enjoys the solitude. For her, someone who has known nothing other than crowded living conditions for a long time, isolation is bliss. She has enjoyed contemplation as long as she can remember, and now she finally has time for it. She lies on the bed with her eyes closed and goes over all of the many questions that she has about life. The only thing she tries not to think about is her future.

After three weeks, she is taken from the subterranean prison realm, half-starved and half-blind from the harsh cell light that never goes out. She is brought to the pre-trial detention facility in Odessa, the city that was the source of her ruin. From isolation, she lands in a crowded cell with eleven women, who fight constantly for one of the eight bunks. Lidia usually sleeps on the ground, but once in a while a young German Communist who has been imprisoned for a second time allows her to shelter with her, where she whispers instructions about how to behave during interrogations. Once, through the bars in the window, she sees Bella Glaser led across the prison yard by two uniformed officers. It is the last time she glimpses her friend.

Lidia writes nothing about her questioning. She merely describes a curious incident. She recognizes that one of her interrogators in Odessa is Slava Bronstein, her erstwhile neighbor and classmate. In school he had shunned her along with all the others, later he approached her—in vain. Now he takes his revenge by raping her in the interrogation room, a tried and tested method used against female suspects. Afterward she asks Slava Bronstein for a pen and paper—she wants to write her confession. He gives her what she asks for, pleased that his method has shown such quick results. However, instead of writing a confession, Lidia writes a denunciation. She reports on his relationship to Trotsky (that he has disavowed), about his hatred for the state and about his father's cooperage which employed twenty poorly paid workers until the revolution. When she is brought to the interrogation cell again the next day, she meets Slava in the hallway. He is as white as chalk. "You bitch!" he hisses. Not so long ago he used to borrow books from Lidia, such as the page-turner *Angel of Love*. She remembers this now. "Of course not, of course not," she answers casually as they pass, "I am the angel of love." A few days later she sees him being dragged across the prison corridor, beaten bloody.

After almost five months in detention, Lidia is led into a small room where she is urged to sign her verdict. Through a crack in the door, she hears a conversation between two prison employees. "We have already overfulfilled the target for doctors and engineers," one of them says. "But with the teachers we have fallen behind, we need to keep at it," the other replies.

It is difficult to imagine that Lidia, twenty-three years old, one meter and fifty-four centimeters tall and only a flyweight after her long detention, is considered to be especially dangerous. Nevertheless, she is brought to Medvezhya Gora by an armed escort of two soldiers in a train compartment reserved especially for her. One wonders if all the others, every single one of the condemned millions, are brought to their destination with so much expense and comfort. The soldiers don't say a single word to her on the way to Moscow. Twice per day, she receives a cup of tea and a piece of bread with bacon fat. When she has to go to the toilet, she is accompanied and forbidden from locking the door. In Moscow, she has to get out of the train and is brought to another station in a prison car. From there, the journey continues toward Murmansk, once again in a separate train compartment with two new military escorts. But there is one improvement: the windows no longer have a screen so she can look out onto the increasingly deserted, snow-covered landscape.

She arrives in Medvezhya Gora on April 1, 1934. She is greeted warmly by a young prisoner who takes down her personal details. It is, she notes in a subordinate clause, her future husband, Yuri.

After the registration, she is "free"; she can go wherever she wants. She stands outside in the snow in her lightweight loafers and thin coat, the night illuminated only by a few large, low-hanging stars. The exiles are simply abandoned in the wilderness; they have to figure out how to get by on their own. It is clear that they cannot escape—as far as the eye can see, there is nothing but forests, swamps, bears, and wolves. A few faint lights seem to flicker in the distance, but Lidia freezes into an icicle after two minutes and she cannot make out a path that could lead to the lights. In her confusion she returns to the registration barracks.

Yuri does not only save her on this night. In the final analysis, she probably owes her survival in the camp to him. From Lidia's son Igor, I know that his father Yuri comes from a well-known dynasty of Russian Orthodox priests, but that he did not continue the tradition because he felt that his calling was to become an engineer. He was exiled because of a disparaging remark he made about Marshal Voroshilov, whom he called a toady. For this, he was sent up for five years. Now, in the camp, he is also just a prisoner, albeit a privileged one. He is a talented young engineer; the camp administration is well-disposed toward him, and he has vital contacts. On this night, he takes Lidia to a heated women's barracks where she can stay for the next few days. There is no bunk for her there, but she can sleep on the floor next to the warm oven. The women give her generous portions of their food rations, stealing almost the entire contents of her travel bag in return.

Lidia is initially assigned to a kindergarten for the children of high-ranking camp officials. The mothers treat her like a serf, but the job helps her to obtain a bunk in a different, better equipped, women's barracks. She receives vouchers for the NKVD canteen and is allowed to finish the children's leftovers. However, her luck does not last long. Unfamiliar with the local conditions, she ends up in one of the swamps that lurk all around while searching for berries with the children. At the last moment, as a few children are already starting to sink, a soldier on guard duty notices them from the distance and leads them out of the death zone. Lidia is fired on the spot, though thankful that her term in exile is not extended. It is unthinkable to consider what would have happened if one of the privileged children had died in the swamp.

In order to avoid an impending assignment as a logger, Lidia takes the initiative and starts looking for a job. She travels across the enormous camp territory with the so-called cuckoo-train from colony to colony and introduces herself. The train consists of a small, rapidly chugging steam engine that pulls a trailer filled with logs. The wood, which is used to fire the locomotive, also serves as seating for the passengers. Once, when the train stalls in the middle of the taiga because it has run out of fuel, another passenger suggests to Lidia that they walk the remaining fifteen kilometers back to the colony instead of waiting for more trees to be felled. Lidia agrees. It is a bright, white night, but in a short time they are in the middle of a swamp again, and they are forced to cover the rest of the distance on the wooden railroad tracks. Lidia's young travelling companion has long legs, the space between the ties is an ordinary step, while Lidia has to jump from one tie to the next. She hops across a stretch of almost fifteen kilometers. Once she misses a tie, and her companion has to pull her out of the cold, black mush that instantly and inexorably starts to suck her in. At some point, one of the giant brown bears that roam around everywhere, and break into the colonies at night in search of food, approaches them. But luckily the swamp separates them from the hungry colossus.

After weeks of fruitless applications (no one wants to hire a political prisoner), Yuri helps her to obtain a position as a teacher in a penal colony for imprisoned minors. By this time, a shy love binds her to Yuri. When she entered the camp, her survival instinct caused her to grasp at the first straw, embodied in the form of Yuri, but now he proves himself to be not a straw, but a strong rope, which helps her to pull herself out of the camp's deadly fields. She could not have endured hard physical labor for long, and from that point of view, a teaching position is her salvation. However, taking the position means she will be separated from Yuri. The Arctic Circle juvenile colony lies directly along the White Sea–Baltic Sea Canal, twenty kilometers from Medvezhya Gora, where Yuri works in the technical administration. They get married before Lidia starts her new job since this is the only way they can receive permission to visit each other occasionally.

The Arctic Circle colony holds two thousand children and teenagers between the ages of eight and seventeen. Street children, orphans, and convicts' children who had already become criminals, and even murderers, in childhood. Lidia is assigned a bunk in a barracks for female school employees. A sack with wood shavings serves as a mattress; she is issued a tin bowl, a cup, and a spoon. The potbelly stove is lit during the night, and the women must go into the forest to collect wood, but there is plenty here. The barracks' door is barricaded shut with a tree trunk overnight to keep out burglars and bears. At lunchtime, Lidia is allowed to eat in the teachers' canteen, and she receives a bread ration, which she brings home for her evening meal. Sometimes the women improve the menu with mushrooms and cranberries, which they collect in the surrounding forests, always careful to avoid getting caught in the treacherous swamps.

The state supplies eighty teachers to re-educate the juvenile offenders. An armed guard is present during the lessons in all the classrooms. Out of ignorance of the situation, Lidia rejects this—she wants to be alone with her students. She is warned, but she is determined, and when she enters the classroom for the first time accompanied by the director, the students stand up politely. Twenty-five boys in white shirts, all clean and well-mannered. The director introduces Lidia, but scarcely has he left the room when a storm of salacious and obscene commentary breaks out, culminating with the cry to "give it to the doll properly." Lidia wants to run away, but the door is already blocked. Furthermore, the escape, had it succeeded, could also have ended badly for her. It is possible that she could have received several days in a detention cell for leaving her workplace without authorization and then been assigned to a logging crew.

She decides to take the bull by the horns. As calmly as possible, she explains to the students that on her own she would not suffice for what they had in mind, but in any case, they would all be shot afterward. At any rate, they would be treated none too gently, and so it might be better to at least give the lessons a try. The pupils provide a convincing counterargument: "We shit on your lessons!" Panic-stricken, Lidia begins to tell one of her fantastic tales, based loosely on Scheherazade. At first there is laughter and mockery, then the classroom grows steadily quieter, the boys' faces become serious and attentive. When the bell rings at the end of the lesson, they protest, "We don't want a break, keep talking." Lidia explains that she is now tired and won't continue with the story until the next day. However, she must also go through the prescribed material, otherwise she will be kicked out. She proposes to complete the mandatory lessons as quickly as possible every day and then continue with her story. The pupils agree to this.

When she enters the classroom the following day with twenty-five notebooks under her arm, she is greeted with a chant, "The cunt, the cunt, the cunt will stay, she's brought us something nice, something nice, hooray!" Lidia ignores the greeting, puts the notebooks down, takes off her coat, and hangs it on a nail. When she turns back around, the notebooks are gone. She expresses her surprise, but the class explains in unison that there were no notebooks there, that she must be mistaken.

Lidia considers how she should respond. The director had urged her to elect a class leader right from the start. One of the boys already caught her eye on the first day because of his lively, intelligent gaze, so she calls on him and he introduces himself as Ivanov 26. Later she learns that everyone in the colony is named Ivanov, they only distinguish one another by their numbers. Their real names are never revealed, and whoever does so anyway is severely punished by the group. Once the camp administration succeeded in coaxing the real name out of one of the young prisoners after having promised him better food, better clothing, and even membership in the Young Pioneers.[3] They tied the red bandana around his neck and sent him back to the barracks after a celebratory dinner with plenty of alcohol. In the morning, they found him under his bunk, strangled with the red neckerchief.

After the lesson, Lidia takes a look at the file of Ivanov 26, whom she has designated as the class leader. This sixteen-year-old with clear blue eyes has already murdered three people. He suffocated his grandmother with a pillow to steal the money she had saved especially for him; during a burglary, he shattered a man's skull with a hammer, and finally, he shot a policeman. He was twelve years old at the time.

Lidia hesitates, but at the next opportunity, she speaks to him about the stolen notebooks. She learns that the pupils manufacture not only playing cards out of the paper but also banknotes. They produce them so perfectly that they are never found out. They are not allowed to shop in the camp kiosk—officially they do not possess any money—so they sell the fakes to other inmates from whom they receive a percentage in the form of cigarettes and cologne, which they drink for its alcohol content. They play cards for high stakes. For example, you can gamble away your voice and then only quack or bark afterward. Players stake their bread ration, their lunch, their only pair of shoes, and sometimes even their lives—not more and not less.

Once, a child who has gambled his life away obediently follows the player who has won it. The two eleven-year-olds go down into a gully, where the winner binds the loser's hands together with a string and starts to saw at his throat with a dull razor blade. The child, accustomed to the merciless discipline of the camp, remains heroically silent for a while, then he breaks loose and runs upward, screaming and covered in blood, to the top of the gully where the guards instantly appear. The child is taken to the infirmary, and the culprit is immediately sentenced. They place the gun barrel to his temple and ask if he has anything more to say. "Uncle, I will never do it again," he says meekly. Then a muffled shot resounds and the boy's body slumps to the ground.

When Lidia tells stories before the end of class, she can observe how these adolescents, who have not heard a kind word for a long time, are transformed. Their faces become soft and approachable. Sometimes they ask naïve questions, make innocent remarks. Over time something like friendship develops between them, but Lidia never forgets whom she is dealing with and she always keeps her guard up.

The polar night and the long twilight cause Lidia to sleep longer and longer in her free time. Sometimes the day lasts only one or two hours, and even then there is nothing more than a bit of gray light along the horizon. Sometimes the snow glows in the darkness, and sometimes one can see large, crystal-clear stars in the sky and the constant magical theater of the northern lights. But Lidia becomes ever more tired, ever weaker. Once, on the weekend, she sleeps for twenty hours in a row. The doctor diagnoses her with early-stage scurvy, and orders her to eat more berries, garlic, and the extract of boiled spruce needles. Long walks before bed are also prescribed. This is easier said than done—no one goes for walks in the colony. Lidia fears the people that she meets here even more than the bears, wolves, and the vicious wild dogs.

One morning she notices that she can no longer get out of her bunk. She knows that she runs the risk of being sent to a detention cell if she misses work without an excuse, but it is impossible for her to get up. Her body is as heavy as cement. She lies motionless and stares at the dark barracks' ceiling. She is certain that she will never get up again. Lidia's barracks mates are familiar with her condition. They give Lidia some of their bread rations, cook the prescribed spruce needles on the potbelly stove, and mix in a spoonful of precious cranberry jam.

On the third day, they revive her with a story from the school: during her absence an influential professor from Leningrad came to the colony. He had already heard a lot about the famous re-education facility in Karelia, and he wanted to use the opportunity to hold a trial lesson with Lidia's students. He had heard through the grapevine that the young teacher refused to hold lessons in the presence of an armed guard, and he wanted to follow her impressive example. No sooner had the director introduced the class to him and left the room than the class leader Ivanov 26 stood up and asked where their pretty young teacher had gone and what such a nasty old man was looking for in the classroom. The question was accompanied by the worst curses and a growing roar. The professor wanted to vindicate himself and start the lesson, but the shouting kept getting wilder. When he finally slammed his fist on the table and demanded silence, the students threw their inkpots at him.

Scared to death and doused in ink, he ran from the classroom. All of the students were put in detention for twenty-four hours, but even on the way there, the boys repeated that they would not allow their teacher to be taken away; they wanted her back at once.

Lidia returns to the classroom on the following day and calls her pupils to order: they not only treated an old man badly but also risked serious consequences for their own future. But the boys remain convinced that one must make short work of such scarabs. They stress that Lidia is under their personal protection and that they will not allow anything to happen to her.

On one occasion, Lidia notices that her students are learning more eagerly than ever before and treating her almost tenderly, not letting her out of their sight. Ivanov 26 explains to her in a whisper that a boy from another class has gambled away all of Lidia's property in a card game, so for the time being she must be kept under guard at all times. In the mornings, when she goes off to school, a few students actually do stand next to her at the door, and after class, they escort her back to the barracks.

Lidia is allowed to visit her husband in Medvezhya Gora for a few days over New Year's. Instead of letting her students know, she slips away unnoticed after the lessons, collects her pass at the office, and is at the fence with the watchtower shortly thereafter. They check her pass and then she is out, in front of the gate. A stretch of twenty kilometers through the polar night lies in front of her. Minus fifteen degrees Celsius, a broad, clear path through the forest, a bright moon, silence. She walks in quick, lively paces, anticipating her reunion with Yuri. In accordance with the laws of the camps, she carries a briefcase containing her belongings and has hidden her pass and her money in her shirt. Branches snap, but she doesn't think anything of it—it is probably just a squirrel since the bears are asleep in their caves at this time of year and the wolves usually stick closer to the settlements. But before she realizes what is happening, someone comes from out of the darkness, attacks her, and throws her to the ground. She can make out the silhouettes of two figures. One of the two men sits on her chest and searches her, the other rummages through her briefcase. "Hand over the money and the pass or we'll kill you!" he quietly commands. Lidia pushes herself down deeper into the snow and starts to scream at the top of her lungs. The second man grabs her leg and twists it so violently that you can hear it crack. Suddenly a shot, then the sound of horses' hooves—it is a mounted patrol. The figures dart off into the forest, Lidia is hoisted up onto a horse and brought to the railway station. They call an ambulance and take her to the infirmary in Medvezhya Gora, where her leg is set. The next day, they bring her two men to identify. She looks at their dirty, vicious faces and the pleading look in their eyes and shakes her head. Lidia knows that they will both get what they deserve even if she does not identify them.

When she returns to the penal colony with a sore leg after her days off, no one asks any questions. Instead, the students curtly inform her that the danger has passed; she no longer needs any special protection. Lidia does not see the connection, but she senses that from now on she belongs to the "Family."

It is often so cold in the classroom that the students have to thaw their inkpots under their clothes before they can start writing. Sometimes snowstorms rage for weeks on end, the world sinks into darkness, and the light is on all day in the classroom. Once, when it is quiet and you can only hear the scratching of fountain pens on paper, a ray of sunshine falls into the room—it seems to have come out of nowhere. Everyone is electrified; they drop their pens and rush to the window. In the eternal, dark gray sky, you can see the thin, shining rim of the sun; it seems so close you can almost touch it. The vision lasts no more than a minute, the glowing sickle sinks behind the horizon once again—a moment of light, a ray of hope in the underworld.

At one point, Lidia is summoned by the camp administration. They ask how she is getting on in the colony, whether she has any complaints. Then they ask her if she loves her country. It is obvious what this question means. They always ask it of anyone whom they want to become an informant. And indeed, they need her help in order to eliminate a "harmful element." It concerns one of her colleagues, the natural history teacher Gennady Petrov. Lidia does not decline the "proposal"; she knows that this would considerably extend her time in exile, but she plays dumb. One week later, she delivers a report to the camp administration that says roughly: Prisoner P. got up at six in the morning, washed himself and shaved, and watered his saplings in their pots. Then he went to the cafeteria to eat his kasha. In the lesson he spoke about the germination of beans in a northern climate and reprimanded one of his students for having dirty fingernails. He complained of back pain and so on and so forth. In the camp administration, they explain that she has misunderstood the assignment; they expect to receive compromising material about Petrov. Lidia nods eagerly and delivers a similar report at the next meeting. This brings her career at the renowned socialist re-education facility on the Arctic Circle to a close. She is dismissed for "limited intellectual abilities."

On her last day, she buys twenty-five fishing hooks at the camp kiosk and gives one to every student as a farewell present. The boys are devastated, but they do not protest. They know that Lidia is also a prisoner who cannot control her own fate.

She still has to work at a lumber mill in Medvezhya Gora for two months before her sentence is complete. Yuri is free as well. They have a child, their son Igor, whom I will find in Siberia's Miass almost eighty years later. Lidia takes a position as a teacher in a free school; her husband works as an engineer in a metal works. They live with their child in an earthen hut with no plumbing or electricity, but they both realize that it is better to stick it out in a remote location for the time being, at a safe distance from the centers of power. She takes stock of her sad life: I have grown coarser, she writes, I have lost a lot of my critical spirit and my finer feelings. The system has won.

While Lidia lives in seclusion with her family in the taiga, my mother holds the fort with her mother Matilda and Tonya in Mariupol.

Meanwhile, her father Yakov has died, her brother Sergey is studying at the conservatory in Kyiv, and Lidia is far away. She probably looks like she did in the old photo that shows her together with her white-haired mother—the skinny young girl with the black pageboy haircut and that startling mixture of innocence and awareness in her eyes. Perhaps during this time, the intimate and always anxiety-filled relationship with her mother develops. By now she is more than sixty years old and still in a politically vulnerable position as the daughter of formerly wealthy and important capitalists. Does my mother nonetheless eventually leave her on her own while she goes to Odessa to study? Does she likewise take shelter at one of her aunts and eat lunch with one and dinner with the other? Is she also required to count the conjunctions in Griboyedov's *Woe from Wit*, and learn how to shoot in the military studies class, move bales of jute around, and teach post office clerks Ukrainian after also learning the language from her nanny? What does it mean that she graduated with honors? Weren't such awards reserved for the children of workers and peasants in those days?

In 1941, there is a small miracle in Lidia's life: she receives a holiday voucher from her trade union leadership entitling her to three weeks' vacation in Crimea. For someone of her social status, it is almost incomprehensible, but I probably owe the fact of my existence to this event. Lidia's husband is working and cannot take care of little Igor by himself, which is why she really cannot go on vacation, but after so many years on the Artic Circle, the chance to travel to Crimea is all too tempting. Lidia sends a telegram to her mother in Mariupol and asks her if she could come visit for three weeks to look after the child, the grandson that she has never seen. And sixty-four-year-old Matilda really does set off for distant Karelia, without realizing that the war will make her return impossible and that she will never see her daughter Evgenia again.

If Lidia had not received the holiday voucher, my grandmother would not have travelled to Medvezhya Gora, and my mother's life would have taken a different course. She would not have married my father;

she presumably would not have even met him, and she would not have allowed herself to be deported to Germany. She would not have left her mother on her own in the middle of the war; she would have hidden from the Germans. She would have stayed in Mariupol, and maybe one day, she would have borne another child, but not me. I am the consequence of a holiday voucher, which some Soviet bureaucrat issued to my aunt, a former counterrevolutionary, for some inexplicable reason.

Lidia's blissful holiday lasts less than a week. On the fifth or sixth day, she is woken up in her hotel room by a distant thunder. It is not a storm, as she thinks at first; it is the start of the war, the German invasion of the Soviet Union. All the guests have to leave the hotel and are brought to Simferopol by bus. From there they continue onward in overcrowded trains. Outside the ripe wheat is burning in the fields. The train moves a bit forward, then back again, forward and back, to evade the bomb squadrons. People scream in fear; the dress of a barefoot young woman sitting in Lidia's compartment suddenly turns red. Her child, whom she is holding in her arms, was hit by shrapnel.

Once the train reaches Kharkiv, it cannot go any further, the tracks have been bombed. The houses in the area around the station are burning; people are lying in the streets. After taking a second look, Lidia realizes that they are not asleep but dead. She gets lost in the panicked pushing and shoving on the streets, and when she is finally in front of the other train station, where the train to Leningrad departs, the platform is already closed. Small and nimble as she is, she climbs over the iron barrier. The train has already started moving; she throws her suitcase in an open window, hands pull her into the train from another window. For three days, the train keeps moving a bit forward and then backward again. The forests are on fire; aircraft debris is falling from the sky. There is nothing to eat, no drinking water, and the overflowing toilets give off an unbearable stench.

As the train finally rolls into Leningrad at dawn, you can already see the burning food warehouses from the distance—flames that leap up to the sky and light up the entire city even though it is raining. Barrage balloons hang in the air; they are supposed to bring down the "Messerschmitts," as the Russians call the German fighter planes. Armed troops belonging to the People's Militia are everywhere in the streets. Lidia just manages to get out of the city; shortly afterward its inhabitants are encircled—a military blockade without parallel in human history that lasts more than two years and results in the slow starvation of about one million people. It is said that there was not a single dog, a single rat in the city anymore. People ate everything, the soles of their shoes, wallpaper paste, and corpses.

Lidia rushes home from the train station in Medvezhya Gora. Everyone is still alive, her little son Igor, her husband, and her mother. Yuri does not have to go to the front after it was discovered at his medical exam that he has tuberculosis. His illness not only saves his own life but also the entire family. Without him, Lidia writes, it would have been impossible to survive the war, which was also raging in Medvezhya Gora, with her small child and her old mother. Daily air raids, airplanes collide constantly and fall from the sky as burning torches. The Soviet soldiers aim their primitive rifles at the German planes; the German pilots respond with salvos of machine-gun fire. Matilda hangs the laundry outside and is infuriated, "Stop shooting, will you! There is a child here, can't you see that?!?"

Once, leaflets are dropped over the area. On one side, a farmer is depicted wearing bast shoes and dressed in tatters, bent over and walking behind a plow. The caption states, "This is how the Russian farmer lives under Soviet power." The other side shows the same farmer, but well-fed, in a felt hat and leather boots, sitting on a brand-new tractor. The caption states, "This is how the Russian farmer will live under the German Führer." Sometimes one of the fighter planes with a swastika on its tail flies so low that you can see the face of the German soldier in the cockpit.

One of Lidia's students is wounded. He lies on the ground, his guts oozing out of his stomach. Lidia bends down and grabs his intestines with both hands so that they do not fall into the dirt. The boy screams bloody murder. Two medics come running up and lift him onto a stretcher—Lidia runs alongside them on the way to the hospital, holding the boy's intestines as he screams. Halfway there she becomes nauseous, she can tell that she is about to pass out, but one of the paramedics snaps at her so sharply that the blood returns to her head. At the entrance to the hospital, a female medic comes up to them and holds out an enamel bowl for Lidia, who puts the now-unconscious boy's intestines inside. Later she hears that he survived.

More and more residents flee. The doors of the abandoned apartments and shops are open; no one cares. Stray chickens and cows wander around the town. A barefoot young woman escapes, shrieking, her sick father in her arms. There are regular reports about villages where the entire population has been wiped out.

In October, Lidia and her family are evacuated to Kazakhstan. The journey in a freight train takes them all across Russia, almost five thousand kilometers, a back-and-forth odyssey of more than a month through the burning country, up to the border with China. Some of the evacuees die on the way, most of the others perish in the snow when they are finally abandoned at night in the Kazakh wilderness and left to their fate. Yuri makes it to Alma-Ata on foot and returns with a horse and cart.

In the end, Lidia writes, they owe their salvation to the war. Yuri and Lidia burn their passports, which contain all the information regarding their previous history as enemies of the people, and claim at the administrative office in Alma-Ata that they lost them in the chaos of the war. Their story is believed, and they receive new passports. Lidia is a blank slate once again, a new person. She can start over from the beginning.

PART THREE

Journey to Germany

On October 8, 1941, when my mother is twenty-one years old, the German Armed Forces occupy Mariupol—Hitler's Operation Barbarossa campaign, which was supposed to decimate the Slavs and provide *lebensraum* for the Aryan master race. When the occupation begins, there are 240,000 people in Mariupol; two years later, there are only 85,000.

I don't know what caused my father to leave Russia and move to Ukraine. I don't know when and how my parents met. But I think it was during the war, that the war created this union. Maybe a hatred for Stalin also played a role; my cousin Igor believes this was the main thing that his parents, Lidia and Yuri, had in common. But the decisive factor was probably that in the inferno of war my mother did not have anyone other than Tonya, that she had to fend entirely for herself. Perhaps, lonely and deathly afraid, she would have simply followed anyone who promised to protect her. The Russian from the Volga was twenty years older than her and possessed the exact skills that she lacked. He could fight, tough things out, and survive. A good-looking, masculine type who was not afraid of hard work, he probably took control of her life right away. For him, she is an incredible stroke of luck—a young woman still enveloped in the aura of the pre-revolutionary elite, to which he had no access as the son of a general store owner. She falls into his hands, a present from the war: young, innocent, and completely lost. Captivated by his strength, fascinated by his coarse, imperious desire for her, she experiences her first passion with him during the war, made all the more existential by the constant presence of death.

When she marries him, does she know about his first wife, a Jew with whom he has two children? This marriage, which I only learned about later by chance, is the most mysterious aspect of my father's largely inscrutable life. He never spoke about his past in the Soviet Union; it was locked within him as though in a vault, to which maybe even he did not possess the key. He also never mentioned my mother a single time after her death—as though she had never existed. My sister and I were left behind alone with him, a man who lived in an impenetrable inner emigration. Apart from his unpredictable outbursts of violence, we knew him only as a silent man, drinking and smoking, while he read from the thick Russian books he received once a month in a large package from the Tolstoy Library in Munich. Occasionally, when he was in a good mood, he would tell us about his life in Kamyshin before the revolution, about traditional religious festivals, weddings and funerals, singing in the church choir, and, over and over again, about the juiciest watermelons in the world, which grew along the endless Volga, compared to which Germany's Elbe was only a brook, though I don't think he had ever even seen it. The only important piece of information that my father ever gave about himself was that when he was thirteen years old, both of his parents died of typhus and that he and his three younger brothers were only able to avoid starvation because he sold his parents' tiny house for a single sack of flour. Decades later, I learn from Lidia's memoir that it

Figure 6. Evgenia in a headscarf, roughly 1943–1944.
Author's private archive.

must have been one of those extortionate deals that her father pursued as an examining magistrate.

I was never able to find out anything about the fate of my father's first family, but their existence is evidence of one thing my mother and I have in common: We were both born into our father's second families. We were the late children of aging men who had abandoned their first marriages and wedded significantly younger women. Yakov's first wife probably stayed behind in Siberia after he took their son to Warsaw, but what happened with my father? Was he already living apart from his first family, or did he abandon his wife and children during the persecution of the Jews and leave for Germany with a twenty-three-year-old? Were his wife and children, who stayed behind on their own, murdered by the Nazis? Or, is it possible that they were already dead when my parents met? I will never find out. My father took this secret, and undoubtedly not only this one, with him to the grave when he died in 1989, thirty-three years after my mother, a blind and mute old man in a German nursing home.

The mass deportation of Ukrainians to Germany begins with a ubiquitous propaganda campaign by the occupiers. At every turn, Soviet citizens are called upon to volunteer to work in Germany—they are promised a paradise. The brainwashing takes place everywhere: in the cinema before the feature film, on all the radio stations, at work, in train stations, in theaters, in all public places and streets. Large, colorful posters show happy Ukrainians at modern German workbenches and smartly dressed domestic workers mixing German Sunday cake. Ukrainian maids are especially popular. In 1942, Hitler issues an order to send half a million to German households in order to reduce the workload for German women. There are daily appeals in the press:

UKRAINIAN WOMEN AND MEN

> The Bolshevik commissars have destroyed your factories and workplaces and deprived you of work and bread. Germany offers you useful and well-paid work. In Germany you will find excellent working and living conditions, and you will be paid according to a pay scale and your performance. Ukrainian workers are especially well looked after. So that you can live in suitable conditions and foster your own culture, special settlements have been built where everything is available: cinemas, theaters, hospitals, radio, baths, etc. Ukrainians live in bright, well-equipped rooms and receive the same meals as German workers. In addition, the company kitchens take national characteristics into consideration and have therefore added *vareniki*, *galushki*, *kvass*, etc., to the menu for Ukrainian workers. Germany is waiting for you! Hundreds

> of thousands of Ukrainians are already working in free and happy Germany. How about you? During your stay in Germany, we will take good care of your family back home.

In the beginning, the propaganda is effective. Not all of the so-called Eastern workers are deported by force, at first many sign up voluntarily. The truth about the utterly hellish work and living conditions in the German Reich only trickles out gradually. Initially, hidden messages arrive in letters; for example, a sixteen-year-old sends a drawing of a flower in a letter to his mother—the flower is a pre-arranged symbol to indicate that the situation is bad. Over time, more and more deportees return from Germany totally destroyed, sent back home because they are no longer of any use in their condition. The stories they tell quickly stem the flow of hopeful volunteers who willingly sign up to work. It is a serious problem for the defense industry as the German labor force is unavailable because all the men are at the front.

Meanwhile, the war's production demands are insatiable; German victory depends upon slave laborers imported from all over the world, especially the Soviet Union and Ukraine in particular. Hitler names his model gauleiter, Fritz Sauckel, as the general plenipotentiary for labor deployment. The son of a Franconian postal clerk and a seamstress, who is later described at the Nuremberg Trials as the "greatest and cruelest slave trader since the pharaohs," makes an appeal to "finally abandon the last remains of sentimental humanitarianism" and issues a command to begin the manhunt. Ukraine is their preferred area of operation. Ukrainians, who make up the majority of the Eastern workers, are considered to be the most inferior of the Slavs, above only the Roma, Sinti, and Jews on the racial hierarchy. They are seized on the streets, in cinemas, in cafés, at tram stops and post offices, anywhere where they can be found; during raids they are taken from their apartments and the basements and shacks where they are hiding. They are driven to the train station and transported to Germany in cattle cars. Countless numbers disappear without a trace, with nothing but the clothes on their backs. Able-bodied young people are especially popular; entire freight trains crammed with Ukrainian teenagers roll into the German Reich every day. But eventually forty- and fifty-year-olds are also hauled off, and later the old and weak as well. Entire villages are deported, including grandmothers with their grandchildren; the deserted villages are burned to the ground. At first, the age limit for slave laborers is set at twelve, then it is reduced to ten. And not only that: in the summer of 1942, a compulsory two-year period of service in the Reich is introduced for all young people between the age of eighteen and twenty from Ukraine. Up to ten thousand future forced laborers are transported to Germany every day, and according to Fritz Sauckel, they must be fed, housed, and treated in such a way that they provide the greatest possible output for the least amount of input.

An East German friend draws my attention to a small volume from Reclam,[1] that was issued in the GDR in 1962. It contains a short text by Franz Fühmann, who was at the front in Ukraine:

> In front of us, pushed up against the wall of the barracks, a silent column stood swaying gently on its hips. They were Ukrainian women and girls, who stood three abreast in front of the barracks' wall and swayed their hips; they were crowded close together and had linked their arms, swaying gently like blades of grass in the wind. Each one of them had a bundle of luggage lying in front of them on the ground, a small bundle: clothes, a cooking pot, a spoon. And they stood, and the wind blew over the roof of the barracks, and then we heard that the column was not silent, they hummed softly, very softly, a gentle song. Sentries in fur coats with guns slung over their shoulders stood guard in front of the women. A sergeant was pacing up and down, smoking; a locomotive gave a shrill whistle and then a black freight train pushed its way onto the track. We had not taken a step further; I stared at the women, and one of the women near us turned her neck and looked at me and looked at Nikolai and Vladimir, the two Hiwis with the "HIWI" armbands;[2]

then she nudged the woman next to her and the row of women slowly turned their heads, one by one, like a book being opened, and looked the Hiwis in the eye and looked at the HIWI armbands. Then they turned away again silently, one by one. The Hiwis stood as white as chalk, their lips trembled. The freight train stopped rattling, gray smoke billowed suddenly, a warm veil; I hoped that the Hiwis would run away under cover of the cloud of smoke, but they stayed put, as though frozen to the ground. The sliding doors of the freight train rattled apart and caves opened up; the women picked up their belongings, and the sergeant screamed: "Let's go, let's go, hurry up!" The soldiers pushed the women forward, then Vladimir suddenly shouted and dropped the cable reel and rushed toward the train, and one of the women who had already turned away turned toward him once again and Vladimir cried out a name, a gurgling cry. One of the sentries jumped forward and poked Vladimir in the chest and roared at us to back off. Vladimir balled his hands into fists; the sentry reached for his gun. I pulled Vladimir back, and Vladimir, since he felt a hand on his shoulder, slumped and turned around and went back behind the barracks, staggering with his head hanging down. Nikolai stood silently, grinding his teeth. The women disappeared into the darkness of the train cars, and suddenly, I saw for the first time what I had certainly seen at the freight station dozens of times and about which I had already sent countless messages via telex: a labor transport went to Germany, to Berlin or Vienna or Essen or Hamburg. But now I saw: my God, they had no shoes on their feet, only bundles of rags, and paper from cement sacks tied around their chests and backs, and none of them had a blanket, and the train cars were not heated, no oven glowed, and there was a thin layer of chaff on the floor and ice hung from the bars in front of the portholes. The sergeant trudged up to us. "What are you gawking at?" he asked quietly. I made my report, then Nikolai and I quickly grabbed the cable reel and left. Vladimir stood in front of the station leaning against a tree; he had closed his eyes and had a shaking chill. I put my hand on his shoulder

> and searched for words, so that I could say something to him; I wanted to tell him that the women from Kyiv would be better off and that they would be well taken care of in Germany, but I could not say anything. I took out my case and gave them a cigarette; we smoked and listened to the thumping of the train, which became faster and quieter at the same time, and then the locomotive whistled once more, and the thumping disappeared into the gray day. Was she his girlfriend or his sister? I wanted to ask, but I did not.[3]

While I was reading, I felt as though I could also see my mother, quietly singing a Ukrainian song with the other women as she leans on a barracks' wall at the train station, but I know that I would not have been able to find her in this picture. She did not leave Ukraine by land, but by sea, across the Black Sea, like her Uncle Valentino before her. My memories correspond with the records from an American occupation authority that were sent to me by an international tracing service. I stare at the papers; they are like ghostly witnesses to a reality of which I was never fully aware. The yellowed pages are undated, but it must be that they contain personal information my parents provided in connection with one of the many applications they made for entry into the United States. The stops on their journey leave no doubt that they were fleeing from the Red Army.

I don't know what my father did during the German occupation in Mariupol. Maybe he had more reasons to flee the returning Soviet government than my mother, but if up to that point my mother's guilt was based on the fact that she came from a family of enemies of the people, capitalists and counterrevolutionaries, now, on top of this, she had become an active anti-Soviet actor by working at the employment office, a cog in the German deportation machine, a traitor and a collaborator. A prison camp was the minimum punishment that she could expect. If she had fallen into the hands of the returning Soviets, she probably would have been shot on the spot.

Before they set off, they get married. The date on the inverted copy of their marriage certificate says that the wedding took place six weeks before the German occupiers withdrew, when it was apparently already foreseeable that the Soviet troops would retake the city. They embarked on the long journey as a married couple to increase their chances of staying together along the way.

One day in August 1943, my mother walks through the weathered archway of her house for the last time. What did the city look like at that time? *All of Mariupol gutted and blown to pieces*, Friedrich Wolf, the representative of the National Committee for a Free Germany wrote to his wife in Germany that same year. The final image my mother has of her city is that of a giant ruin. It has long been clear that the war is lost, but at the last minute, the German soldiers obliterate what remains of Mariupol. In a blind rage, they blow up one building after another, aim flamethrowers at the windows and doors of previously undamaged apartment houses; they destroy schools, kindergartens, libraries, the granary, and water tanks in order to leave behind as much scorched earth as possible.

What could my mother have taken with her on the journey into the unknown? I know about the old, gilded icon crowded with the most important Russian Orthodox saints that now hangs on my wall at home—my only valuable family heirloom. I know about the three photos, including her picture in a headscarf, which shows her alone and that she took with her as a memento. I know about the marriage certificate and the papers that I destroyed as a child, as well as two slim volumes of Russian poems and tales from which she had read to me so often. I have lost these books, but to this day, the torn, almost earth-brown paper, with its musty, bitter smell, is like a part of me. I still know it by heart, Pushkin's famous poem about the learned tomcat on a golden chain who circles around a green oak tree day and night, Lermontov's poem about a lonely sail that flashes white amid the blue mist of the sea and does not know what it is looking for in the distance. All of this lies together with her other things in her bag, when for the last time, she goes through the archway of her house, which has long since been taken over by strangers. The nanny Tonya probably helped her pack, most likely she still accompanies her for a bit and carries her bag. Tonya, the good soul, her second mother, who changed her diapers, held her in her arms, and taught her Ukrainian songs—she also says goodbye to her forever.

The papers from the Americans show that Odessa was their first stop as they fled. Perhaps when they left Mariupol, they did not yet have any intention of going to Germany. Maybe they only wanted to reach Odessa, where at that time the German occupiers were still fully in control. Regardless, they stay in the city on the Black Sea for a full eight months, or at least, this is what is written in the American papers. My father's profession is listed as "bookkeeper"; there is no entry for my mother. I had always thought that my father landed in Ukraine from Russia through the chaos of war, but now it turns out that he had lived in Mariupol since 1936 and already worked there as a bookkeeper. The papers from 1947, which were about to disintegrate, gave me information about him that he had never provided himself and raised entirely new questions.

My first name suggests that my parents find refuge with my aunt Natalia in Odessa. Natascha is the nickname for Natalia, and I suspect that out of gratitude my mother named me after this aunt, a shy, girlish woman with a futile expression in her eyes. She gave me, her first child, the name of the last person under whose roof she lived in Ukraine.

Odessa is retaken by the Red Army on April 10, 1944—my parents leave Ukraine at the last minute. The question of whether they left voluntarily or if they were deported from Odessa remains unanswered. It is impossible that at this time they did not know what awaited them in Germany. They probably only have a choice between plague and cholera, between forced labor in Germany and death in Ukraine. Conceivably, they also leave with the hope of reaching America via Germany. This is what they always wanted, for as long as I knew them. America may have been their actual goal from the start. Germany was only an unavoidable detour; forced labor was the price they had to pay to get there. Or is none of this true? Did they really only want to go to Odessa, and were they hunted down and deported like so many others?

As my mother gets closer to Germany, she moves further away from me. The curtain on her life in Ukraine opened completely unexpectedly, although I could never find out anything more than I already knew about her forced labor in Germany, and I only knew what was written on my father's employment card. The papers from the Americans still help me to navigate as I reconstruct her route to Germany, but after that, the historiography is all I have. The American records do not tell me anything about how they reached Romania from Odessa, but here a memory helps me. They often spoke about a voyage on a ship, and the Soviet bombs that threatened them.

As I picture it, the people in Odessa are herded in droves onto the ships waiting in the harbor and pushed onto the decks. Shortly thereafter, my mother sees the Black Sea coast swim away, sky-blue Ukraine disappears from her eyes forever, sinking in the waves of the stormy April sea. She has no time to cry. She knows that she could die in the next few hours since the German naval units, which have been driven back in retreat, are being bombed mercilessly.

The actual cargo of the German ships that depart from Odessa for Romania usually consists of strategic raw materials destined for the German war industry. Forced laborers, who are transported along with this cargo, serve as a human shield against the Soviet Army, which attacks the enemy ships from the air and sea. Hundreds and thousands of terrified people shelter on the decks, some on top of each other, covered only with tarpaulin against the rain, cold and wind. Sometimes, the Soviet bomber pilots do not detect the human cargo; sometimes, compatriots are knowingly sacrificed in order to sink a German ship. After all, they are traitors and collaborators who surrendered to the enemy and whose lives have no value. In one attack, eight thousand people die in the waters of the Black Sea.

My parents' ship reaches Romania, but I do not know where it docks. In the records of the US authority, the next stop on the way to Germany is listed as "Transit Camp Brailov." Brailov is the English name for the city of Brăila, in the interior along the lower Danube. Maybe the ship sailed all the way there, but maybe it docked in the major Romanian port of Constanţa, and from there, they traveled onward by train to Brăila, about two hundred kilometers away. Regardless, in Romania, my parents are already on the other side of the world. Romania and Germany are allies in the war, and on Romanian territory, the Soviets can no longer reach her. My mother still can't believe it, but what she always held to be impossible has occurred: she has escaped, truly escaped. She has been saved; she is free. This is how it may have seemed to her.

As expected, I get no answer when I search the internet for various terms to find out about the transit camp in Brăila. Who should have recorded them all, the countless transit and filtration camps across Europe! From an atlas, I learn that Brăila is located in Romania's Wallachia, and I remember that my finger had searched for something here before. My great-grandmother Anna von Ehrenstreit's possible ancestor, Jacob Zwillach, Lord von Ehrenstreit of the First Wallachian Infantry Regiment, whom I found in a nineteenth century register of Austrian nobility came from here. Did my mother know that Brăila, her first stop in the other world, was located in Wallachia, the possible ancestral home of her relatives on her father's side? Did she know her family history? Or did I know more about the family by that time than she had ever known? Did she know as little about her origins as I had for my entire life? Was she not only a person without a future, but also one without a past?

I spend hours looking at photos from transit camps in hope of suddenly spotting the face of my twenty-four-year-old mother in the endless stream of people. Young women, girls with headscarves, cardboard suitcases and bundles of cloth, some of them practically still children, dressed in rags. They are all frightened, from towns and villages, and they do not understand where they have been taken. A mass of nameless people, too many to count, who exist only as numbers. Each one of them is my mother.

After arriving in the transit camp, known as a *Dula*,[4] the new arrivals are registered, counted, examined for their ability to work, and sorted. They are disinfected by spraying a petroleum-like liquid on their clothing where it covers the hairy parts of their bodies, or they are forced to strip naked, after which their clothes and baggage are deloused in a so-called disinfection chamber. If there are showers available, they are allowed to use them. But maybe the *Dula* in Brăila is one of those camps that are nothing more than a wasteland, simply a piece of land where people wait under the open sky for their onward transport. Already weak from the journey, many fall ill as they do not get anything to eat and are forced to sleep out in the open, in the dirt, in the cold, in the rain. The mortality rate in these camps is correspondingly high, so that many of the deportees never reach their destination.

On my father's employment card, it says that he arrived in Germany on May 14, 1944, but the card itself was not issued until August 8, a gap of almost three months which, once again, I can only fill with conjecture. Are they, like many others, sent from *Dula* to *Dula* as chaos reigns? Registration and re-registration, again and again new checks, filtrations, roll calls, disinfections, and examinations of fitness for work? The employment offices are overwhelmed by the incoming crowds; they cannot find assignments for all of them. In addition, the deportees are supposed to be demoralized, to become accustomed to the fact that they are no longer subjects, but objects that can be treated in every conceivable manner. However, it is also quite possible that my parents were spared this odyssey through the transit camps and brought straight to Leipzig from Brăila. In this case, the employment office issued the cards three months late.

The American documents also do not reveal how my parents reached Leipzig from Brăila. Either they continue by boat on the Danube through Serbia and Hungary into the German Reich somewhere near Passau, or they are transported in one of the cattle cars that convey the never-ending quantities of human cargo to Germany from all over the world. They are, above all, Ukrainians, but also Russians, Poles, Latvians, Lithuanians,

Estonians, Belarusians, Azeris, Tajiks, Uzbeks, Greeks, Bulgarians, Yugoslavs, Hungarians, Czechs, French, Italians, and many others, even Chinese. On her first trip abroad, my mother is part of an international community.

One thousand eight hundred kilometers from Brăila to Leipzig, the city of Gottfried Wilhelm Leibniz, Friedrich Nietzsche, Karl Liebknecht, and Johann Sebastian Bach. Now it belongs to the National Socialist barbarians. Except for one hall, the famous railway terminus has been destroyed, hit by forty-six tons of American bombs on a single day. What does my mother see in the city? Presumably only flags with swastikas on them, waving in the ruins. Ruins and camps, camps everywhere. She has long known that her journey did not lead to paradise, but to hell, straight to the heart of the Gulag, which she thought she had escaped forever.

Some forced laborers are lucky. Occasionally, at small businesses, private households and farms, they are not treated badly; in exceptional cases, they are even integrated into the family. But my mother is not assigned to such a workplace, and it would probably not have worked out for her there. Since she was not capable of doing ordinary work, especially in a German household or on a farm, she would certainly have incurred the wrath of her German employers. And young Slavic women were particularly exposed to sexual exploitation in private workplaces that were hidden from public view. To a great extent, it was commonplace.

I remember a long time ago when, in order to work in peace and quiet, I rented a small house for a summer from a Franconian farmer on the outskirts of a village. My boyfriend at the time visited me on the weekends, and during the week, I was mostly alone. The landlord, who had an idle farm in the neighboring village and had retired early due to alcoholism, stopped by every now and then. He brought me a few eggs from his remaining chickens or a piece of bacon—this was the pretext for his visits. His alcoholic gaze, however, revealed a different motive. Staggering and breathing heavily, he stared at me greedily with his glassy eyes. Although I probably could have dealt with him easily in an emergency since he was almost too drunk to stand, I always panicked whenever he appeared, usually in the evenings, when the lonely house on the edge of the village was already enveloped by the shadow of the nearby woods. He called me "Russla" in the regional dialect, and at some point, it dawned on me. The word did not spring from his own imagination; he knew it from earlier times, when almost every German farmer had his own Russla on his farm. That is what they used to call them in those days in Franconia, people like my mother, not maliciously—they could have also named their dairy cow Russla. If I had been in my mother's position, the farmer would not have needed to woo me with eggs and bacon to win my favors; he would not have had to go to the trouble.

My mother is spared an assignment on a farm, but nevertheless, she has bad luck, and it even comes in threes. She and my father not only arrive at a place that is constantly under Allied bombardment, not only are they assigned to the dreaded armaments industry but also to a plant belonging to the Flick Group, of all things, a company known for its especially inhuman working and living conditions. They are sent to ATG, Allgemeine Transportgesellschaft mbH, in Leipzig, 101 Schönauer Street, an assembly plant for military aircraft, which German fighter pilots glorified frenetically:

Let the song of the engines roar,
The hour of freedom resounds.
And where your proud birds fly,
Be victorious in your flight.

The "proud birds" are manufactured at the Flick plant by 9,500 workers, including 2,500 forced laborers, who must participate in the production of death machines that will be used against their own countries. My parents are separated; my father is placed in a men's camp, my mother in a women's camp. From now on, they no longer have names, they are only the numbers, which are written on their respective employment cards. They have to wear a badge that says "OST" on the right side of their chest, three white letters on a blue background, the abbreviation for "Eastern worker," the worst designation after the Jewish star. It is a punishable offense for workers of other nations to speak with them.

The new arrivals are given a leaflet in Ukrainian, Russian, and German:

> The following regulations are applicable to workers from the occupied territories of formerly Soviet Russia:
>
> 1. Supervisors' orders are to be followed at all times.
> 2. Anyone leaving the camp must be accompanied by a supervisor.
> 3. Any sexual relations with persons holding German citizenship, with other foreign workers or prisoners of war, is prohibited and punishable by death. Women will be sent to a concentration camp.
> 4. Anyone who strikes, incites other employees, abandons the workplace without authorization, or supports subversive activities will be sent to a concentration camp as a forced laborer. Especially serious cases are punishable by death.
> 5. The compulsory badge with the label "Ost" must be worn on the right side of the chest of the respective article of clothing. Good workers who behave in a well-disciplined manner will be treated well.

In his secret speech in Pozen, Heinrich Himmler leaves no doubt about his purely utilitarian view of the Slavic forced laborers: "How the Russians are doing, how the Czechs are doing, is of no interest to me. . . . If they are dying of hunger, this is only of interest to me to the extent that we need them as slaves for our civilization. Whether or not ten thousand Russian women collapse from exhaustion while digging an anti-tank trench interests me only to the extent that the trench is completed for Germany."

It goes without saying that forced laborers are not allowed to resign and that it is not possible for them to change employers. And of course, they are not allowed to return home.

The ATG workers are distributed among twenty residential camps, twenty out of a total of six hundred, which exist in the greater Leipzig area. ATG is a huge company, a small city of workshops, secret underground production facilities, residential barracks, industrial barracks, kitchen barracks, laundry barracks, lavatory barracks, and canteen barracks. Female forced laborers are prohibited from setting foot in a men's camp, and vice versa. Does my mother even know in which camp my father lives and where he works on the sprawling factory grounds? Do they have opportunities to cross paths, see each other, and exchange a few words? Is it possible for them to meet at meals in one of the canteen barracks, or in some areas where men and women are allowed to linger together? Are there some secluded places on the camp territory where the forced laborers, divided by sex and nation, can come into contact with one another?

The camps have quaint names such as Sunflower, Birch Grove, Meadow Green, Papyrus, Weissflog, Fairy Tale Meadow, Rawhide, Good Luck, Serenity, Black Rose, Brunhilde, Hawthorn, Cloverleaf, and Lowland, to name just a few. Which one was my mother in? The records that could provide me with this information no longer exist. The ATG company archive is no longer available, perhaps it was destroyed in a fire, or maybe the American or Russian occupiers took it with them; most likely, the company management destroyed it at the end of the war in order not to leave any evidence behind. I receive a small amount of information from a memorial site, including a sketch of the ATG compound and the camps. Once again I encounter the same phenomenon that I come across constantly during my search for clues: of the twenty camps, only a branch of the Buchenwald concentration camp, which held five hundred Hungarian-Jewish women who worked for ATG is documented. There is a considerable amount of information available about this camp, and a memorial plaque was also placed where it stood. Not a single word is written about the others, ATG's two thousand, mostly Slavic, forced laborers, to say nothing of dedicating a memorial plaque to them.

I look at the sketch of the compound over and over again, and retrace the lines of the streets with my finger. I can rule out the camp for Hungarian Jews, but there are still nineteen others where my mother could have lived. She went here somewhere in the mornings, in the winter darkness, on her way to work in the assembly hall; in the evenings, also in the winter darkness, she returned to the barracks. When the days were longer, she may have read the German street signs: Asternweg, Rosenweg, Dahlienstrasse[5] . . . Does she pass by garden plots on her way to work, a colony of private homes and lawns, or should I picture the gloom of a war-damaged industrial terrain where streets named for flowers are only remnants of a past that is no longer visible?

There are labor gangs that are allowed to walk independently, and there are others that are accompanied by guards and driven on with shouts and beatings. The wooden shoes that the women wear on their feet clatter in the streets. The dreaded wooden shoes, for which there is no alternative after those brought from home wear out. Then there are only the expensive wooden shoes, which you must purchase from the management; hard, boat-like clogs that deform your feet, and hurt and chafe with every step. If you have bad luck, your feet become inflamed and abscesses develop, and those who can no longer make it to work, who fall ill, soon run the risk of being filtered out and left to die. A few women hold their shoes in their hands and walk barefoot as they are otherwise unable to keep pace. Sometimes they sing quietly as they walk, as is customary at home; there people almost always sing, in the fields, in their apartments, and on the streets. My mother sings as well in her beautiful, clear soprano, which I will later still hear her singing with so often; now it is probably more of a humming, just as Franz Fühmann heard at the train station before the women were loaded onto the cattle cars. Like all the women, she wears a headscarf, and perhaps she still has her own dress which she brought with her from Mariupol. But maybe all of her things are already worn through and torn, and work clothes made of cotton drill hang from her thin, half-starved body, while the rigid wood chafes her feet. Don't the gangs of forced laborers wake the German residents every morning with the clatter of their many wooden shoes on the roads they take to work?

Twelve-hour days await her on the factory floor. I remember her never-ending dispute with my father, who demanded that she go to work in order to earn extra money like most of the other women in the houses. My mother cried because she did not think she would be able to do it. The labor camp had probably destroyed her health and her nerves permanently, even the word factory caused her to panic. Once she tried it nonetheless and took a job in a factory that made window blinds, but after a week she collapsed.

How does she manage not to collapse now? Day after day, twelve hours on an assembly line, six days a week, on Sundays as well if they don't have enough workers. At the same time, she has been severely weakened by hunger and the restless nights in the cold, overcrowded barracks, teeming with vermin. And she does not do any old job, but is required to participate in the assembly of fighter planes, deployed to kill her own people. The supervisors have the right to inflict corporal punishment, and she is probably not infrequently beaten for working too slowly.

There are lone saboteurs who risk their lives by deliberately making mistakes at work to harm the German war industry. My nervous and frightened mother could hardly have been one of them. She would have been more likely to try to conform as much as possible in order not to attract attention. This mindset had probably already become second nature to her in Mariupol—remaining inconspicuous in order to survive.

Harassment and punishment are part of everyday life; the Ukrainians suffer the most as they are at the bottom of the racial hierarchy, held to be lazier, less willing to work, and more deceitful than the other Eastern workers. They are punished for not wearing the OST badge, for not saluting the commander, bartering, stealing food, allegedly loafing on the job, damaging property, and many other things. The mildest punishment is a box on the ears, then the lash, additional work, reduced rations, and hourly wake-up calls at night. Occasionally workers are doused with cold water in winter and locked in a detention room where they die of hypothermia. One minor offense is enough to land in a re-education camp. This kills two birds with one stone: the forced laborers are punished along with the Germans who are imprisoned in these camps, as they are supposed to feel further humiliated and degraded because they receive the same treatment as the Slavic *untermenschen*. The chance of survival is especially low; in some the conditions are said to have been more brutal than in the concentration camps. Fritz Sauckel, the general plenipotentiary for labor deployment, encourages the supervisors to punish the forced laborers: "If they are guilty of the slightest offense in the factory, then please report it to the police immediately, hang them, shoot them dead! I don't care at all."

The Slavic workers live in the worst barracks, receive the lowest wages and the worst food. Their staple is so-called Russian bread, which consists of coarse rye meal, slivers of sugar beet, straw meal, and leaves and causes gastrointestinal diseases. Instead of the promised *vareniki* and *galushki*, there is a liter of cloudy water every afternoon and evening from which they can fish out a few cabbage leaves, peas, or beet slices. To add some variety, there is spinach soup with worms swimming in it. The menu is supplemented with one hundred grams of margarine and eighty grams of sausage or meat per week, usually low-grade raw horsemeat. The workers have to stand in line at the food counter with their aluminum bowls—those who come too late get nothing.

In order to squeeze even more output from the workers despite their starvation-level rations, a so-called performance diet is introduced. Whoever works more gets more to eat. This does not lead to increased costs for the Flick Group, as they are merely redistributing the food. What the high performers receive is taken from the rations of the weaker ones. Thus they inevitably grow even weaker, their productivity declines further, and they fall into a dangerous, downward spiral. This does not present any problems for Flick. Replacements are readily available, fresh, still unspent human material from the occupied countries. Slavs are considered to be especially robust. "Some living things are so resilient because they are so inferior," Joseph Goebbels said. "After all, an alley cat is more resilient than a champion German shepherd."

I remember a doctor who examined my eyes in the eighties. He knew about my ancestry and was shocked by what he saw in my eyes through his diagnostic device. Instead of the hardy genes and indestructability that he had assumed he would see, there were so many constitutional defects and weaknesses in my iris that he no longer wanted to believe that I was a Slav. Forty years after the end of the war, his world was shattered. He looked at me with such concern and mistrust; it was as though he thought I was a fraud.

Destroying as many Slavs as possible through labor also aligns with Hitler's plan to decimate the Slavic people to make room for the Aryan master race, and put the remaining Slavs at their service. They should be individuals without any education or ties, without their own culture or national identity. They should be treated well, given plenty of food, and be permitted to amuse themselves with song and dance so that their work ethic is strengthened and they are of as much utility as possible to the Thousand-Year Reich. Accordingly, universities and other post-secondary schools in the occupied territories of the Soviet Union are quickly closed—domestic animals do not need to be educated, they merely have to follow orders. Four years of basic education are more than enough for future domestic workers, Hitler said at one of his famous "Table Talks."

The forced laborers' wages are laughable, and women earn even less than men. If I calculated correctly, my mother has less than six Reichsmark left per week after taxes, social security, the Eastern workers' deduction, and room and board are paid. She can buy next to nothing with this. A loaf of bread costs about ten Reichsmark at this time, and in any case, money barely has any value outside the black market since you can hardly buy anything in the shops anymore without a voucher.

Sometimes the workers in the camp scramble like animals for scraps of food, for a few frozen or rotten potatoes or beets; others risk their lives to slip out of the locked and guarded barracks at night to steal what can be had in the surrounding fields. A few, who still have the strength, hire themselves out to local farmers on their Sundays off (which are increasingly rare in the last year of the war), to earn some extra money or to eat their fill for once. Others make decorations or toys out of the scraps they find on the factory and camp grounds, which they exchange for food on the black market. If they are caught, there is a serious risk that they will be sent to one of the re-education camps from which very few get out alive.

My mother has been used to hunger all her life, but now, because of the twelve-hour days that are the norm in the camp, her body begins to consume itself. Doubtless she finds herself in that degrading state of malnutrition where her thoughts revolve only around eating. Her swollen legs sting as she stands at the conveyor belt, her back aches, her eyes burn; the machines drone in her ears, and their echo follows her as she sleeps in the barracks. She probably suffers from impaired vision, dizziness, and intestinal cramps, but all this merely encourages her obsessive thoughts about the hard, mortar-like piece of Russian bread that she keeps in her pants pocket so that no one can steal it from her. If she were to give in to temptation and eat the bread saved for dinner right away, she would not be able to sleep at night from hunger, and in the morning, she might not be able to get out of her bunk. And that could be the end. She works in order to survive; she knows that her labor is her only asset, and that if she slackens and succumbs to her weakness, then she is lost.

The bright living quarters, equipped with radio sets, bathrooms, and other comforts that the propaganda posters promised to the gullible and impoverished Slavs are nothing more than run-down wooden barracks; in addition, they are desperately overcrowded as ever more camps are destroyed in air raids and more and more people are crammed together into increasingly cramped spaces. My mother, who was born not only into hunger but also into the tightly packed conditions of Soviet life, is accustomed to its involuntary communities of strangers. Anything like a private sphere would only be a vague concept to her, but in the camp, her entire living area consists of a wooden bunk. For hygienic reasons, the straw sacks were replaced with paper mattresses filled with wood chips, but this does not impress the vermin, who continue to harass the exhausted women all night.

In the war's final winter, the temperatures are exceptionally severe. Although there are stoves in the barracks, there is nothing to heat them with. The women look outside for discarded wood, branches, foliage, for anything that burns. Little by little, they take apart the wooden stools that have been placed in the barracks, and eventually they tear the boards from their bunks and burn them for a few minutes of warmth. Presumably, my mother only has a thin, tattered blanket with which to cover herself. She probably wears all her remaining clothes at night before covering herself with her gray overcoat and the camp blanket. She has a cold for most of the winter, her dry skins burns and flakes, her hands are raw and cracked, and her lips are bloody. She has shiny red chilblains on her feet that torture her every time she slips on her shoes and itch unbearably when her feet warm up during the day. The rheumatism which she develops during her time as a forced laborer will torment her until the end of her life, as will the liver damage caused by the contaminated camp food.

Waking up is the worst part of the day, a reveille from the trill whistle at five in the morning. Maybe my mother is torn from a nightmare, but no nightmare can be worse than the reality of the camp that is right in front of her from the moment she awakens. Every day is endless, a piece of time—you don't know how long it will last or if it will ever end. Prisoners know when their sentence ends, while in the German labor camps, there is no release date. My mother not only lives without a future, but the past also seems so remote, as though she had abandoned it somewhere away from the world, on another, infinitely distant star, to which she will never return. She has to fight against the homesickness that tears at her with all her might because, if she surrendered to it, her emotional defense system would collapse. In her previous life, she did not know how precious the ordinary aspects of daily existence that everyone takes for granted were—how delightful it was simply to be able to go out onto the street, to lock the door behind you in the bathroom, to turn the electric light on and off at night when you felt like it, or to put on a clean, ironed dress. As she stands at the assembly line constantly repeating the same motion, which has become something like an unconscious movement, she thinks of these things as an inestimable happiness that is lost forever. Again and again, almost obsessively, the faces she once knew pass before her inner eye, the faces of her parents, siblings, friends, and acquaintances. She has dialogues with each of them in which she searches for herself, for the person that she used to be.

Everyday life in the camp is governed by unpredictability and despotism. New orders continually come from above, the supervisors' moods shift from day to day, the regulations change constantly. Sometimes the barbed wire is removed, and then later, it is replaced for some inexplicable reason. Sometimes the rations are slightly increased, then reduced again. Sometimes you are allowed to leave the camp, then it is prohibited again for a long time. It happens repeatedly that a worker is beaten to death or shot for no apparent reason. Hunger, fear, and the unbearably cramped conditions in the barracks lead to denunciations, theft, and prostitution. For a piece of bread, for a bar of soap, women risk their lives and sell their emaciated bodies to Germans or better-off foreign workers who have a higher standing in the racial hierarchy. For a sandwich—a year in jail. A kiss—two years. Sexual intercourse—off with your head, according to Fritz Sauckel's maxim.

The Eastern workers present the Nazis with a dilemma they are unable to resolve. They are essential in order maintain the German war industry, but their presence is incompatible with National Socialist racial theory as it endangers the genetic purity of the German people. German men are strictly prohibited from having sexual relations with Slavic women;

nonetheless, rape is a part of daily life in the camp. Why would my mother have been spared, especially as she was more beautiful than the simple, coarse girls who had been abducted from their Russian and Ukrainian villages in large numbers? But visual differences among the workers were probably irrelevant, they are all one body, a single sex organ that is always available. A German man who is caught red-handed gets away with a light sentence or goes unpunished, while the victim receives the death penalty or is incarcerated in a concentration camp. Whenever there is evidence that German women are having relationships with Slavs, they are expelled from German society, their heads are shaved, and they are labelled as whores and driven through the streets. A Slav who has dared to approach a German woman is publicly hanged. His corpse is left dangling on the gallows for several days as a deterrent to anyone else.

Typhus and dysentery are rife in the camps. Workers who fall ill are sent to the overcrowded infirmary barracks, where they receive a minimal amount of medical care. In the beginning, invalids were sent to their home countries, but now they no longer go to the trouble. If the sick do not recover quickly enough, they are in danger of being classified as permanently disabled, which is almost always equivalent to a death sentence. The patient no longer receives treatment as this would take too much desperately needed medicine away from the German people. He is left to his own devices and only receives the so-called diet ration; usually he dies after a short time.

Tuberculosis epidemics are also common in the camps. Due to their weakened immune systems, a majority of the workers are infected, but the disease does not break out in everyone. Only those who have already reached their limit can no longer put up any resistance to the "White Death." Those who are too sick to work are committed to so-called sanitoria where they are given excess doses of medicine and liquidated, provided they have not already died of their own accord due to malnourishment and the failure to provide medical assistance. Moreover, in September 1944, Heinrich Himmler orders that all Slavs in psychiatric hospitals should be murdered. Since German hospitals are overcrowded, it is irresponsible to treat Slavs who will not be able to contribute their labor to the Reich for the foreseeable future. Other sources show that not only Jewish prisoners but also Slavic forced laborers were used as human guinea pigs in medical experiments. They were experimented on in tanks of cold water, pressure chambers, injected with trial vaccines, and exposed to powerful X-rays and other, for the most part, deadly tortures.

Over time, the misery of the forced laborers increased more and more. An official of the Foreign Office noted at the time:

> The Eastern workers find themselves in such a state of general apathy that they no longer hope for anything in life. For example, women are hit in the face with nailed boards. Even for the most minor offenses, men and women are locked in concrete punishment cells in the middle of winter with their outer garments removed and deprived of their rations. For "hygienic reasons," Eastern workers are sprayed with cold water from a hose on the camp yard in wintertime. Hungry Eastern workers are executed in front of all the camp inmates in the most inhuman way over a stolen potato.[6]

The Eastern workers' lack of rights was so extreme that any German could beat them if they felt it was justified. Toward the end of the war, they could not, as a rule, expect any sanctions, even in the event of manslaughter.

The Allied bombings are also becoming increasingly merciless. If my mother's workplace is located far from the camp, she has to endure long, exhausting marches on a daily basis. If she lives nearby, possibly even right on the factory grounds in Camp 1, she is directly exposed to Allied air raids, whose targets include the German armaments industry. The air raid shelters are generally reserved for Germans; countless Eastern workers perish during attacks on the barracks when they are locked in at night. A Russian forced laborer who also worked in a factory in Leipzig described the situation:

> The British air raids happened at night; the Americans came during the day. . . . You could set your watch by them. As soon as it got dark, the sirens began to howl. Well, then they bombed us. There were an incredible number of airplanes; they called them "flying fortresses." If you looked up, there were so many that you couldn't see the sky. Our camp was only hit by small incendiary bombs that came down like hail in the sun. They exploded on the ground, scattering phosphorous. Once we stayed awake until midnight waiting for the next air raid, but it never came. We were surprised, and then we fell asleep anyway. And suddenly without any warning, the bombs fell at four o'clock in the morning. And you know, half the city or more . . . those were the big bombs that weighed at least a ton. The whole city was on fire. During the day, it was dark from all the smoke; at night, it was light. The blaze was huge. At some point our factory was hit too, though we of course lived further outside the city. Production stopped, and we were brought into the city under guard and forced to clean up the ruins. Things were better for us there. We could find food in the ruins, and naturally it made its way to our stomachs, in addition to our rations. Once SS men with machine guns took us to work. We had to fill up the craters that the bombs had made. There was a fascist there whose entire family had been killed in the bombing. He took a sip from a small bottle, just a sip, you know Germans don't drink much, then he took off his swastika armband and blew his nose in it.[7]

A stranger who shows me what my mother must also have seen: the flying fortresses, the glow of the burning city. After the German bombs that fell on Mariupol, after the Soviet bombs that threatened her life when she sailed on the ship to Romania, she now finds herself in a hail of American and British bombs. In Mariupol at least, she could hide in the basement of her house; in the German camp, she is completely exposed to the inferno. She cannot even run out into the open but is trapped in the barracks, which could go up in flames at any moment.

Is it during these nighttime bombings at the height of the war that she begins to lose her mind? Or did it already happen somewhere along the way, during this catastrophic stretch of her life that must seem like one long nightmare? She was raised to believe by her mother, who, though a Catholic, was deeply rooted in the Russian Orthodox folk religion and the belief in God as a savior and protector. Does she pray during the air raids and call out to her patron saint, the martyr Evgenia, whose icon must have once been attached to her crib? Does she pray, or is she already fighting her hopeless duel with God, the merciless, indifferent authority, whose silence will destroy her. If she still has hope at this point, then it must lie with the Allies, who are both her potential murderers and liberators.

It was only several decades after her death that I came upon the idea to do the math. The result was unequivocal: my life began in one of the Flick Group's barracks, in the final phase of the war. How did it happen? Were married couples allowed to have sexual relations? Were there opportunities for them to meet alone and unobserved? It is difficult to imagine, since children were not welcome among the slave laborers, especially from the inferior Slavs.

I imagine that it is a Sunday, the day most workers spend sleeping, doing laundry or taking care of their hygiene. But on this Sunday in early March, spring is already in the air; it is a red-letter day for my parents. They have received a pass and leave the camp together. The pass gives them the right to go into the city unsupervised. They can finally spend a few hours together away from the omnipresent eyes of those who watch over them day and night. My mother is dizzy from hunger and so much open space—she is no longer used to it and takes my father's arm. Her emaciated body sinks into her grey overcoat, perhaps she still owns a pair of patched-up shoes that she has brought with her from Mariupol and spare her from having to shuffle along in wooden clogs. It is still cool; she is probably wearing a headscarf, with her thick hair pinned up underneath. When she lets it down, it falls to her shoulders like a black cape—now it has been cut off, her head shaved because of the lice. A worn jacket flaps on my father's body, he has tied the only tie he brought from home to his thin neck to mark the occasion. They both wear the mandatory OST badge on the right side of their chests. Maybe they have a few marks[8] on this Sunday so that they can buy something edible to eat. Many of the stores in the bombed-out ghost town do not serve the ragged slave laborers; sometimes, it says on the door that they are not allowed to enter, while other shopkeepers don't care where the money comes from. Perhaps they can afford a roll made of real flour and a soda? It is possible that my father also barters on the black market, maybe my mother is only able to survive thanks to her husband's clandestine activities.

Those who walk along the devastated streets face hidden dangers. At any moment, the sirens could wail to announce another air raid, at any moment my parents could be stopped by one of the military vehicles that patrol everywhere, the Volkswehr or the SS, organizations that can do whatever they want to them, especially toward the end of the war, when violence against forced laborers becomes increasingly arbitrary. With a nervous hand, my mother checks if she can still feel the pass in her coat pocket; without this certificate, they would be lost—arrested immediately and possibly shot. It is possible that you can already see a few green buds, the first timid gorse blossoms, snippets of nature, about which my mother forgot during the never-ending camp winter.

Maybe it happens on that day, maybe they find a hiding place somewhere in the ruins or behind the bushes on the outskirts of the city? But perhaps I am also the result of a rushed and breathless embrace somewhere in the camp, when they could have been discovered at any moment, possibly sniffed out by one of the German shepherds who help the guards search for escapees? It is possible that my conception can be blamed on a moment of recklessness because the war's end is already in the air, because euphoric rumors are circulating through the camp that liberation is imminent, especially as Allied air raids become ever more aggressive.

In any case, one day my mother notices that she is pregnant. Her body has been sending her signals for quite some time, but she did not understand the message. Many women in the camps miss their period due to exhaustion, and morning sickness can be mistaken for a symptom of permanent hunger. Her ravaged body has long been alien to her. It is no longer hers; it belongs to the Flick Group. But at some stage, she suddenly realizes that there is a child growing in this body, a second living thing with whom she must now share her rations. A child who wants to live through her, who demands her vitality and protection and a place in the world. She does not even possess these things herself.

Does she know what happens to children who are born in the camps? Had she become pregnant with me earlier, I probably would not exist. In the beginning, pregnant forced laborers are sent back to their home countries, but Fritz Sauckel changes his tactics after more and more women get pregnant intentionally to escape the camps. German women are supposed to have as many children as possible in order to strengthen the Germanic race; abortions are prohibited and punished severely. For Slavic forced laborers, on the other hand, abortions are not only allowed but mandatory; their racially inferior offspring are not welcome. Thousands of "primitive short-legged Slavic women," as Hitler calls them, are pressured to have abortions under threat of punishment; if they refuse, they are eventually forced to do so.

Women who do manage to give birth do not receive any legal protections. According to the Nazis, Slavs do not require any special treatment because for them pregnancy and childbirth are just as straightforward as they are with an animal. After they are born, infants are taken away and brought to a facility that is sometimes called a "Foreign Children's Care Facility," a "Foreign Children's Foster Home," or a "Foster Center for Bastard Children." For the most part, these names are used to conceal facilities for infanticide. Some of the newborns are treated mercifully and killed immediately after birth by lethal injection; most have to die on their own, slowly and in agony. They are covered in boils, eczema, and impetigo. They starve, freeze, or die of poor hygiene and neglect, negligence and a lack of love. In the barracks, which are filled with excrement, bedbugs, and maggots, the babies' corpses are stacked on top of each other and stored before being buried in margarine boxes. According to sources, 100,000 to 200,000 Eastern workers' children perished in the Nazi facilities, though the actual figure is considered to be significantly higher.

In August, 1943 SS-Gruppenfuehrer Erich Hilgenfeldt writes to Heinrich Himmler:

> It is an either-or situation. Either we don't want the infants to survive—in which case we should not let them slowly starve and, through this method, remove many liters of milk from the overall supply; there is a way of doing this painlessly, without torture. Or, we plan to raise the children in order to use them later as workers. But then we must feed them in such a way that they are able to work adequately.

Apparently Himmler follows the SS Gruppenfuehrer's second proposal, since at least a few nurseries are set up where newborns receive sufficient food and care. It seems that in the final stage of the war, those responsible for the labor force do not seem to realize that this effort is being made in vain and that very soon they will have no more need for slave laborers.

Chaos reigns in Leipzig. Camps and factories are being hit with bombs and destroyed with ever greater frequency. Abandoned forced laborers wander through the city's thick smoke in search of shelter and something to eat. It is assumed they are looters, fair game for the drumhead court-martials of the SS and the Wehrmacht. Thousands are shot for abandoning workplaces that no longer exist, or out of fear of revenge or the possibility that they will provide eyewitness testimony.

But then they finally arrive, the Americans. The GIs enter the barracks and say: "You are free." They laugh: "The war is over," they say, and hand out cigarettes and chocolate.

ATG's management and their employees have already cleared out. The workers ransack the company's offices; they storm the barracks and throw themselves on the food supplies, the tubs of marmalade, the loaves of bread, and wheels of cheese. In the city, they plunder German shops, and stuff themselves with anything they can find, roasting meat on fires, which they light in the street. They pour out of all the city's camps into the open, fraternize in the streets, Russians with Italians, French with Poles, Ukrainians with Serbs, everyone with everyone who is not too weak for the ecstatic celebration. The Germans are afraid, and barricade themselves indoors. The tables have turned; the masters have become losers, and the slaves winners. They wander through the streets by the thousands, forced laborers who have become unemployed; no one has any use for them anymore. Some set off for home on foot; others drift about aimlessly—ungoverned people, desolate, shabby figures, who often travel in groups, in hordes. Overnight, a new category of people has emerged: displaced persons, or DPs for short. Millions of Slavic nothings and nobodies, who will soon also make the American liberators suspicious. Like Stalin, they suspect them of collaborating with the Germans, and in the army newspaper *Stars and Stripes*, they are referred to as criminal vagabonds, fascists, and Bolsheviks.

For this reason, the agreement made at the Yalta Conference to forcibly repatriate all Soviet citizens is not only beneficial for the Germans, who have no more need for the burned-out workers and fear revenge. It also suits the Americans, who want to restore order as quickly as possible. Millions of deportees start their return journey, millions who face Stalin's sanctions—a miserable existence until the end of their lives. For Stalin, the former forced laborers are traitors and collaborators, who did not resist the enemy's efforts to exploit them, but submitted, while millions of their compatriots gave their lives in defense of the fatherland. Some are shot after they return home, others go straight from a German to a Soviet labor camp. Most are condemned to spend the rest of their lives on the margins of society; they cannot find work and depend upon parents or relatives to get by. Attending university is certainly out of the question. They live not only in poverty but also in isolation, because everyone is afraid of associating with returnees who have been declared to be traitors; moreover, former female forced laborers are regarded as the Germans' whores.

It would take several decades for the issue of compensation payments to former forced laborers to arise in the Federal Republic of Germany. Repatriates seeking redress are required to provide evidence of the forced labor they performed. Very few are able to do so since their papers were either lost in the chaos of war or destroyed out of fear of the Soviet state. For those who do receive compensation, the amount is a mere drop in the ocean considering how long they suffered.

Terrible scenes are played out during the repatriation. Soviet DPs throw themselves at the Americans' feet and beg to be shot rather than sent home. Some commit suicide, hanging themselves from a beam in their barracks for fear of Stalin's revenge. They were deported and worked to exhaustion, and now they are being sent back to face the madness of a merciless despot.

An exception is made for Balts, Belarusians, and Ukrainians who lived on Polish territory before the war and were deported to Germany. They are free to choose if they want to be repatriated, to remain in Germany, or emigrate to another country. My parents are saved by this loophole. An American hand writes "Cracow" as their hometown in their papers, although only a few lines above this it says that my mother lived in Mariupol and my father lived in Kamyshin and Mariupol and that they were both deported from Odessa. There is no trace of Poland. Nonetheless, Cracow is registered as the place of deportation. The great mystery of the American papers, my parents' lie, and perhaps the American soldier's act of mercy, or possibly his ignorance of geography—the little word Cracow must in any case have saved my parents from deportation and resulted in me being born in Germany instead of the Soviet Union.

In July 1945, the Americans withdraw from Saxony and leave this part of Germany to the Red Army. Once again the Soviet government has caught up with my parents, it followed them all the way to Germany. They flee again, this time toward Nuremberg, the closest major city in the American zone. The war crimes trials will also take place here soon, and forced labor will be declared a crime against humanity. The Flick Group is charged as well. An ATG employee testifies under oath that no distinction was ever made between German and foreign workers; the foreigners were put up in high-quality accommodations and the German camp commanders were very well liked. He continues:

> Certainly, the life of a foreign worker was no paradise, as he was separated from his home and family. But I have to be honest and state that the company management did everything possible to make life easier for the workers. . . . Considering the circumstances, the food could be described as good. . . . In order to feed the foreigners, the management took the initiative and procured large quantities of foodstuffs, especially potatoes and vegetables, in the rural area around Leipzig. The workers' other various needs were also given real consideration. . . . There was also no lack of regular cultural offerings for the foreign workers. For a long time, the ATG camps were held up as models, and it was only after a few were destroyed in air raids and consolidation became necessary that they did not look especially attractive anymore as they were no longer surrounded by newly planted green spaces.[9]

The prosecutors come to a different conclusion:

> Conditions were especially bad in all of the Flick Group's plants; in many cases, the accommodations were squalid, and the working hours were exceptionally long; fear and forced confinement, physical suffering and disease, abuse of all kinds, including flogging, were the norm.[10]

Fritz Sauckel, my parents' ultimate superior, is also one of the people charged by name in the trial. I grow up in Nuremberg with exactly the same Franconian dialect that Sauckel, the general plenipotentiary for labor deployment, spoke; his German is the first that I learn. His

Franconian dialect was said to be so pronounced that during the trial he had to be asked repeatedly to speak more intelligibly. When he was sentenced to death by hanging, he burst into tears. He believed that his conviction had been due to translation errors.

Friedrich Flick denies that he is guilty in any way and presents himself as a victim of National Socialist tyranny. The verdict against him is mild. He is sentenced to seven years in prison and released after three years, advancing quickly to become one of the richest men in the newly founded Federal Republic. His company will remain the only one that never pays the former slave laborers a single mark of compensation. Leipzig's ATG is dismantled by Soviet troops: the machines are transported to the Soviet Union, and the factory buildings are blown up.

I ask myself again how my parents managed to get from one city to another in their flight from the Soviets, on this occasion from Leipzig to Nuremberg, three hundred kilometers across the devasted country. Do they simply buy tickets and sit on a train? Do they have enough money for this? Are the trains even running, or have the tracks been destroyed? Do they move forward in stages, one stretch by train, one stretch on foot? Millions of others are on the move with them, displaced persons; forced laborers from all nations; liberated concentration camp inmates and prisoners of war; German evacuees who want to return home; countless expellees from Silesia, East Prussia, and Bohemia. Everyone is moving west with whatever possessions they have left, alone or in convoys—one of the greatest human displacements of all time, the *Götterdämmerung* of the Thousand-Year Reich.

My parents teamed up with another Ukrainian couple whom they either met in Leipzig or afterward, on the run. Only when they arrive in Nuremberg, do the four of them realize that not much is left of the city. In their final air raid, the Royal Air Force dropped six thousand bombs and one million incendiary munitions on the Franconian capital in half an hour. A world of ghostly ruins. And yet—my parents had escaped the Soviets once again.

They wander about for hours; it is raining and getting dark. They find an unlocked storage shed on the grounds of an out of the way factory situated exactly where the twin cities of Nuremberg and Fürth meet. Apparently, it belongs to an adjacent iron works. They slip in, hoping to remain undetected so they can sleep for a few hours between the rusty scrap metal containers stored in the shed. My mother has no way of knowing that her brother Sergey is also in Germany, that he is in the Soviet zone from which they have just escaped, singing arias from Russian operas for the soldiers of the Red Army. She has no idea that her mother is still alive, and that together with her daughter Lidia she was driven to the other side of the world, evacuated to Kazakhstan's Alma-Ata, practically all the way to China. Wet, hungry, and almost unconscious from exhaustion, she falls asleep on the hard wooden floor. The child inside her is still alive; it is moving. The terror that she feels because of this child extends all the way into her dreamless sleep.

PART FOUR

Displaced Persons in Postwar Germany

One stolen night under the roof of a storage shed in a Nuremberg factory yard turns into almost five years. The shed belongs to the factory owner, who seems to be an exceptional German. He does not chase off the Slavic *untermenschen*; instead, he has sympathy for them and grants them asylum on his territory, although this violates the Allies' laws. Displaced persons are not permitted to choose where they stay; they must reside in special DP camps where they are once again under guard, though they also receive meager provisions. But apparently my parents and their companions prefer an uncertain, outlaw existence to another camp.

I don't know how they manage to survive in the initial period after their escape without any access to a food and other essentials. Perhaps the German factory owner not only allows them to stay in his shed but also helps them find food and the "furniture" I still remember: field beds,

Red Cross blankets, a petroleum lamp, and a table, which I can still see silhouetted beneath the shed's crooked, cloudy little window. There must have been an oven as well, or we could not have survived five winters in the dilapidated dwelling.

My mother lives in a constant state of fear. The factory owner can dispossess us at any time, the authorities can become aware of our presence, or someone can report us; in short, a Damocles sword is always hanging over us in the form of expulsion and confinement in a DP camp. For five years, we stay in the shed, five years during which the German factory owner holds his protective hand over us, covering us repeatedly, although it makes him liable to prosecution. Why does he do it? Is it possible that he has been so captivated by my mother's mysterious beauty that he doesn't have the heart to chase off this so obviously defenseless, forlorn woman and her companions? Perhaps he had also engaged forced laborers, and now he wants to make up for it by helping these Slavs who have no place to stay.

On a December night in 1945, my mother goes into labor. Since my birth certificate says I was born in Fürth, I know that she could not have given birth to me in the shed, as it was located within the Nuremberg city limits. I probably came into the world in a hospital in Fürth, and I can only speculate how my mother got there. It is only a few hundred meters from the border to Nuremberg; maybe she goes on foot, accompanied by my father, in the darkness, snow and ice, between two infrequent contractions. Maybe someone also calls an ambulance—it could only have been the factory owner who lives at the other end of the yard and has a telephone.

Perhaps she has never been more afraid and never felt more lost than she does in the maternity ward of the German hospital where she eventually stays behind alone, delivered up, come what may, to those who see her not only as a Slavic *untermensch* who contaminates the delivery room with her bad blood but also as the embodiment of the victorious Soviet power, the Communists and the Bolsheviks, who killed millions of

Figure 7. Evgenia's grave with her two daughters and their father standing behind it, 1957. Author's private archive.

German fathers and sons and fell upon Germany as murders, looters, and rapists and who occupy a large part of its territory. Naked and bursting with pain, she lies as a perpetrator in front of the victims and forces them to welcome her child. Can she have felt all of this, or is the birth such a force of nature that it drowns out all her other feelings? At around seven in the morning, a malnourished woman marked by physical exhaustion and exile delivers a surprisingly strong and healthy girl into the world, who only suffers from neonatal jaundice, which was common at the time.

When she sees her baby for the first time, she is taken aback by this sulfur-yellow, froglike creature that screams constantly; it has white-blond fuzz on its head that could not have come from either her mother or her father. From the beginning, she has the feeling that something evil has hatched from her body, that she has given birth to a little monster—a child that cries almost nonstop and does not allow anything to calm her. It becomes a torture for her, a new variety of the violence that she has always faced and cannot combat with her shattered nerves. A child, who bites painfully at her breasts, from which hardly any milk flows. Everything else that she offers is refused: carrying, rocking, cajoling, singing, kissing, hugging—all of it only seems to increase the screaming. Is the child in pain, is it filled with her mother's sense of horror, was it transmitted into her body? Perhaps it is sick, seriously ill, and about to die? She cannot understand or interpret the child's continuous, violent demands; sometimes, it seems that the child hates her and that it is screaming for a different mother. She rocks it in her arms and cries from despair and exhaustion; she is afraid of herself, of losing control and doing something terrible so that it would finally be quiet, so that she can finally sleep for an entire hour.

And then comes the night when she and her husband are arrested by the American military police. It is not possible that I actually remember it; the image must come from my imagination, inspired by later accounts of the incident, and yet I feel like I saw it, as through a small hole in a black curtain. Two naked figures with their hands up stand against the wooden wall in the dark shed. They are illuminated by an eerie light which doesn't seem to come from anywhere. They could be puppets, but I know they are my parents, whose strange, waxy bodies I see from behind, pushed against the wooden wall by an invisible force. It is only for an instant, then the light is extinguished and everything sinks back into primordial darkness. But the image of the two people against the wall, naked and defenseless, is burned in me forever. Whether I truly saw it, or invented it, for me it is the beginning of the world.

It is likely they are arrested because the Americans suspect them of collaborating with the Nazis, as they do all Soviet forced laborers who are still in Germany after the war, but strangely only my parents are picked up, not the second Ukrainian couple living with us in the shed who also managed to avoid being forcibly repatriated. My starving father goes on a hunger strike in prison to force the release of his wife, whose child cannot survive without her milk while she remains with the other lodgers. If she didn't have to worry about me, the prison would have been almost like a paradise for my mother. For the first time in a very long while, she can get enough to eat, it is warm, the screaming has stopped, and she can finally sleep. But her husband's hunger strike is successful, and she is released after just a week. And my father is also freed shortly thereafter.

Whatever my parents are suspected of doing apparently cannot substantiated. No one even arranges to confine them in a DP camp; on the contrary, my father goes to work for the Americans. His powerful tenor, trained from childhood in Russian church choirs, becomes his principal asset in Germany. His first engagement is at a Nuremberg theater, where, together with other displaced persons from the Soviet Union, he sings famous Russian songs which the American soldiers want to hear. He is paid in kind, receiving delicacies, which the vast majority of the postwar German population can only dream about. White bread, canned cheese, salted butter, milk powder, Lucky Strike cigarettes, and Hershey's chocolate, which comes in bars and cans. Chocolate in solid and liquid form is the staple food of my childhood.

The storage shed in the factory yard consists of two small rooms. My parents live with me in the front room, which opens onto the yard; the other couple have set themselves up in the back room, which directly abuts the factory wall. The moment that I recount this, their long-forgotten name rises from the bottom of my memory and surprises me with its familiar sound. The Zyganenkos—I no longer see their faces in front of me, but the remembered name proves to me that they were real, and real for me a long time ago as well.

We, the occupants, have to share the space in the small shed with each other as well as with the dusty scrap iron containers, which are kept here for some incomprehensible reason and give off a pungent, rusty smell. Everything smells of rust: our clothes, hair, sheets, blankets, and the white American bread we eat. We don't have any cupboards or shelves; all of our possessions are stored on the iron, which turns our fingers red when we touch it. All day, the shed vibrates silently to the rhythmic stamping of the machines in the iron works; we have gotten used to it, we hardly hear it anymore. Nor do we hear the thunder of the trains that drive over the nearby railway embankment at short intervals, mostly freight trains with heavy, iron wagons, which transport unseen goods to unknown destinations, the wheels rumbling and pounding on the dilapidated postwar tracks.

There is no electricity or water in the shed. A kerosene lamp hanging from the window handle gives off light, and water must be fetched from the signalman's house on the other side of the factory yard. My mother always takes two buckets with her so she can go there as infrequently as possible. The signalman has remained loyal to the Nazis and makes no secret of his hatred for Russians. The fact that he allows the *untermenschen* from the factory yard to use his water tap is due solely to the authority of the factory owner, who has created a situation which the signalman does not dare oppose, since he allows us to stay on his property. Still, from time to time, my mother does not know how he will react, if she can fill up the buckets with the vital water once again or not.

The specter that haunts us is called Valka, the largest camp of its kind in Bavaria, infamous for the catastrophic conditions that prevail there, the embodiment of terror for all DPs. The camp is practically around the corner, in Nuremberg-Langwasser, and that is exactly where we would end up if we were no longer able to stay in the shed. As the lord of the water, the signalman has the final say over whether we must go to Camp Valka or not. He seems to be gathering the necessary anger and courage within himself to defy the factory owner and possibly even report him. At once greedy and hostile, he stares at my young mother in her worn little dress while she stands before him and waits for the thin trickle of water from the tap to fill her two buckets, expecting at any moment that something will happen to tear the silk thread on which her life outside Camp Valka depends. She often returns in tears with the two heavy buckets that pull her shoulders down, and her resigned "I-can't-take-it anymore" face. My father has no understanding for her sensitivities; he thinks she is hysterical, self-pitying, and good-for-nothing. He has to do almost everything himself: cook soup on the gasoline stove, mend holes in his clothes, and earn a living. He expects his wife to at least keep the shed clean and fetch the water.

Besides the signalman, there are other people who have something against the Russian riffraff living on the factory grounds. At night one often hears footsteps, whispers, and the crunch of gravel; suddenly a flashlight shines in the window or sometimes someone rattles at the door. The child begins to cry; her mother jumps up and covers her mouth in panic. No one knows who is spying and sneaking around outside. Are they thugs or perhaps burglars? But what could they take? Most likely they are people who hate Russians, like the signalman, who frequently harass the squatters in the shed, wake them from their sleep, scare them to death, and may even want to murder them.

Despite everything, we do have some sort of daily routine. In addition to his job as a Russian entertainer for American soldiers, my father also pursues other activities. He barters some of the American cigarettes and chocolate that he receives as a salary on the black market, and he also collects scrap metal, as many others did in those days. He brings coals to Newcastle, as we are surrounded by scrap metal, but it does not belong to us. In the evenings, while my father sings for the Americans, my mother and I have to sort the scrap that he found on the streets during the day. We sit on the floor and work by the light of the petroleum lamp. There is a fascinating object called a magnet which separates the good metal from the bad. My mother shows me that you can not only make the iron jump but also walk it on the ground without having to touch it—it always follows the magnet. This is the good metal that we have to fish out from the bad; the next day, my father takes it to the scrap metal dealer who pays him something for it. We use the money to buy dark German bread, cabbage, beets, and salt.

Once my father brings a heavy, old men's bicycle home from the black market, on another occasion a small, graceful wristwatch for my mother. She has never owned anything like it and hardly dares to wear something so valuable. By now I understand that the Germans look down on us, and I want to prove to them that they have misjudged us, so one day I hold the pretty wristwatch with the gold-colored chain out to a complete stranger in the factory yard. At first he laughs and shakes his head, but after I make it clear to him that he is welcome to take the watch, that we have many, he looks around carefully and snatches the unexpected gift, puts it in his pocket, and quickly rides off on his bicycle. Weeks later my mother is still looking for it; she is more worried about my father than the watch—he is convinced that she has lost his present. The watch's mysterious disappearance is talked about for a long time; my father repeatedly cites it as an example of my mother's carelessness and incompetence.

The people around her, first in Ukraine and then in Germany, had probably long convinced her of her inferiority, but if she had ever tried to gain at least a minimal amount of self-confidence, then her husband undoubtedly took the last wind from her sails. There doesn't appear to be much left of his former love for her, apparently she is only a burden to him now. In Germany, I am the only living thing whose love she can still hope for. Maybe she wants to comfort me when she says she is not my real mother and, at the same time, provoke me into protesting. My real mother, she says, is just as blond as I am, a beautiful German lady who lives in a real house with furniture and her own faucet who will come to pick me up someday. She tells me about a child named Moses who was placed in a basket by his mother and abandoned along the Nile before the daughter of a king found him in the reeds and rescued him. She sings me the Russian song of the cuckoo, the *kukushka,* who has lost her children and never stops calling them in her sad voice. All of this encourages my belief that I am a foundling, and I am torn. On the one hand, I would like nothing more than to be the child of a German mother and live in a house that is as fancy as the factory owner's, which stands at the other end of the yard in a garden with fruit trees and roses; on the other hand, I am filled with incredible sadness because I am apparently not my mother's child. I start to cry, to scream and to rave; my mother should say that she lied to me, that she is my real mother, but she never does.

Sometimes she also tells me a mysterious story about a glass city. A city, in which everything is made of glass, the houses, the furniture, the streets, even the shoes on the feet of its inhabitants. Everyone walks around with a snow-white cleaning cloth and polishes the glass, removing every piece of dust, every condensed breath. I don't know what she is trying to tell me with this story, what this immaculate city represents. Perhaps it is her counter-image to the poverty and filth in which she lives; maybe she feels that she is a piece of dirt, maybe even at that point the image was an expression of her longing to feel numb, to die.

Most of the DPs live in hope of being able to emigrate to America, just as we do. They have set up a temporary representation of the American Consulate General in a gray barracks in the American occupation zone, where they house DPs seeking to emigrate while their applications are being processed. The drive there is probably the first trip of my life, but I don't remember that. I only remember the run-down barracks and the American woman I see after standing for days in drafty, overcrowded corridors. As she asks my parents questions in broken Russian, her fingers hammer on the keys of the cast-iron typewriter with breath-taking speed, her long red fingernails flashing. She has a silver-blond perm, and a cigarette smolders in the corner of her mouth, her large lips are painted bright red; the smell of smoke mixes with the indescribable scent of a perfume—my first glimpse of America.

It is winter, it is cold in the barracks, everyone is coughing; I get sick and develop pneumonia. At night we sleep in a hall filled with strangers; a large, black rabbit sits on my chest and stares at me out of the darkness with evil, yellow eyes. It is so heavy that I can't breathe anymore; I am being smothered, I am hot, I am wheezing, gasping for air—and then I feel my mother's cool fingers rubbing the green, miracle lotion into my chest which the American doctor prescribed for me. I have never desired anything like this ointment. The sharp smell hits my nostrils, and I am instantly released; air rushes into me immediately, and the horrible rabbit disappears.

The Russian twins are the only people I can find in the depths of my memory from our time in the processing center for the thousands of DPs who wanted to emigrate to America. I have recovered from pneumonia, and I am holding my mother's hand on the street as they approach us with their thick, honey-colored braids. They are the chosen ones who have received a visa that will allow them to go to America with their parents. Even now, on this desolate postwar German street between the dilapidated, dirty barracks, they are surrounded by the nimbus of the other, distant world, the glamor of the life that awaits them in the mythical kingdom of freedom and happiness, where there are probably miracle ointments against everything.

My mother has a subliminal fear that we will also receive a visa. She is certain that the ship will sink en route, that she will suffer the fate she managed to escape when crossing from Odessa to Romania. But her fear is completely unfounded: we belong to the overwhelming majority whose visa applications are rejected. Only a few lucky applicants are granted entry into the promised land; all the rest must return to their respective DP camps, while we go back to our factory yard. At bottom, my mother never believed we would receive a visa. She never had any luck in her life; it would have seemed like another betrayal of those she left behind, the imprisoned and oppressed people in Ukraine. In this respect, the trip back to our shed is perhaps akin to a homecoming for her.

Our housemates, the Zyganenkos, are sensible enough to assume they have no chance of getting an American visa; they apply to immigrate to Brazil instead and receive a visa after a short wait. I remember the wild, incomprehensible pain that came over me when the rattling Goliath[1] drove out of the factory yard with our housemates and all their belongings, and I had to recognize that what I had thought of as a game had become serious. Someone who belongs to me and is understood to be a part of my inviolable world can depart and abandon me forever, whether I want them to or not. I want to die, and press myself into the dark gap between our shed and the factory, where the rats are and where everything vibrates and there is nothing but the pounding of the machines. My mother runs across the yard for hours looking for me. Only in the evening, when she is already thinking about calling the German police, does she shine a flashlight into the gap and discover me. She is certainly very thin, but not thin enough to squeeze into the gap; there is just enough space for a child's body. She has to beg and plead with me to come out on my own. And no sooner am I out, dirty, tear-stained and numb from the cold, than my father's blows start raining down on me. My mother tears at his jacket and screams for him to stop, but he beats me until I am lying on the ground and warm blood is dripping from my nose. My mother throws herself on top of me and screams, and she keeps on screaming even after my father is already sitting in the shed again and drinking. He has been doing that more and more recently.

The Zyganenkos promised to write to us, but we never hear from them again. All of my mother's misgivings seem to be confirmed—the ship that was supposed to bring her unfortunate companions to Brazil must have sunk. Later we hear from somewhere that they died an even more gruesome death—murdered and eaten by Brazilian cannibals. But these are probably just an eruption of the sort of violent Russian fantasies, which I will encounter so often in the future.

My mother stays behind in the shed with her husband and child. She has lost the only people who protected her in a foreign land; they were her little Ukraine in Germany. Perhaps she has a sudden, rude awakening, when, in her heart, she understands that she is truly separated from Ukraine forever, that there is no other place for her on earth than this shed, which she only has thanks to the graciousness of a German factory owner; that she is forever doomed to live in a country where she will remain a foreigner, ostracized and delivered up to a man who seems to hate her. It is likely that even then I already feel she can no longer endure her life, that at any time she is about to disappear, to slip away from me. Probably our roles were already reversed by then; perhaps as a four-year-old I carry her on my shoulders, in constant fear of losing her, a fear I had from birth.

I spend most of my time outside in the factory yard. I play with iron scraps, or I sit in the doorway of the shed and watch the trains go by, trying to imagine where they come from and where they are going. My mother is homesick, and I suffer from wanderlust. I am obsessed with the question of what the world looks like behind the factory yard, which I am not permitted to leave, because the big, dangerous Leyher Street is right behind it. When someone walks across the yard, I take the opportunity to show off a few of the German words I know. I say "hello" and "goodbye" in rapid succession, and I don't understand why the Germans laugh.

Sometimes, I can't stand it anymore and I walk out to the big road via a narrow, dirt path. Then I stand there and stare. I behold the German houses, real, big houses made of stone, which I marvel at as though they are palaces. The Germans have white curtains in their windows with green leathery plants behind them in flowerpots. I look longingly at the strange, sugar-coated pastries in the window of the bakery, where, when we can afford it, my mother buys dark German bread which tastes so different than the fluffy American white bread. I examine the Germans' faces, their glasses, hair, bags, umbrellas, and hats. Most of all, I am amazed that there are also German children. They draw chalk boxes on the sidewalk and jump from box to box. I listen intently to the foreign language, the other, with incomprehensible sounds that I sense are the key to the German world, the world with faucets and electricity.

I usually pay a high price for my excursions. If my mother catches me, as is ordinarily the case, I receive ten lashes from a belt on my bare bottom as a punishment. It is an agreement between us, I have a choice between pain and renunciation. My mother doesn't scold me, she is not angry, she is only fulfilling the obligation required by our agreement. I have chosen pain, and I receive it. The blows from the belt burn like fire, but just as unrestrained as I screamed as a baby, I have learned to play dead in the meantime. I never show my mother with a twitch, or a cry of pain, that her punishment affects me, that I am vulnerable.

One day I discover a little girl behind the green thicket in front of the factory owner's house—the first living thing of my age in the factory yard. It is true that I am expressly forbidden from approaching the house, but the unknown girl, who stands behind the garden gate and waves me over, exerts an irresistible attraction. We stand in front of each other and eye each other with curiosity. The girl has curly brown hair and wears a light-colored dress with cap sleeves. She smiles and opens the gate, and I enter the terra incognita behind the fence for the first time, the realm of our lord and ruler, upon whom our existence depends. The girl shows me a doll which is alive; it can open and close its eyes and say "Mama." The fact that I can take the doll and hold it makes me dizzy with delight. The girl owns a scooter as well; she shows me how to ride it and urges me to try too. But I don't have the chance. My mother grabs me by the collar and drags me out of the garden. I can't keep up with her; I fall down and get dragged across the entire factory yard, across scrap metal and shards of glass, my knees fester for weeks afterward. I never see the girl behind the fence again, no matter how often I look for her; only a scar on my right knee reminds me of her to this day.

The inevitable day finally arrives, which my mother had dreaded from the start. We do not know what caused it, but the German authorities order us to be interned in Camp Valka. The factory owner cannot do anything more for us; he has exhausted all his options. As a farewell present, he gives my mother a valuable old brooch: a golden salamander with small, sparkling green emeralds on its back.

For a long time after my mother's death, I wore this piece of jewelry, which for whatever reason my parents never converted into cash, no matter how bad things were, until one day I lost it. But I still ask myself today who this fearless German factory owner was, who sheltered us illegally on his property for almost five years and also, in the form of a valuable brooch, gave my mother the compensation that Friedrich Flick denied his forced laborers. I either forgot the name of our mysterious benefactor, or I never knew it. Once I drove to the city limits between Nuremberg and Fürth in order to search for traces of our shed, but there was nothing there; the factory was gone. All I saw were hypermarkets and highways and the embankment from back then, trains still racing across it.

During the war, Camp Valka's barracks in Nuremberg-Langwasser served as accommodation for participants in the Nuremberg Rallies, with their massive parades and Blood Flag consecrations.[2] Soviet prisoners of war were also held there for a short time. When we move there, the barracks have become a small city where four thousand DPs from thirty nations are crowded together, most of them already since the end of the war—four thousand people who don't know what to do with their rescued lives. A few dozen languages whirl around in a confusing mix, almost no one can speak German. Everyone has only one thing in common: they were forced laborers in Hitler's empire. The slave laborers, once so much in demand, are now unemployed, an annoying relic of the lost war.

The American camp is named after the Latvian-Estonian border town of Valka, but the Russians put an "s" in front and say "Svalka," or dump. Like the Baltic city of Valka, the camp was also divided in two until recently: high Nazi Party officials were interned in the eastern half up until 1949, and the western half was already reserved for DPs. Victims and perpetrators lived almost next door to each other, in the slipstream of the neglected Nazi Party grounds, which shared our fate: it was no longer needed. In the stony desert, under the giant tribune where Hitler once gave his speeches, American GIs now played rugby.

The Allies had expected gratitude and obedience from the freed slave laborers, but that turned out to be a mistake. The labor camps robbed them of their faith in law and order in Germany; they are demoralized and still considered to be aggressive and almost impossible to control. Camp Valka is known far and wide as a dangerous place due to its anarchic criminality, as a melting pot of friendly and hostile nations and as a Sodom and Gomorra. It probably has the worst reputation in the world. Everyone is on the hunt for a job, for an income, a livelihood. Every sort of imaginable, and unimaginable, transaction takes place. Some rummage through heaps of rubble for scrap metal and other useful rubbish; others smuggle duty-free cigarettes, trade in pornographic photos, insulin and other medicines, break into market stalls, make money as card sharks, and live from theft and fraud. Disputes and fistfights are constant; there are stabbings, murders, and suicides. The Germans view the Slavs as savages, and all their prejudices are confirmed. The Nazi propaganda machine portrayed them as wild and dangerous animals, sometimes with horns and tails. Germans still live in fear of acts of revenge, although these hardly ever take place. The camp inhabitants keep to themselves, in their own world, separate from the Germans, with the exception of the police, who are deployed constantly. Raids take place almost every day. My father is also involved in some sort of shady deals that we are not allowed to discuss. My mother lives in constant fear that the police will also pay us a visit.

The DPs receive three meals per day in prepared containers that must be picked up at an issuing point. In addition, they are entitled to a monthly camp allowance of 12.50 marks. Electric power is supplied every other day, switched between the wood and the brick barracks. About thirty people live in every barracks, each of which is equipped with a toilet and a faucet.

We live in one of the wooden barracks, together with mice and bugs that torment us all night long. When it rains the water runs through the leaky roof, so we have to rush to put every available receptacle underneath. The warped window doesn't close properly, the oven doesn't draw well and gives off clouds of smoke, we freeze and cough throughout the winter. During this time I catch almost every childhood illness, from measles to mumps and chicken pox to whooping cough.

One of the highlights from this period is my mother's pregnancy. She is only a little over thirty, but in this picture from my memory, she looks old, withered and sick; her hair is parted in the middle and tied into a tight knot in the back. She wears a green and white patterned dress, its creased hem jutting out in front, raised by a curved stomach which looks like an outsized ball glued onto her skinny body. When I ask why she has such a large belly, I see her exchange a tiny complicit smile with my father—a moment of intimacy between my parents that remains almost singular in my memory. I am not aware of ever having seen an embrace between them, let alone a kiss or another act of tenderness. Since I slept in the same room with them for almost my entire childhood, I must have usually been present when they did what in their case could hardly be called making love. But either it happened in an entirely secret, silent way, or I found the proceedings in my parent's dark bed to be so frightening that my naive brain immediately suppressed them.

The noise level in Camp Valka is a daily torture for my mother; she cannot get used to it. In the labor camp the acoustics were probably not so harsh because everyone fell into their bunks after the exhausting workday and slept. Our Valka barracks host the clamorous life of those who have nothing to do all day and suffer, for the most part, from what we now call posttraumatic stress syndrome: sleeplessness, nightmares, anxiety, irritability, depression, delusions, unchecked aggression, and much more, along with all sorts of physical complaints, from which no small number of DPs perished even after being liberated. The tiny barracks' rooms vibrate with tension. No one speaks softly; everyone has to shout in order to be heard amid the surging waves of noise. There are constant arguments; wailing and loud laughter cancel each other out, every word is heard, every sneeze and sigh from next door, the sounds flow into each other to create a great, never-ending cacophony. Especially in winter and when there is bad weather, the long, dark corridor becomes a playground for the children; they are always being chased away by someone who is on his way to the toilet or must fight his way through with his container to the only faucet at the end of the hallway.

The tumult causes my mother to feel even more uprooted than she already is. She covers her ears, jumps up, and runs out of the barracks, where, in addition to the torture from the racket, she is pestered by a paranoid neighbor, an old Estonian woman who curses madly in Russian through the thin wooden walls. For some reason, the confused woman has transferred all her mental images of the enemy onto my mother, whom she curses as a Communist, a Jewish whore, an American spy, and a Nazi floozy. My mother is unable to defend herself; sometimes she cries all day long, in fact, she cries all the time. Her worst illness is homesickness. It torments her incessantly; it seems to be something like a thirst that never subsides, but grows ever stronger, until one day it kills you.

For me, Camp Valka is, above all, the place where I begin attending German school. A photo from the first day proves it: twenty-nine children arranged in three rows against the shabby backdrop of a barracks. Two rows of girls and a row of boys sitting cross-legged at their feet in the front. Four children do not have a cornet of sweets and presents to mark the start of lessons. I am one of them. The blondest of them all, radiant despite this deficiency.

It is a camp school for camp children, who must all first learn German. Since I was already taught by my mother in the shack on the factory grounds, I can read and write in Russian when I enter the German school. I know the fables of Ivan Krylov, the magical children's stories of Samuil Marshak, and I can recite at least a dozen poems by Alexander Pushkin and Alexei Tolstoy, but German is still a kind of background noise. This changes abruptly when I enter the German school. German words appear in my mind like sheet lightning, as though they were dormant inside me for a long time, merely waiting for the moment of awakening. The German language becomes a strong rope that I grab immediately in order to swing over to the other side, into the German world. It is indeed still unattainable, but I know that it is waiting for me and that one day I will be a part of it.

A language war breaks out with my parents. They refuse to understand my German. My father truly does not understand, and he will not understand it his entire life. My mother, who speaks better German than everyone else around me, refuses to understand. And I don't want to understand her Russian anymore; I don't want to have anything to do with her at all. There are constant fights; she tries to hit me, but I escape, and in any case her hands are far too weak to hurt me. She is powerless against me, because I am not afraid of her; I am only afraid of my father's hands. He rarely beats me; it is only as a last resort, when my mother turns me over to him. That is the only weapon that she can use against me, the only one of her threats that frightens me: "I will tell your father." Sometimes she pardons me, when, weeping, I apologize in Russian for my lies and bad behavior, but most of the time the sentence is carried out in the evening when my father returns home, usually drunk, from his clandestine activity. He is a person whom alcohol makes aggressive, so a complaint from my mother suits him well. He calls me *cholera, parasitka, kretinka*; he holds onto me with one hand while the other falls on me like an ax. My mother is the judge; he is the executioner, the enforcement authority.

Most of the time, I roam around the camp territory after school. I don't remember other children, only something desolate, gray; a scorched territory, as it were, where, in my memory, there is not a single tree. I cannot go farther away to escape my parents—the camp territory is much larger than the factory grounds, but it is a prison, surrounded by a wall topped with barbed wire. You can only enter or exit when a guard opens the barrier at the entrance.

My father is not the only one who pursues a secret income; I do it too. A repulsive, bloated man who speaks broken Russian and always wears a hairnet beckons me inside from his window to the barracks' room where he lives alone. I have to take off my underwear and dance for him while lifting up my dress. It sickens me and I am afraid of the man, but it is not without exhibitionistic pleasure that I show myself to him, not without an awareness of the dark power that I have over him while he devours me with his eyes and moans as he shakes an incomprehensible trunk that towers out of his fly. I don't know why he does this, but I know that very soon a milky liquid will shoot out of the mysterious part which the man will catch up in a handkerchief. With that, my performance ends. He sticks the shrunken trunk back into his pants and admonishes me not to tell anyone about my visits and gives me ten pfennigs. I take my wages and run to the kiosk to buy a cherry lollipop and chewing gum. This repeats itself until the day when the man grabs me and attempts to push his trunk into my mouth. He promises me fifty pfennigs if I am willing; it is a fortune, but I cannot overcome my revulsion. I escape with difficulty and abandon my secret job, controlling my craving for sweets from then on.

Sometimes my mother tells a story about how once, when she still lived in Ukraine, she wanted to enter a convent and become a *monashka*, or nun. She cries and says that her current life is God's punishment for not having followed his call. I know that nuns do not have children, so I ask her, "And me? Would I not have been born, if you had become a *monashka*?" She looks at me with her darkened eyes. "Maybe it would have been better if you hadn't been born," she says. "If you had seen, what I have seen . . . " And once again her eyes peer off somewhere I cannot see, where I do not exist.

In the daytime, when my father is not there, a holy man frequently comes to visit us, a Russian, who looks like the picture of Leo Tolstoy on our calendar, which we have hung on the wall in our barracks' room in Camp Valka even though it has been out of date for a long time. Andrey Zakharovich is a small, frail man with a vegetarian skin tone and a thinning white beard. He was a forced laborer in a mine and always carriers a Bible wrapped in newspaper with him. My father says he has a bad influence on my mother, that he encourages her mental illness, and in addition he suspects them both of adulterous secrecies. He forbids her from continuing to meet with him. When she once again threatens to hand me over to my father for a beating, I threaten in response: "Then I will tell him that Andrey Zakharovich visited you again."

In my observation, the relationship between him and my mother is purely mystical and religious—the relationship between a messiah and a would-be *monashka* who has lost her faith. My mother wants to be converted by him, to once again be able to believe that there is a beneficent and loving God, of whose existence she was once convinced. She hangs on his every word when he speaks or reads aloud from the Bible, but their encounters almost always end in an agitated dispute, whose contents I do not understand. I only understand that Andrey Zakharovich defends God, and my mother accuses Him, probably for what she saw and I would like so much to see just once to comprehend what she feels and grasp wherein the secret of her incessant, immeasurable pain lies. I fear this pain, but I would like to experience it a single time. Therefore, my fervent bedtime prayer is almost always as follows: "Dear God, please allow me to feel what my mother feels, only for a moment, so that I can understand her."

Andrey Zakharovich brings not only the Bible with him when he comes to visit us but also usually warm little cakes, which are, likewise, wrapped in newspaper, and, baked at home on his petroleum cooker, come from a completely different world than our daily camp fare—the gooey soups and porridge, of which I can never eat more than a few spoonfuls. As a result, I have become dangerously thin—one of the undernourished children of the postwar period for whom the Red Cross finances rest and relaxation holidays. I will also have to complete two more of them at feeding centers somewhere in the Bavarian Alps, from which I will return even thinner than before since I can't keep the strange German food down: meatballs, blood sausage, hash of lung, and enormous yeast dumplings. I immediately vomit up everything that is forcibly stuffed into me.

But Andrey Zakharovich's creamy, sweet Russian cakes are the most delicious I have ever tried. It is how I imagine the taste of manna that God let fall from heaven in the desert for His people, the Israelites, as my mother told me. However, Andrey Zakharovich not only brings sweet things but also something bitter, a yellow-green powder that is called quinine. It is supposed to cure all diseases, my mother's rheumatism, her headaches, her heartaches, her stomachaches, all of the many pains that constantly torment not only her soul but also her body. I am also required to take a pinch of it regularly, though my mother and I can only do it if we drink a large cup of water right afterward, because the powder is so indescribably bitter. However, Andrey Zakharovich swallows it without water and does not flinch. "It is not bitter," he says. "We only believe that it is bitter."

I notice an effect from the quinine; I can run even faster and even further—there is a new, unknown energy inside me, something almost like invulnerability. Maybe that contributes to the fact that the fights with my mother become increasingly aggressive. I no longer let anyone tell me what I can and cannot do; I am almost never at home anymore, and above all, I lie constantly. Lying is the badge of shame of my childhood, a curse that I cannot escape. I lie compulsively, without cause, without any sense; I simply lie because the truth, for whatever reason, never crosses my lips. My desperate mother, who no longer knows what to do with me, employs a punishment from the Old Testament. She writes on a piece of cardboard in big black letters and pins it to the wall. *Natascha lies to her mother*, it says in Russian and German. I am not allowed to go outside, but am forced to endure my public exposure, burning with shame every time someone enters the room and looks first at the writing on the wall, then at me. Most of all, I am afraid that Andrey Zakharovich will come, under whose gaze, as it seems to me, I would immediately go up in flames. And he actually arrives. He stands in front of the cardboard, puts his glasses on, and studies my mother's inscription attentively for a long time. Then something unbelievable happens. He takes his glasses off again and tears the cardboard from the wall. "What are you doing to your child, Evgenia Yakovlevna?" he says angrily. "You, an intelligent woman. . . . Are those Stalin's godless methods, or Hitler's? What has become of all us?!" he adds sadly. I see how my mother blushes. The tables have been turned, and now she is the one who has been humiliated. Her eyes lowered, she turns toward me and says softly, "You can go outside and play."

My sister is born while we are moving to a new home. Although Camp Valka is not closed down until the mid-sixties, we are resettled in 1952, the year when the displaced persons are turned over by the Americans to the newly founded German refugee authorities and given a new status. Effective immediately, they are no longer known as displaced persons but instead as "stateless foreigners." They are stateless, but have temporary residence status in Germany. In a provincial Franconian town, north of Nuremberg, a settlement for a handful of them is built, something like a small Camp Valka. Only now it is not a question of provisional, temporary accommodation anymore, but a permanent residence, for most of the DPs the first and last in Germany, the final stop. The locals call the apartment blocks built for us on the Regnitz "the houses"; a new enclave that is far more comfortable than we could ever have imagined. No more barracks, but real houses of stone, four blocks in a square, a landscaped courtyard with three young birches, which are supposed to remind the Eastern European inhabitants of their homeland. Everyone receives their own apartment with running water, electricity, a cast iron kitchen stove with an oven and a reservoir and—an unbelievable luxury!—a bath with a boiler. Our ghetto lies behind the last houses of the city, which are small, crooked, and likewise located beyond the asphalt-covered street; topographically they almost belong more to us than to the city. Especially on hot, windless days, the air is thick with the stench of decay, which the locals call "the gas," spread by the so-called bone factory, where animal bones are processed into glue. Its emissions mix with the sweet, sticky smells that escape from a nearby chocolate factory. A dizzying, unmistakable cocktail of aromas.

The city was left unscathed by the war; for me, the old center is a German fairy tale. There is a medieval city hall, whose half-timbered facade sinks behind bright geraniums in the summer; silent, labyrinthine alleys, which are like passageways between the small, half-timbered houses that lean together, their windows and doors always shut; a swift little river, a wooden mill wheel turning in it; a moss-covered town wall with watchtowers and embrasures; a weather-beaten, former imperial palace with a moat. The so-called gateway to Franconian Switzerland, a remote backwater where only the many disabled veterans remind one of the catastrophe gone by, men, who in contrast to me, had seen Russia, and now walk around with one arm, an empty jacket sleeve, or with a black eyepatch, others drag themselves along on one leg using homemade wooden crutches. Everyday life also includes American tanks that push through the narrow streets singly or in columns and make the little city shake again and again. From open top jeeps, American soldiers throw candy and chewing gum to children, who are already waiting for them expectantly by the roadside. Farmers' wives from the surrounding villages who come to shop in the city still wear the old, traditional Franconian costume. In a few years, an American movie will be filmed here called *Town without Pity*, whose theme is the double standards and persecution mentality of provincial city dwellers. The film's protagonist, played by Christine Kaufmann, has something in common with my mother: in the end she also drowns in the Regnitz.

My mother does not move with my father and me; she arrives later, straight from the hospital. I stand at the window of our new kitchen and see her get out of a car in the courtyard. She doesn't seem to be happy about our new apartment; her face expresses something between hysterical despair and quiet hopelessness. In her arm, she holds a white bundle that hides my sister, who—it will later emerge—is a quiet, sensitive girl with a black tuft of hair and, even as a small child, a striking resemblance to my mother. To me it is a mysterious little creature, that almost never cries, but lies contentedly in its little bed, evidently completely satisfied; it sleeps most of the time.

In our new residence, meals are no longer served to us; instead, we have to pick up our welfare payment from the city administration once a month and provide for our own sustenance. Caritas gives us a few pieces of furniture, including a kitchen cupboard with little windows, an imposing steamer trunk which smells of mold and incense, and an ornate old commode, which would be thought of as an antique today, but was considered junk in those days. It is the time when everything in Germany becomes new: the houses, the furniture, the people; it is the time of rebirth, of forgetting after the war. That's why the houses on the outskirts of the city are not well-liked, they are a reminder of something that no one wants to hear about anymore. Camp Valka's reputation has pursued us this far; here we are considered barbarians once again, a pack of criminals.

My mother must feel herself a foreigner twice over. In Camp Valka, despite the large-scale forced repatriations, there were Russians, Ukrainians, and other Soviet citizens who spoke Russian. There are no such people here. We have landed, once and for all, in an Eastern European Babylon, a cacophony of languages in which one merely understands individual words of one's own language that are similar in other languages. Except for us, there is only a single Russian, a one-legged invalid, but he doesn't stay long. He is so homesick that he does not even fear death, and one day, after he has saved up the money for a ticket, and despite my mother's entreaties, he makes his way back to Russia with his crutch. He promises to write us, but we also never hear from him again, and his fate remains as unknown as the Zyganenkos.

As Russians, we are not only the avowed political enemy of the Germans, even in the ghetto we remain outsiders. One evening something sinister is cooked up against us, a sort of pogrom. Drunk men gather under our windows, words such as "Communists," "Bolsheviks,"

"Stalinists," are uttered, words that are the same in all languages. A stone flies into our room, together with shards of glass.

Individual, still recognizable figures emerge from the gray swirling mists of my memories from the houses. There was Marianka, a Pole, whose large, alcohol-swollen body seemed to flow in the hands of anyone who touched her. Apparently, she had no place of her own in the houses, but lived here and there, moving from man to man with her passel of children. They all impregnated her, beat her, and chased her off again. In the end, she lived with our neighbor, a Romanian with a glass eye. When she died of an intestinal obstruction, he was left all alone with her children. He didn't know what to do with them, so he kept them. He was usually in the courtyard drinking beer, aggressively defending his honor, and searching for the fathers of the nameless children he had to feed.

There was Farida, my secret Serbian friend, with whom I was forbidden to play because I enticed her into making adventurous trips with me to the city or across the river meadows and gravel pits in the summer until it got dark. Nobody knew about our blasphemous crime: we opened the door to a small chapel that was surprisingly unlocked. Outside in the river meadow the sun was burning hot, inside we were surrounded by a cool shady silence and a stuffy, musty smell. We observed the old, hand-made chairs, the German Madonna dressed in light blue with a halo of stars and the heavy bronze candlesticks; we touched the fine, white altar cloth, dipped our fingers in a basin filled with stale, foul-smelling water and examined the German Jesus with protruding ribs hanging high above the altar on a wooden cross wearing only a loincloth and who was even more foreign to Farida, who had Muslim parents, than he was to me. We didn't know what to make of our discovery; in an outburst of courage, Farida put her finger on the open wound where a nail had been driven through the crucified victim's foot, but strangely nothing happened, the German Jesus didn't even flinch. He failed to react when we shook the cross; our curses also left him cold. I hit him on the shin, and he shook silently in his inaccessible heights, but after lightning still failed to strike, we began to spit on the Germans' silent sanctuary; we tore the flowers from the vase which stood on the altar and pelted it with the slimy, half-rotten stems. We rampaged until the crown of thorns fell from the clay savior's head and shattered on the stone floor. Only then did we wake up from our destructive delirium; we saw what we had done and fled across the fields, through the ripe grain, which made us invisible to our persecutors, whom we were certain would have put us behind bars forever for our outrage.

There was a gloomy, silent man of unknown origin, a Hercules, who always walked across the courtyard with a tiny woman from the gypsy barracks. She disappeared into one of his jackets, which reached down to her ankles, with the black hem of her gathered skirt peeking out. I never saw them speak to each other, presumably they did not speak the same language, or maybe they had nothing to say to each other. Gold-colored jewelry jingled on her body, and she wore a fake, red rose in her oily and shiny hair. She always walked by like that, in the giant men's jacket, with the silent, menacing-looking Hercules at her side; she had managed to avoid the gas chambers by a stroke of luck.

There was a young Czech, who, like many in the houses, suffered from tuberculosis, which was still a life-threating disease among the poor after the war. He had recently married a German, but more often than not, he was in the courtyard playing the accordion: "Rosamund," "The Blue Danube," and Czech pieces that we did not know. I was a little bit in love with him because he played so beautifully, always alluding to the sadness in his eyes with an indefatigable, almost obsessive gaiety. One day when his wife came home from work, she found him dead on the floor. He lay with his face down in a pool of blood, which had burst out of his consumptive lungs.

There was Jemila's mother, who let her lament resound for days through the courtyard from her open window, her lament for her little daughter, whom the German children pushed into the Regnitz. It was dead quiet in the courtyard; no one was outside. I sat on the threshold in front of our door alone and listened to the strange wailing that emanated in waves, rising and falling, sometimes wordless, at other times in a language I didn't understand, from the dark square of Jemila's window, behind which she had lived. On the lamppost in the courtyard, where all the important announcements were put up, there was a note announcing when Jemila's funeral would take place. It was a murder that was never punished and never prosecuted, which the German police never investigated.

Little by little, a few Germans also started to move into the houses. We did not like them; they were intruders, reducing the already limited space that was promised exclusively to us. Undoubtedly, they took offense at being billeted in the houses. Although they lived on the margins of society, among former forced laborers they must have felt like they had been thrown onto the garbage heap.

I remember the German twins, two young men with blond crew cuts, both in fashionable houndstooth jackets, house painters with impenetrable faces who went to work and came home together every day. Their mother, a quiet, chubby woman with a proper topknot, pushed her disabled husband across the courtyard in a wheelchair. The four of them lived in complete seclusion, never saying hello or speaking to anyone.

The most violent thug in the houses was certainly Mr. Kreller, who lived on the floor above us with his family. He was a heavy drinker who regularly beat his wife and adult daughter, Anneliese, with such force that our ceiling was in danger of collapsing. My mother and I cowered beneath the thunderous banging; it seemed that furniture was being broken, the shrill screams of Mrs. Kreller and her daughter could be heard across the entire courtyard. Anneliese worked as a hairdresser and hid the money that she earned. It was all about this money; Mr. Kreller was looking for the hiding place, which, as his wife had told my mother, was in the sewing machine. The beautiful, ambitious Anneliese soon succeeded in switching sides. She married into the large, respected leather business on Main Street and rose from the lowest underclass into the city's respectable and affluent bourgeoisie—at that time it was, to my mind, the most distant of all stars, the greatest joy, that a person could experience. Holding her groom's hand and wearing a wedding dress that was like the crest of an ocean wave, she stepped out of a sky-blue convertible Opel Rekord on our doorstep—a sensation which was the first and last of its kind in the houses. Shortly after his daughter's wedding, Mr. Kreller had a stroke; it became quiet above us. We only heard him utter some hoarse curses now and then or moan softly.

A German woman with a colossal mammoth's body who was missing her front teeth lived in the housing block across the street. It was said that she stole coffee beans and schnapps from stores so that she could entertain her lovers. She was married to a spindly, consumptive little man who spent most of his time out in the courtyard, drinking beer from a bottle, coughing and spitting blood while he warmed his emaciated body in the sun. Their roughly ten-year-old daughter with a thin neck and fawn-colored hair was her mother's maid. She could be seen mopping the staircase and sweeping the courtyard, lugging home the groceries, and cleaning the windows. In the wintertime, she had to get coal from the coal dealer, though always only in small amounts, because they did not have enough money to buy more. She was thin and pale –perhaps she had caught her father's TB—and all winter long she pulled a small handcart behind her across the courtyard, loaded with a pile of anthracite and a few briquettes.

The custodian was German as well, an inconspicuous older man who leaned out the window from morning to night and watched over the lawn in the courtyard suspiciously, the green German sanctuary in our midst. There would be trouble if one of us dared to set foot on the lawn when a ball rolled onto it or simply decided to take a shortcut across it. In the summertime, when all the windows were open, you could hear Mr. Hensch barking admonitions all day—he simply couldn't manage to teach us to behave properly.

For my mother, moving to the houses marks the beginning of another difficult period. Her first child had already been a disaster, but now she has two to look after, and having her own apartment means that she must finally take on the role of a housewife. My father's patience is at an end; he no longer helps her with the housework. From now on, she must do everything herself: cooking, cleaning, washing, darning socks, ironing—everything, which in her time and place, belonged to the inherent duties of a woman.

In Camp Valka, there were a few people she could talk to and share memories of her homeland, above all Andrey Zakharovich, who single-mindedly opposed her desolation with his belief in God; he may have been something like a father to her. Now there is no one left. She is completely alone, an outcast everywhere, not only in her German surroundings, not only in the houses where she, as a "Russian," cannot fit in, but also in her marriage, which becomes a living hell.

I am enrolled in the second grade at the Evangelical elementary school after the Catholics categorically refuse to admit me. The Evangelical school does not want me at first either, since I am Russian Orthodox, but eventually the director takes pity on me and gives me special permission to attend. In the camp school, I was a child like any other, here I experience my exceptional status, my negative attribute, from the very first day.

The school building lies behind the city park with the imposing old city wall; the city's coat of arms with two trout is displayed above the school gate. Every morning, it is the entrance to Tartarus, populated with twenty-three children who were born at the end of the war like me, who drank hatred for Russians with their mother's milk and who already know from the age of seven or eight that Russians are *untermenschen*, the ultimate evil in the world. Miss Schorrn, the teacher, is a Germanic blond with steel-blue eyes, who always keeps a cane in her hand and uses it liberally to apply the dreaded blows; she does not offer me protection, quite the opposite, in fact. With her stories of the Russians' atrocities, from their lust for murder and brutishness, she directly encourages my classmates to attack me. I am a welcome outlet for the pent-up aggression of the children, who are suffocating from the complete silence of the postwar period and for whom the spirit of National Socialist discipline still rules at home. Their violent outbursts against me allow them to come up briefly for air.

Even more than being assaulted on the playground and hunted down after school, I fear being teased by my German schoolmates; it is the least time-consuming and most effective weapon they can use against me. Miss Schorrn never calls me by my first name, but only by my last name, which she cannot pronounce. Instead of Wdowin,[3] she says Dowin, and my classmates turn this into Doofus. That is my nickname in school. They laugh at everything about me, my feet, my hair, my nose, and my clothes. They shout "Piss-Liesl" at me after I wet my pants once out of fear in front of the blackboard; "Stink-Liesl," they shout. "The Doofus doesn't wear underpants, the Doofus doesn't bathe, the Doofus smells and Russians clean potatoes in the toilet bowl." If something goes missing from the classroom, an eraser or a pencil sharpener, suspicion always falls on me. There is a saying in German, those who lie, steal, and since I constantly lie, I must also be a thief. If someone merely says the word "stealing," blood rushes to my head, and I sit at my desk with burning cheeks, providing visible evidence to confirm their suspicions, although I have never misappropriated German property.

If I steal, then it is only money from my mother's change purse, so that I can buy an *Amerikaner* glazed cookie or at least a roll from the bakery on the way to school. This is my substitute for the packed lunch the German children bring and that my mother cannot manage to prepare since she is unable to cut slices of bread properly and we don't have toppings or even any butcher paper; she feels so weak and sick that she can't even get out of bed in the morning when I have to go to school. Most of all, it seems to be the never-ending, mysterious disease of homesickness that weakens her more and more. She talks about her father, who died when she was still young, almost every day, and about the brother she loved so much, and most of all about her mother, whose fate remains unknown. And at the same time she cries, cries constantly; it seems to me that she dissolves into tears more and more often, and I cannot understand what sort of loss can cause such lasting, unimaginable pain. Sometimes, she sits at the kitchen table and draws faces with a pencil, in fact it is the same face over and over again. This is how I imagine the inhabitants of the glass city that she told me about look, glass people with cold eyes who stare into space. The drawings pile up in the drawer of our kitchen table; a new one is added almost every day.

Singing is the only thing that can briefly pull her out of her depression. It is our counterspell, which temporarily chases the ghosts away. Our repertoire includes not only Russian and Ukrainian music but also German songs, which I learn in school and my parents also love: "Evening Silence Everywhere," "If I Were a Little Bird," and "There in the Snowy Mountains." My mother usually sings the first voice with her light soprano, I sing the second, and my father the third; he, who is really a tenor, accompanies our singing with his wordless bass modulations, since, unlike my mother, he cannot sing along to the German texts. With his bim-bam-bom, which is like a deep bell, he lends a Russian flavor to the German songs. In the summertime, the neighbors often gather under our open windows and listen and applaud. These private concerts provide a brief moment of reconciliation with the Russians, just as we feel a sense of reconciliation and belonging to each other when we sing.

If I am not being chased to the houses after school, if my classmates don't feel like it and decide to leave me alone, I take a detour via the cemetery, which leads me through the city park past the mighty weeping willow, the tips of its green fronds hanging down in a dark, muddy pond, and past where the Germans sit under colorful umbrellas and eat ice cream. My destination is the mortuary, where you can look at the dead who were still laid out in open coffins in those days; for me, they have a magical allure. I look closely at the faces of the dead Germans, who lie silently in state behind the window, with dark cypresses and white candles on either side of their heads. I study the closed eyes, the mouths, the hair, and the folded hands on the white funeral pall. Once I see how a fly walking on the tiny, shriveled face of an old woman disappears into one of her nostrils and emerges shortly thereafter from the black chasm of her wide-open mouth. I am plagued by the idea that the dead are not really dead, but that they hear and feel everything and are buried alive without being able to call out to anyone. I always wait for one of them to bat an eyelid or twitch at the corners of their mouth, like my mother when she falls down and lies on the ground as though dead. From my father, I know that she has not only inherited her mental illness from a relative but also a heart that is too small and weak. She suddenly grabs at it and sinks to the ground. I already know the game, but I can never tell if it has finally become serious. I try to wake my mother up; I pinch her, throw things at her, pull her hair, increasingly panicked since she doesn't move. I scream and torment her until a smile appears on her mouth, and she straightens up with ease before punishing me for the outrageous blows I struck. I don't know what is stronger within me—the hope that she will really die, or the fear that this is exactly what will happen. That one day I won't be able to wake her up anymore or that she will make good on her constant threat to go into the water. At night I don't dare fall asleep since I am afraid she won't be there anymore when I wake up. I tie a rope to her foot and take the other end with me to my bed and hold it tight, constantly worried about her and afraid of her at the same time.

Once she asks me whether I would rather stay with my father or go into the water with her, together with my little sister. "It doesn't hurt," she says, and since I don't want to stay with my father under any circumstances and it doesn't hurt either, I immediately agree. It almost seems like a badge of honor that she wants to take me along.

The water seems to have grown tired of waiting for my mother, my sister, and me, and so it comes to us. After days of torrential rains, the small and otherwise harmless Regnitz swells into a huge, dirty brown stream that sweeps up trees and debris and constantly expands. Soon the water is also in our courtyard, at first forming a few puddles, to the delight of the children who jump around in them barefoot; next they turn into a closed body of water that reaches up to our door, still and smooth, then gradually stirred by currents and eddies. Again I lie awake at night, afraid to sleep. Maybe we are already in the water, maybe it is already at our windows and will break into the room at any moment and bury us. Yet, the water was only threatening. It sloshes around in the courtyard for a few more days and then slowly retreats, just as mysteriously as it arrived; the Regnitz turns back into the peaceful, idyllic little river that snakes through the countryside behind our houses, blue and glistening as ever before. Only the fields and meadows are devastated, including our little garden on the riverbank, whose cucumbers, tomatoes, and pumpkins sustained us all summer.

And then comes the day when my parents are sitting in front of the radio listening to a Russian voice during a static-filled broadcast, news interspersed with Bach. Stalin is dying. There was no one my mother feared and hated as much as him, the short Georgian with the stiff arm, the son of a shoemaker and a serf, who was actually called Dzhugashvili, but renamed himself Stalin, the "man of steel"—my mother had never spoken of him as anything but a monster. Now that he is on his deathbed she suddenly feels sorry for him. She listens to Bach and wipes a tear from her eye. "But he was evil," I object in astonishment. "Yes, he was evil," my mother says, "but we don't know what he is going through now. He is about to face God's judgement." As far as I can remember, that is the last time I hear something come out of her mouth that indicates a belief in a just God.

With Stalin's death, something incredible has happened, something that can change everything. Can we go back to Ukraine now? Will the world start all over from the beginning? Is Ukraine free again? I don't know if my parents asked themselves these questions, but if they did, they must have soon realized that Stalin's death did not change anything for them. Even during the so-called thaw, the Soviet Union remains a totalitarian state, sealed off from the outside, where people like my parents are considered enemies of the people, traitors of the fatherland, and collaborators. Nonetheless, every time they are summoned, the German authorities urge my parents to return home soon; what would happen to them in the Soviet Union is of no interest. My mother always comes back from these meetings in tears and looks like she has been beaten.

And soon our hope of emigrating to America is also extinguished. We had already submitted a number of applications for a visa, but now, following an obligatory medical exam, my father is told that he has TB. It is known that America only welcomes people who are in perfect health; a TB diagnosis means the visa application will be rejected, and such decisions are final and irreversible. And it could be fatal for my father, perhaps for all of us, since we might be infected without even knowing it. Suddenly my father, who, aside from occasional malaria, has never been sick, is the weakest of us all, closer to death than my infirm mother.

The four of us have to go to the public health department, where they take blood samples and X-rays to determine if we are contagious. A few days later the doorbell rings and to our great surprise, the German medical officer is standing outside, not in his white lab coat, but a gray suit and tie. He has come to the houses to tell my mother in person that she has nothing to worry about, we are all healthy; the American doctor's diagnosis was incorrect, her husband only has an old, harmless spot on his lungs, probably from the pneumonia he caught many years before. My mother invites the medical officer in and offers him a cup of tea with *varenye*, which she made from the raspberries in our little garden by the river; the handsome young doctor even drinks a second cup and converses in a very kind way with my mother, a way I have never heard a German speak before. Later she says that God sent her this man. My mother is certain that the TB diagnosis was not a mistake, but a malicious lie by the Americans, who do not shy away from using such a horrible disease as a pretext to get rid of people like us forever.

But the shock cures my parents. They abandon their attempts to emigrate, and my unemployed father comes up with an idea for a business.

He wants to start a chicken farm. He plans to buy at least one hundred laying hens and a few roosters in order to supply German shops with eggs and deliver meat to the big hotel at the train station. With the help of my mother, who, as always, must act as a translator between him and the Germans, my father applies for a loan at the Stadtsparkasse on Main Street. My mother doesn't believe that we will receive a loan from the Germans, but after a few weeks in which my parents have to go to the bank and the authorities several times, it is granted. An unbelievable, dizzying figure of one thousand marks.

The city allows my father to set up his chicken farm on a piece of fallow land far out on the Regnitz that he leases for a minimal amount. An old man from Azerbaijan with a stomach ailment assists him with the project. In lieu of any payment, he is allowed to stay in a shed that he builds on the property in addition to the chicken coop—in the houses he lives with his daughter, her husband, and four grandchildren in a two-room apartment, which is just as small as ours.

From then on, my father is no longer at home during the day, but more than ever, we live in fear and horror, dreading the moment when we see him through the window coming back from the building site on his bicycle, usually drunk. Now that he is working, it has become all the more important for us to fulfill women's household duties.

Every day my mother and I carry out a hopeless battle against the dirt and disorder in our apartment. My father calls it a pigsty. None of us have ever set foot inside a German apartment, but my father repeatedly holds German women up as an example to my mother, claiming that where they live, as he knows from somewhere, it is so clean you can eat off the floor. For us, that would be completely impossible; the sand always crunches under our soles, no matter how often we mop the floor or sweep it with the ruffled goose wing that serves as a broom. We are unable to shift the substance from the wrong location to the right one—it resists all our efforts and immediately escapes from our rags and mop water. It is likely that the old, half-rotten furniture in our apartment is disintegrating so quickly we can't keep up with it; the furniture itself is probably the source of the dust that we constantly remove from it. Then there is the disorder, against which we are entirely powerless. We always have to search for everything, although we are constantly tidying up; we simply can't find a permanent place for our things, and we don't know how to organize everything in order to best fight the chaos.

My father doesn't like my mother's cooking either. Once, he finds a ragged ten-mark note in his borscht, which inexplicably ended up in the pot and then landed in his soup plate. My mother turns pale, as do I. My father looks at her as though he is about to beat her to death. Then he sweeps the plate off the table. *Cholera*, he yells, *kretinka*, *parasitka*, *debilka*, while my mother picks up the shards from the floor, her hands shaking. He kicks her so hard that she falls face down into the pool of soup and cuts her cheekbone on a piece of the broken plate. Her red blood drips into the red broth on the floor.

I vaguely remember another ominous incident with my father: we—my mother, sister, and I—are huddled together on the bed in the bedroom, hiding from danger. Suddenly, the door is pushed open, lighting up the dark room. My father stands, staggering and obviously very drunk, in the illuminated doorway, babbling about my mother's "little white hands," her "blue blood," and her "hereditary mental illness." She hugs us, my sister and me, with both arms and screams: "Not the children, please, not the children! Hit me, but leave the children alone!" In Ukraine, she could have left him, fled from him and gotten a divorce, but in Germany, she has no alternative; she is at his mercy.

My little sister remains the delicate, quiet, withdrawn child that she has been from the beginning. She has my mother's black hair, pale skin, and blue, slightly veiled eyes. She annoys me because I have to take care of her so often, and I don't really know what to do with her. Once I tie her to a table leg in order to have some peace. She endures this without complaint, like almost everything else. Whenever we have a rare delicacy, a few cherries for example, I usually get double the pleasure. I gulp my portion down at once, while my sister devours them with her eyes for a long time. She picks up the cherries one by one and looks at them for a long time from all sides, lost in thought; she arranges them on the table in mysterious patterns, reverently exchanging one cherry for another as though she is playing solitaire. She delays the pleasure longer and longer, although she must already know how it will end, since it is the same every time. I don't have to take anything away from my sister, I only have to ask her—actually not even that. She gives me the first cherry entirely on her own, then the second and the third; she gives me each one with a gracious smile, only hesitating over the last one. She would like to eat at least one, it would be enough, but she cannot defend her property, she cannot manage it. The mere knowledge of my desire forces her to hand over the last cherry with an expression of perfect noblesse.

There is a constant hunger inside me, an inadequacy, that my sister doesn't appear to experience. Most of all an envy of the other children burns within me, not only the Germans but also those who live in the houses. I would also like to have a mother who can fry potatoes and bake a cake, who sews the curtains for our window and doesn't leave her change on the counter because she is too embarrassed to take it. At school, they laugh at me because I have holes in my stockings and a failing grade in needlework. "You're not a real girl," Miss Schorrn says. "Your top marks in the other subjects aren't going to help you." It's another blot on my reputation: I am not German, I lie, I steal, and now I learn that I am not a real girl either. The German children have mothers who can knit sweaters and mend their clothes with a sewing machine; my mother doesn't even know how to sew on a button—there is nothing she knows less about than needlework. She cannot show me how to cross-stitch, how to knit purl stitches, or how a knitting doll works. Apparently, I have also inherited her "little white hands," because my stitches keep falling off my needle, and I have to untie everything again. While everyone else is already knitting socks, I am still poking about on my potholders.

At the beginning of summer, my father completed his work on the chicken farm. One hundred white Leghorn chickens and a few outsize white roosters with fat red combs stroll on the distant property along the Regnitz. The wooden coop, which is similar to the Valka barracks, has two flaps that open to allow the chickens to go outside via narrow ladders. The Azerbaijani's shed, which includes a homemade bed, is simply a part of the coop that is partitioned off and includes a small window. My father also plants a small vegetable garden, and he shows me how you can carve your name into a pumpkin when it is small and then watch the letters grow all summer. A German shepherd, which my father names Ada, lies on a chain in front of her hut and licks my bare feet.

My mother, my sister, and I often go to the farm together since we have to help out our father. On the long journey, my mother pulls my sister along behind her on a board with a handle and wheels as she is still too young to walk that far. We walk and we walk, always along the Regnitz; it is hot, we are tired and thirsty, but the trip never ends. Once, when we finally arrive, my mother stops in front of the gate and stares at the wooden swing set my father built for me and my sister. "There is a skeleton hanging in the swing," she says in a flat voice. I can't see anything, but my mother stands motionless, pale as chalk, as though hypnotized in front of the wooden frame with the board that dangles in the air on two pieces of rope.

During this period, my mother doesn't speak very much anymore. She becomes stranger and increasingly absent, announcing with greater frequency that she will go into the water. And yet, just prior to this she had been so carefree and happy, like I had never seen her before. She had suddenly started to comb her long black hair and to try out new hairstyles; often, she simply stood in front of the mirror and looked at herself for a long time in amazement, as if she had forgotten what she looked like, or as though she was seeing herself for the first time. If she was waiting for the German doctor, who stopped by many times after his first visit (always in the daytime when my father was at the chicken farm), she wore her black floral dress with the ruffled peplum along with the salamander brooch which the Nuremberg factory owner had given her. She suddenly started joking with my sister and me, and sang "*Poviy, Vitre, Na Vkrainu*,"[4] and the song about the light blue cloth that the singing wind plays with on the river. Sometimes she sang "*Na Sopkakh Mandzhuriy*,"[5] an old Russian waltz, which her mother must have sung as well, and twirled to the beat; then she stopped abruptly and looked at her feet, again astonished, as though she didn't understand what they had just done, or as though she had to check whether her feet really belonged to her.

The young doctor, Wilfried, was so tall that I had to lift my head up as though I was peering at a church tower if I wanted to look him in the face. Everything about him was fair and light: his hair, his suit, and his eyes behind his glasses. He brought something with him every time, oranges and chocolate, a small, dark blue bottle of perfume for my mother, and on one occasion, a ticking wall clock that hung in the kitchen above the radio from then on. Sitting on one of our Caritas chairs, he listened to my mother as she told him about her life. Probably, he was the first German who asked her questions, the first person to inquire about her in an eternity. A German had also never been so nice to my sister and me. He named us Snow White and Rose Red, joked with us, and put my little sister on his knee and played "Hop, Hop, Rider," with her, which she enjoyed with great enthusiasm. At some point my mother sent us out into the courtyard where we were supposed to play, or into the other room if the weather was bad. From there I heard some half-whispered German words, sometimes louder, sometimes quieter, that I could not understand except for the startled and defensive "No! No!" my mother kept repeating. And then once again the whispers and sighs.

Eventually, Wilfried did not come back. My mother did not say a word about it; she only started to fade away again. It was like she was freezing to death, as though her body was shrinking. She stopped looking in the mirror, she stopped singing, and stopping speaking almost entirely.

In the meantime, it has become clear that my father's business is not going according to plan. Not a single store in the city wants to buy eggs from his chicken farm, no one needs them, they all have their regular suppliers. Apparently, he hadn't even considered such a possibility, irrespective of the fact that his eggs are too expensive for the German shopkeepers. He wants to charge extra for freshness, although our eggs are anything but fresh, as they pile up in our cellar for weeks since nobody wants to buy them. We eat most of them ourselves, and share them with the Azerbaijani and his large family; every now and then, someone rings at our door, one of our clients from the houses, though we can count them on one hand. Here too, most people prefer to buy their eggs in German shops than from us.

At least the big hotel at the train station takes a few chickens from my father every now and then, as he had hoped. An awful spectacle always precedes these transactions. My father chases the chickens, who run away from him, seemingly aware of what he has planned. When he finally catches one, he chops its head off with an ax. He has to hold onto the chicken when its severed head is already on the ground since it still tries to escape, wildly flapping its wings. Once one of them manages to break free; it flutters away without a head and flies a short distance, blood spurting in the air, until it dives into the grass, one hundred meters away from its head.

Every Saturday after school, I am required to go and sell eggs. I ring the doorbells at the Germans' doors and say, "Fresh eggs from the chicken farm." The stairwells are cool and dead quiet and really so clean that you could eat off the floor. Through open doors, I catch a glimpse inside German apartments for the first time, the carpets, lampshades, rubber trees, and other things that we do not have. The German women have perms; they wear aprons and slippers, which are also unknown to us and must be part of the secret of German cleanliness. Only—most of them don't want our eggs either. "Which chicken farm?" they ask. "Where is that, anyway? Oh, you come from the houses . . . But these eggs are much too expensive, at Wiemann's they cost three pfennigs less." I am ashamed of my expensive eggs from the houses; most of all, I would like to give them to the German women for free and even thank them for taking the eggs.

However, I contribute to my own humiliation by always adding one or two pfennigs on top of the price set by my father. If, on a Saturday afternoon, I have sold thirty eggs after wearing myself out by trudging from house to house with my heavy basket, then I have earned thirty or even sixty pfennigs. With this I can buy a *granatsplitter* chocolate cake at the bakery and save the rest for a pencil case, a real German pencil case, which everyone in my class has except for me. One day I earn so much that I can secretly go to the cinema for the matinee screening of *It Is Midnight, Dr. Schweitzer*, which tells the story of the famous doctor's hospital in the jungle. It is the first time in my life that I watch a movie, and for days afterward, it is as though I am in a trance.

Even without my scams, my father's chicken farm is a flop—as a nine-year-old I can understand that much. We no longer have enough to eat, and at night we often go to bed hungry. Our temporary salvation once again appears in the form of piecework, which my mother takes on. She is good at what this work requires of her. Every week we receive a large package of material, and then my mother and I sit at the kitchen table and glue flowers, small pale roses, which must dry with a green leaf on a perforated board before we tie them together into bouquets of twelve. We hardly do anything else besides gluing flowers; school becomes a minor matter for me. I hardly go outside anymore to rove about in the wilderness that has been given to us near the gravel pits and the floodplains; instead I sit at the kitchen table and work, although my fingers and eyes burn from the glue. My mother and I go all out, we get faster and faster, but no matter how much we glue, we never earn more than a starvation wage.

We cannot go on like this. My father decides to make another attempt at a singing career by joining a Cossack choir that tours all year round, filling concert halls and churches across Europe. He hands over the chicken farm, with a drastically reduced number of chickens, to the Azerbaijani, packs a big, old cardboard suitcase he obtained with my mother at Caritas, and makes his way to Dusseldorf, where the choir's directors are based and the tour bus is waiting. I don't know if there were really any Cossacks in the ensemble or if they only chose the name because it sounds so romantic to German ears. In any case, Ivan Rebroff was a member of the choir; later he became famous for his extensive vocal range and his embodiment of the Russian soul, although he had absolutely nothing to do with Russia. He was a German, whose name was neither Ivan nor Rebroff, but Hans Rippert.

The life my father now leads is inconceivable to us. He is in a different city almost every day, sleeping in hotels and eating in restaurants. He sends us money and colorful postcards: the snow-covered Alps with tiny houses in the valley, immense Dutch tulip fields, the Eiffel Tower, a Spanish flamenco dancer with castanets in her hand. My sister uses the postcards to set up her mysterious game of solitaire on the floor, which we stopped sweeping a long time ago. My mother doesn't read the postcards, and she leaves the money he sends carelessly on the table—my sister and I help ourselves to it to our heart's content. We buy enormous quantities of Franconian ring bologna, cherry lollipops, and ice cream cakes and stuff ourselves until we throw up. I used to have to be home in the evening when the streetlights came on; now my mother no longer pays any attention. I hardly go to school at all and roam about outside until it is dark. Every now and then, my mother still goes to the chicken farm to collect the eggs, but she is really only keeping up appearances. The eggs that I no longer try to sell around the neighborhood pile up in our cellar and rot. When a client from the houses rings the doorbell, my mother doesn't answer the door, she has stopped answering it entirely, she doesn't even seem to hear the doorbell. When a neighbor, who apparently senses something of our family disaster, stops by once to bring us a cake, our mother forbids us from eating it. She says the cake is poisoned and throws it in the trash.

We have given up cleaning; occasionally I wash a few plates under the tap or take the trash down to the dumpster in the basement, everything else is covered in dirt, and my sister and I don't have any clean underwear. It is already autumn; in the evening, it gets chilly in the apartment, but we can't heat it since there isn't any wood or coal.

When we, my sister and I, kneel down in the evenings to say our prayers before we go to sleep, as we are accustomed to do, our mother says, "There is no God," and forbids us from praying. The next day she crosses herself, starts to cry, and tells us to pray again after all. Many times she sees things that I can't see—nuns dressed in white passing by the window, the birches on fire in the courtyard, or on one occasion a snake that moves closer to her in the kitchen, so that she recoils and presses her back against the wall and screams. Usually she sits on a chair in the kitchen and stares straight ahead. There is no point in shaking her, pinching her, or pulling her hair; she puts up with everything and no longer reacts. "Mama, when are we going into the water?" I ask once. And then she finally says something. She says, "Soon."

One day her eyes suddenly become lively again, she leaps up from the chair, takes my jump rope, ties it around my neck and starts to strangle me. She is convinced that I am a child of Satan, evil that she has brought into the world. She must kill me; God has commanded her. Another time she pulls me out from under the bed, where I am hiding, and holds a knife to my neck. I scream bloody murder, and she lets me go.

After that, I try to kill her. I secretly put needles in my mother's bed so that they will pierce her while she sleeps and flow with her blood to her heart. She told me herself that this can happen if you play with needles. I hold my breath all night, but the next morning, my mother gets up just like always. She seems not to have noticed the needles in her bed at all.

I know that something terrible is about to happen, but I am entirely alone with this knowledge; I can't tell anyone, there is nowhere to sound the alarm, there is nothing to do. The entire time I hope that someone will notice something on their own, but no one notices anything. I don't know where my father is, and it would never occur to me to call him, of all people, for help.

My mother has a Russian friend, Maria Nikolaevna, who does not live in the houses, but in her own home with her German husband on Weingartsteig. There, in a room with carpets on the floor and paintings on the walls, I once heard my mother play the piano—something so unspeakably beautiful and sad, like nothing I had ever heard before. On the way home, my mother held my hand and said it was the "Raindrop" prelude by Frédéric Chopin, a Polish composer who died young and poor. I would like to run to Maria Nikolaevna and ask her for help, but I know that I cannot. For a while she and my mother visited each other regularly, but then Maria Nikolaevna's husband put a stop to it. He had his law firm's reputation to think about, and for this reason, he did not want his wife to associate with people from the houses.

When my mother calls me "Satan's child" again and shakes me so hard that I almost lose consciousness, I tear myself away, rush into the bedroom and lock the door from the inside. Then I take our scissors and with burning hatred I cut up all of my mother's clothes, one after the other, everything that I find in the closet. I rage until there is nothing left, so that the only piece of clothing she owns is what she is wearing. When I realize what I have done, I want to escape out the window, but it is already dark outside and it is raining. Eventually, I have no other choice but to unlock the door again. I stand with the scissors in my hand and wait for my mother to enter. When she finally comes in and sees the pile of shredded clothing on the floor, she stops short, but immediately thereafter a pensive smile crosses her face. "Well done, my girl," she says, and strokes my head tenderly. "You did that very well."

From that moment on, she stops speaking entirely. I beg her, I plead with her, I shake her, but she says nothing more. She sits there again with her frozen, absent gaze, revealing nothing about what she sees somewhere in another reality.

Finally, the tenth of October arrives. That day I go to school, and no one questions me about my poor attendance, including the new teacher, who apparently does not even count me as one of her students. I come home and start babbling out of habit; I am like a waterfall, talking like crazy without periods or commas. I tell my mother that on the following day we will take a class trip to Walberla. And then she suddenly speaks. "You won't go along tomorrow," she says. Only those five words, and then she falls silent again. I explain that I have to go, that it is compulsory; I scream, I stamp my feet. "I have to go along!" I shriek. "Everyone is going!" But she can no longer hear me.

Furious, I run out of the apartment, slamming the door loudly behind me. It was always like that. I was constantly forbidden to do everything that was routine for German children; not only what they were allowed to do, but what they had to do. My parents always said: we are not Germans. I cannot know that this time my mother's words are not a prohibition, but a prophecy. You won't go along tomorrow—the last words that I ever heard her speak.

I come home late, even later than usual; it is already nine o'clock when I turn the key in the lock on the door of our apartment. But the door does not open. I push harder; the door gives way a little bit, and suddenly I hear my younger sister break out into pitiful screams. She has barricaded herself inside, creating a bulwark by piling up all of our chairs next to and on top of each other in front of the door. I push against it one more time, and all the chairs fall to the ground with a loud crash. I squeeze into our hallway and notice at once that my sister is sick. Her eyes glisten feverishly, and her arms are covered with red spots. This is exactly how I looked when I had the measles.

My mother is not at home. It is the first time that this has happened so late. If she goes somewhere, then it is only to the chicken farm to get eggs, but she must have come back by now. It is so dark on the path along the Regnitz that you can't see your hand in front of your face. My sister no longer knows when she left, she has a fever and seems to be totally confused. We sit at the kitchen table and wait. It is dead quiet; we can only hear the ticking of the wall clock above the radio, which the doctor gave my mother. My eyes are glued to the big hand that jumps every minute. Today's date is crossed off on the calendar hanging under the clock.

Later I go into the bedroom to get a blanket for my sister, who has the chills, and right away I see what has changed. An enlarged portrait print of my mother in a Ukrainian headscarf has hung on the wall ever since I can remember; she always considered it to be outstanding evidence of her beauty. Now the photo has been taken down; it is lying on the bed, torn in half.

I run over to Farida's parents and tell them that my mother has disappeared. Farida's father rings the doorbell to wake up the German custodian; he has a telephone and calls the police. Farida's mother takes my feverish sister out of our apartment and packs her off to bed at her place. I have to show the two policemen, who come in a car, the way to the chicken farm. It is the first time I sit in a car, and for that alone, it is already a historic occasion for me. The night is cold and clear; the moon sparkles on the dark Regnitz as we drive by.

The Azerbaijani emerges from his shack, bleary-eyed and shocked by the sight of the police. No, he hasn't seen my mother, she wasn't there today, she hasn't been around much lately. Ada whines on her chain; her amber eyes are the only thing that can be seen in the darkness. The stupid rooster crows in the middle of the night.

"My mother is in the Regnitz," I tell the policeman. They exchange glances and say, "Oh, that's nonsense." However, on the way back, they point the searchlight they have brought with them onto the river and drive very slowly along the bank. I am terrified that my mother will suddenly appear in the beam of light, lying dead at the water's edge. But all you can see is black water.

I spend the rest of the night at Farida's; the next day Maria Nikolaevna picks me up and takes me to Weingartsteig and her house with the paintings and the piano, which my mother played. I am afraid of her German husband, he'll definitely get angry when he sees me, but he only stares at me through his glasses with a long, sad look.

During the next two days, Maria Nikolaevna is repeatedly on the verge of telling me something, but then she shakes her head and starts to cry. "I can't," she sobs. "I can't. Your mother has only gone away to visit friends, she'll be back soon." I am puzzled. Whom would she have gone to visit? She doesn't know anyone. Besides, she would have worn her good shoes, but they are at home in the hallway.

It is a long way from Weingartsteig to the cemetery, but I am an experienced sprinter. I run from one end of the city to the other without stopping until I am panting in front of the mortuary. And there she is, my mother. I had no hope of not seeing her behind the glass. I had long known that I would stand here one day and look at her, that the evil game she played with me so often would one day turn serious. Now there is no longer any point in shaking and pinching her; I can no longer coax a smile from her. There is nothing I can do anymore to prevent her death. I had always been haunted by the idea that in reality the bodies behind the glass only appear to be dead, and that they cannot call out to anyone, although they hear and feel everything, but my mother doesn't feel anything anymore, this I know. Now she is really dead.

How happy she must be that it is like this, I think; she no longer feels anything of the life that tormented her so terribly. Or, would she have swum back to shore if she had known how to swim? At the last moment, did she die against her will after all? For some reason, what scares me most is the thought of the cold October water. I think it is likely that she did not drown at all, but that her small, weak heart stopped first, that it probably burst when she ran into the cold water.

She looks strange with her black hair loose on the white cushion, like Snow White from the book of German fairy tales. She has a bruise on her right cheek, under her eye. What did she bump into in the water? They had folded her hands over the funeral pall just like the other two dead laid out that day, but they did not put a cross between her hands. There are also no wreaths or flowers in front of her coffin. She lies completely unadorned, and entirely apart, in a different place from the two dead next to her.

Only later do I learn that her gray coat with the frayed velvet cuffs, her last article of clothing from Ukraine, had been found on the riverbank only a few hundred meters from her lifeless body, washed up by the current. She had taken off the coat, folded it neatly and laid it on the grass. She had probably selected the location well in advance, maybe on the day that she crossed off the tenth of October on the calendar. Those were the signs she left behind: the cross on the calendar, the torn photograph, and the coat on the riverbank. Why did she take it off? Didn't she realize that its weight would help her drown?

At the time of her death, no gravesites were available at the bucolic municipal cemetery, and the new cemetery had only just been established. Today this cemetery looks like a private neighborhood with pretty gardens, but at the time it was a construction site. For a long time the gravestone with the Russian inscription stood in a wasteland plowed through by excavators and bulldozers. Now, the grave no longer exists. There is nothing left except for a few old black and white photographs, an inverted copy of her marriage certificate, and an icon she brought with her from Ukraine long ago. Presumably it is a piece of family property that, by chance, had not been expropriated.

I look at her for a long time behind the glass, until it gets dark and they close the cemetery gates and I have to leave. Her face is distant and closed; it reveals nothing about the circumstances of her death, nothing about why she didn't take us, my sister and me, along with her, nothing about why she went alone in the end.

Acknowledgments

I would like to thank everyone who helped make this book possible. First and foremost, Igor Tasiz, who supported me so tirelessly and knowledgeably during my search.

I would also like to thank Oleg Dobrozrakov, Alexey and Dmitry Dobrozrakov, Lyudmila Dobrozrakova, Tatiana Anochina, Evgenia Ivashchenko, Irina Yakuba, Elena Suetina, Dmitry Morozov, Olga Timofeeva, Roman Levchenko, Elena Levina, Maria Pirgo, Svetlana Likhacheva, Tatiana Matytsina, Dr. Tim Schanetzky, Alex Köhler, Barbara Heinze, Bettina von Kleist, Dr. Elke Liebs-Etkind, Gabriele Röwer, and Anne Friebel of the Leipzig Nazi Forced Labor Memorial. Special thanks go to Volker Strauss.

Last but not least, I would like to thank my ancestors from Ukraine, who helped to write this book: Matilda De Martino and Yakov Ivashchenko; Lidia and Sergey Ivashchenko; Epifan Ivashchenko and Anna von Ehrenstreit; Valentina Ostoslavskaya; Olga Chelpanova; Georgy Chelpanov; Natalya Martynovich; Elena Perkovskaya; Leonid Ivashchenko; Teresa Pacelli and Giuseppe De Martino; Angelina, Valentino, Federico, and Antonio De Martino; Marusya and Volodya Pitschachtschi; Ledya Suetina; and Eleonora Zhubranskaya. I owe special thanks to my Aunt Lidia Ivashchenko, whose life story was a gift of immeasurable value.

Berlin, Autumn 2016

Notes

Part One. Answers in the Internet

1. Penny and Lidl are German discount supermarket chains.
2. The German Democratic Republic (GDR) was the official name of East Germany, which existed from 1949–1990.
3. Registry office.
4. Göring was a leading member of the Nazi Party who served as president of the Reichstag and minister of aviation in the Third Reich. He received a death sentence at the Nuremberg Trials but committed suicide before it could be carried out.
5. Originally published in Russian as *Nagrudnij Znak "OST,"* or Badge "OST." During World War II, slave laborers in Nazi Germany were required to wear a blue and white badge with the German word Ost, or east, written in large white letters. The German title translates as *A Distinguishing Mark*.
6. *Die Zeit* is a German weekly newspaper.
7. A seventeenth-century administrative division of the Kingdom of Poland that later became part of Ukraine.
8. This appears to be a mistake in the original certificate, the actual title of Alexander Borodin's 1890 opera is *Prince Igor*.
9. CPSU is the abbreviation for the Communist Party of the Soviet Union.
10. The Kurfürstendamm, known as the Ku'damm, was the leading commercial street of Cold War Berlin, and it retained its status as the Champs-Élysées of the city into the 1990s.
11. Hartz IV is system of unemployment benefits introduced in Germany in 2005, named after Peter Hartz, who led the committee that designed it.
12. "How young we were," is a hit song from the 1975 Soviet film *My Junior Year Love Affair*.
13. The Maidan Nezalezhnosti, or Independence Square, is the central square in Kyiv and the traditional meeting place for political rallies including the 2013–14 Euromaidan which culminated in the overthrow of the government.
14. The Allgemeiner Deutscher Automobil-Club, or General German Automobile Association, is the largest automobile club in Germany, with its own fleet of mobile mechanics.
15. Anna Akhmatova, "Requiem," *Sochinenija v dvux tomax* (Moscow: Izdatelstvo Pravda, 1990), 196–203.
16. This 1872 opera is known as *Black Sea Cossacks* in English.
17. The Russian language uses two separate pronouns for the word "you." *Vij* is used in formal contexts and *tij* is used between friends and acquaintances.
18. Georgy Ivanov, *On the Border of Snow and Melt*, trans. by Jerome Katsell and Stanislav Shvabrin (Santa Monica, CA: Perceval Press, 2011), 113. Copyright © 2011, used by permission.

Part Two. Aunt Lidia's Journals

1. The American Relief Administration, or ARA, is a US government program which distributed food aid in the USSR from 1921 to 1923.
2. Narodniy Kommisariat Vnutrennich Del, or People's Commissariat for Internal Affairs, established in 1917, was the USSR's interior ministry. It was responsible for political repression as well as the Great Purge, and it ran the Gulag. In 1946, its name was changed to the Ministry of Internal Affairs.
3. The Young Pioneers (1922–1991) was a Soviet youth organization for children aged nine to fifteen, known for the distinctive red neckerchiefs they tied in their shirt collars.

Part Three. Journey to Germany

1. Reclam Verlag is a well-known German publishing house, founded in Leipzig in 1828. During the Cold War, the Reclam family relocated to Stuttgart in West Germany, while the German Democratic Republic (GDR) nationalized the original business and continued to publish books under the Reclam imprint.
2. *Hiwis* were former prisoners of war and others who served alongside the Nazi forces in occupied Eastern Europe during World War II.
3. Franz Fühmann, *Jedem sein Stalingrad* [To each his own in Stalingrad], in *Autorisierte Werkausgabe in acht Bänden* [Authorized works in eight volumes], vol. 3 (Rostock, Germany: Hinstorff Verlag, 1993).
4. *Dula* is a German-language abbreviation for *Durchgangslager*, or transit camp.
5. Daisy Lane, Rose Lane and Dahlia Street.
6. *Notat eines Beamten des damaligen Auswärtigen Amtes* [Notes of an official of the former Foreign Office], in Ulrich Herbert, *Geschichte der Ausländerpolitik in Deutschland. Saisonarbeiter, Zwangsarbeiter, Gastarbeiter, Flüchtlinge* [A history of policies toward foreigners in Germany: Seasonal workers, forced laborers, guest workers, refugees] (Munich: C. H. Beck, 2008).
7. Report from a Russian forced laborer who was deployed to a factory in Leipzig, audio recording, Foundation Remembrance, Responsibility and Future (EVZ), Berlin, https://www.stiftung-evz.de/eng/the-foundation.html.
8. This is a reference to the Reichsmark, the currency of Nazi Germany.
9. Testimony by an ATG employee at the Nuremberg Flick trial, in National Archives of the United States, RG 242, National Archives Collection of Foreign Records Seized, M 891-33 (excerpt).
10. Testimony by the prosecutor in the Nuremberg Flick trial, in Th. Ramge, "Total War, Total Profit" [*Totaler krieg, totaler profit*], *Die Zeit*, no. 34 (August 8, 2004).

Part Four. Displaced Persons in Postwar Germany

1. Goliath was a brand of trucks manufactured by Bremen-based Goliath-Werke Borgward & Company, which ceased operations in 1961.
2. The Blood Flag consecration ("Blutfahnenweihe") was a ceremony for SA and SS units at Nuremberg in which a flag allegedly carried by the Beer Hall Putsch rebels in 1923 and soaked with the blood of one of their members was used to consecrate new SS flags by pressing them against the original flag.
3. Natascha Wodin's birth name is Natalja Wdowin.
4. "Blow, Wind, to Ukraine," is a poem by nineteenth-century Ukrainian writer, Stepan Rudansky, that was set to music by Lyudmila Alexandrova.
5. "On the Hills of Manchuria" is a waltz composed in 1906 by Ilya Shatrov.